Return on Customer

Thomson University

Learning Centers

THOMSON

Other books by
Don Peppers and Martha Rogers, Ph.D.

*The One to One Future: Building Relationships
One Customer at a Time*

*Enterprise One to One: Tools for Competing
in the Interactive Age*

*The One to One Fieldbook: The Complete Toolkit
for Implementing a 1to1 Marketing Program*
(with Bob Dorf)

*The One to One Manager: Real-World Lessons in
Customer Relationship Management*

*One to One B2B: Customer Development Strategies
for the Business-to-Business World*

*Managing Customer Relationships:
A Strategic Framework*

Don Peppers
Martha Rogers, Ph.D.

Return on Customer

**Creating Maximum Value from
Your Scarcest Resource**

Return on Customer[SM] and ROC[SM] are service marks of Peppers and Rogers Group, a division of Carlson Marketing Group, Inc. Registration pending.

First published in 2005 by:

Marshall Cavendish Business
An imprint of Marshall Cavendish (Asia) Private Limited
A member of Times Publishing Limited
Times Centre, 1 New Industrial Road
Singapore 536196
T: +65 6213 9300
F: +65 6285 4871
E: te@sg.marshallcavendish.com
Online bookstore: www.marshallcavendish.com/genref

and

Cyan Communications Limited
119 Wardour Street
London W1F 0UW
United Kingdom
www.cyanbooks.com

A CIP record for this book is available from the British Library

ISBN 981 261 808 2 (Asia & ANZ)
ISBN 1-904879-34-9 (Rest of world)

Designed and typeset by Cambridge Publishing Management

Printed and bound in Singapore

Contents

Acknowledgments

We have navigated uncharted waters in developing the ideas within *Return on Customer*, but we have had help. Lots of it.

Special thanks to Steve Skinner, who helped us think through the basic concept of Return on Customer early in the process, and led some of our firm's first client work in this area. Thanks also to Christian Neckermann, Marijo Puleo, Vernon Tirey, Chris Bassler, Stephen Fraser, Christopher Helm, Tom Schmalzl, Lorenz Esguerra, James Vila, Sophie Vlessing, Robert Wadman, Trish Watson, Lisa Goodmaster, Scott Lochridge, Dave Johnson, Bob Langer, Michael Lengel, Elizabeth Weisser, Simon Jury, Patrick Winterbottom, Tom Spitale, and Tim Shorrocks for helping us figure out how to turn the ROC concept into a workable tool for helping companies create value, benefiting their customers, employees, and shareholders by balancing the demands of short-term performance with long-term growth. The Peppers & Rogers Group Centers of Excellence in Organizational Transformation, Analytics, Strategy, Customer Experience, and Practice Design have been invaluable, and we thank every member of each of those teams for input and reaction. We also thank the Decision Sciences experts at Carlson Marketing Group, especially Taylor Deursch and Vice President of Decision Sciences Linda Vytlacil, as well as the "ROC and Roll" practice leader, Lane Michel.

We are very grateful for financial and accounting expertise brought to bear on the nearly finished manuscript, especially by Preeti Choudhary from Duke University (and thanks to Rick Staelin for introducing us!). Thanks also to Doug Smith, our intrepid advisor about all things financial.

We appreciate the encouragement and support we've received from everyone at Carlson Companies. Marilyn Carlson Nelson, Chairman and Chief Executive Officer at Carlson Companies, epitomizes the kind of corporate leadership we expect many companies will be trying to cultivate as their firms strive to act more and more with their customers' interests at heart. Curtis C. Nelson, President and Chief Operating Officer at Carlson Companies, is a visionary as well as a true leader. Thanks, in addition, to Steve Geiger and the other members of Carlson Marketing Group's Executive Committee.

For countless hours of behind-the-scenes research and digging out the background we needed, a special thanks to the entire team of information specialists at Carlson Companies, including Wendy Stotts, Kristin Hektner, Phyllis Lindberg, Julie Smith, Susan Skrien, Cathy Schlifer, and Karen Martin. Additional thanks for the help with details provided by Holly Daniels, Perry Bjornrud, Carolyn Filbert, Jenny Smith, Judy Lindgren, Sara Messier, Patricia Plugge – but a very special thank you goes to the intrepid Tom Lacki, who not only led the overall research effort but also provided a challenging and stimulating intellectual commentary on the implications ROC held for a variety of other economic concepts and ideas.

Kudos to Marji Chimes, the tireless and relentlessly optimistic leader of Peppers & Rogers Group's media team, and to Jenn Makris, and to the entire media and marketing group. Thanks also to Jamie Sachs, Brian Weaver and Dave Messler for keeping the computers running (even nights and weekends). Thank you, Mike Kust, Barry Wegener, and Steve Solmonson for making us look good (and for all your other help and support). Thanks to our literary agent, Rafe Sagalyn, and to Roger Scholl and Chris Fortunato at Doubleday.

We'd like to express our deepest gratitude to our truly amazing executive assistants – Jenny Smith, Mandy Kraike, and Donna Munns – who have seen us through the various stages of frustration and triumph, and to our patient, supportive spouses, Pamela Devenney and Stuart Bertsch.

But most of all, our thanks go to the pioneers in this field – to those academicians who are now writing the first books and articles that will help build better companies, to those financial analysts and shareholders who are constantly seeking better, more balanced ways to understand the true value of their investments, and to those visionary business executives who intuitively know that their companies can only create lasting, genuine value for investors by delivering lasting, genuine value to customers.

Don Peppers, Martha Rogers, Ph.D.
April 2005

1. An Open Letter to the Financial Community

Businesses succeed by getting, keeping, and growing customers. Customers are the only reason you build factories, hire employees, schedule meetings, lay fiber-optic lines, dispatch service trucks, stock inventory, file for patents, operate call centers, negotiate contracts, write software, or engage in any other kind of business activity whatsoever. Without customers, you don't have a business, you have a hobby.

The problem is that business success is extremely difficult today – probably more difficult than it ever has been. All the easy growth has now occurred. Every household in the industrialized world already has one or two or more cars, a washing machine, television sets in different rooms, and a cellphone (or several). Once an economy matures, customers are no longer so hungry to buy, but businesses are even hungrier to make sales.

Yes, we've all benefited from the unprecedented improvements in productivity over the last couple of decades, but higher productivity has also put renewed pressure on margins. No matter how much streamlining you do today, you're just keeping up. Everyone in your firm is already doing a job and a half. The cost cutting you thought was a temporary inconvenience has now become a permanent hardship.

And then there's the impact of globalization. Offshoring and business process outsourcing may help you control your costs but globalization, too, comes with a price tag. Your products are being reduced to commodities, as more competitors find their own opportunities in your section of the globe, and at least part of the reason you can't get any pricing traction is because someone in the Far East is already undercutting you.

Even though price increases may be nearly impossible to sustain, the cost of selling and marketing is still going up. The more you spend on marketing, the less you have to show for it. Response rates decline, sales effectiveness erodes, and customers continue to become more demanding. New and improved products may temporarily solve your problem, but knock-offs and competitive innovations now appear in days. And we've seen a *lot* of new and improved products introduced, as companies all try to innovate their own way out of the same problem.

In category after category, in market after market, companies are wrestling with the fact that their products and services are simply in over-supply. Too many personal computers chasing too little demand; too many airline seats chasing too little traffic; too many varieties of fresh fruit in the produce section, too many kinds of bottled water, flavored popcorn, and coffee beans; too many accounting services, consultants, systems integrators, and executive-recruiting firms; too much advertising space chasing too few advertisers; too many frozen foods, breakfast cereals, skin creams, razor blades, cold remedies, and hair rinses; too many trucking services, wireless minutes, and drums of chemicals.

What's the only thing in short supply these days? Customers: Customers are difficult to find and hard to keep.

The scarcest resource

In today's business world, customers are even scarcer than capital. If you have a customer for your business, you can almost certainly get the capital you need to serve him. But the market – any market – contains only a finite number of customers, who will each do only so much business in a lifetime, with *anybody*. Even if there are *lots* of customers, it's still a finite number.

To remain competitive, you must figure out how to keep your customers longer, grow them into bigger customers, make them more profitable, and serve them more efficiently. And you want more of them.

Unfortunately, the financial metrics you learned in business school are not easily adapted to account for the value companies generate from this scarce resource, with the right balance between current-period sales and customer lifetime value. But striking that balance is necessary if you want to know whether you're better off investing in

Note: Beginning on page 254, you'll find the endnotes and citations for this book.

customer acquisition or in customer retention, or in product development, or opening new stores, or plant efficiency, or better qualified
personnel, or more service, or cost reduction. While you may believe in
your heart that a particular decision creates shareholder value, there's
no financial metric currently available to tell you how much shareholder
value you actually created, or even whether you created any at all.

But Return on Customer[1] can help you. Return on Customer is a
breakthrough financial metric that can *quantify* the actual shareholder
value you are creating (or, possibly, destroying) with your various business actions and initiatives.

Thinking long-term

Let's face it: Businesses gauge their success today almost entirely in
terms of current-period revenue and earnings. Financial analysts
demand that a firm "make its numbers," or the stock price will likely
founder. Certainly, public-company CEOs think this is the case, and
they'll go to great lengths to meet analysts' expectations.

A 2004 survey of American executives revealed that meeting short-
term Wall Street expectations is such an urgent need at publicly held
firms that three out of four senior executives say their company would
actually *give up economic value* in exchange for doing so! More than half
said they would "delay starting a project to avoid missing an earnings
target." Four out of five executives said they "would defer maintenance
and research spending to meet earnings targets."

Quarterly reporting of financial results has certainly created a highly
competitive business landscape. But it also drives executives to pursue
contradictory business goals. Company managers are expected to
strive for long-term value and growth, in order to increase true shareholder value, even while they are also pressured to deliver against more
and more aggressive short-term goals. Moreover, as financial systems
become more sophisticated, we measure performance with continually
shortening yardsticks. Some companies now boast about their ability

---

[1] Return on Customer[SM] and ROC[SM] are service marks of Peppers and Rogers Group, a
division of Carlson Marketing Group, Inc. Registration pending.

to close a quarter in one day. Stock-market analysts focus on short-term results as a proxy for long-term potential.

The problem is that the more short-term a company's focus becomes, the more likely the firm will be to engage in behavior that actually *destroys* long-term value. The obsession with current revenue and earnings at many firms has generated a pervasive culture of bad management.

Don't get us wrong. It's a *good* thing for listed firms to respond to investor demands, and it's *good* that a free market for a company's stock can discipline an errant management. The real problem has to do with the way a firm's future earnings and cash flow are evaluated by investors, and by the stock analysts who interpret the firm's numbers for them.

Investors are in fact very interested in understanding a company's long-term value, but at present there is no better or more reliable indicator of long-term value creation than, well, short-term financial performance. The discounted-cash-flow (DCF) method for valuing a business is based on forecasting the firm's future cash flows, but in the end even the most sophisticated predictions rely mostly on aggregate business trends, projections of market growth, and competitor activity, and in any case all such projections begin with today's numbers. So, like the butterfly whose wings cause a tornado a continent away, small fluctuations in current earnings or revenues wreak massive changes in projected company valuations and share prices, as their effects are extrapolated and magnified years into a company's financial future.

Tightrope: Balancing short-term reporting with long-term success

This creates a difficult problem for managers, because any firm's current earnings are likely to go up and down frequently, due to unexpected and unpredictable events. The natural noise of commerce is hard to dampen out of a firm's "earnings trajectory" from quarter to quarter, but investors' preoccupation with current numbers requires a firm to try, simply in order to preserve its listed value.

One symptom of this malaise is the rash of executive scandals and questionable accounting practices that have plagued the investment community in the last few years. Senior managers know they can "game" the price of their own company's shares by pumping up their current sales, or by smoothing out their short-term results, and then all they have to do is sell their own stock or cash out their personal options some time before reality catches up with the market.

As bad as the most recent round of corporate scandals has been, however, this obsession with current numbers has had a far more corrosive effect on overall management decision-making. Focusing on the short term to the exclusion of other concerns allows managers to shirk their primary responsibility altogether – which is to preserve and increase the value of the enterprise.

Think about it: Almost every senior manager at any listed company has had the experience of attending a meeting called for the express purpose of hitting the year-end numbers, or even quarter-end numbers. Perhaps at this meeting they decided to put off some valuable R&D work, or maybe they trimmed a costly but important service improvement. Chances are the attendees knew full well that taking these actions would do more actual harm to the company than good, but they went ahead anyway – because *they weren't being held accountable for creating enterprise value.* They were being held accountable for short-term results: Wall Street results. Bonuses depended on it. Jobs depended on it. Many of these managers probably also figured they'd be long gone before the company tabulated the actual bill.

And why is it that in business magazines and surveys, lists of the most admired and successful companies seem to include a disproportionate number of privately held firms? Obviously, the market for private companies' equity is less liquid, so private companies have some disadvantages relative to listed firms when it comes to raising capital. But their equity values are also considerably less volatile, with the result that private firms do not have to dance to the financial community's tune. At private firms, cynicism does not trump economics.

Surely there is a message here. Surely this has some significance. Is there anything financial analysts could do to address the difficulty that listed companies have in paying serious attention to the long term? Well – yes, actually. And that's why we're addressing this open letter to the investment community.

The desperate push for organic growth

Investors today want executives to demonstrate that their companies can actually make money and grow the old-fashioned way – by earning it from the value proposition they offer customers. They want a firm's customers to buy more, to buy more often, and to stay loyal longer. They want a firm to show it can go out and get more customers. They want *organic growth*.

Managers read this message loud and clear. As one CEO put it, "I believe that you don't get better by being bigger, you get bigger by being better. And so [we want] organic growth." According to another, "We don't create shareholder value by getting larger through acquisitions, but rather through organic growth." Of course, sometimes an acquisition does create shareholder wealth, but it has to be the right kind of acquisition – a business combination that increases the power of the customer value proposition, allowing the combined entity to achieve genuine, organic growth.

Managers push for growth because it is essential to protecting and improving shareholder value. All management's thoughts and actions, from strategizing with respect to competitive positioning, to cutting costs and streamlining operations, to creating an attractive and productive environment for employees – everything, in the end, is designed to preserve and increase the value of the firm they are managing, and organic growth is the key.

Growth fuels innovation and creativity, generating new ideas and initiatives, and stimulating managers in all areas to "think outside the box." Growth keeps a company vibrant and alive, making it a good place to work – a place that provides employees with economic benefits and opportunities for advancement. Organic growth is, in the words of one HR executive, "the fountain of youth" for a company.

Most business executives would agree, intellectually, that *customers* represent the surest route to business growth – getting more customers, keeping them longer, and making them more profitable. Most understand that the customer base itself is a revenue-producing asset for their company – and that the value it throws off ultimately drives the company's economic worth. Nevertheless, when companies measure their financial results, they rarely if ever take into account any changes in the value of this underlying asset, with the result that they

are blind – and financial analysts are blind – to one of the most significant factors driving business success.

Think about your personal investments. Imagine you asked your broker
to calculate your return on investment for your portfolio of stocks and
bonds. The broker would tally the dividend and interest payments you
received during the year, and then note the increases or decreases in the
value of the various stocks and bonds in the portfolio – current income
plus underlying value changes. The result, when compared to the amount
you began the year with, would give you this year's ROI. But suppose the
broker chose to ignore any changes in the underlying value of your securities, limiting the analysis solely to dividends and interest. Would you
accept this as a legitimate picture of your financial results? No!

Well, this is how most investors assess the financial performance of
the companies they invest in, because this is how companies report their
results. More ambitious analysts can examine comparable firms, they
can try to estimate growth prospects, and they can even try to evaluate
the benefits of loyal customers. In the final analysis, however, they are
still just counting the "dividends" from these customer assets, while
ignoring any increase (or decrease) in the value of the underlying assets
themselves. But just as a portfolio of securities is made up of individual
stocks and bonds that not only produce dividends and interest but also
go up and down in value during the course of the year, a company is, at
its roots, a portfolio of customers, who not only buy things from the
firm in the current period, but also go up and down in value.

Return on Customer: Measuring the value created by customers

Return on investment quantifies how well a firm creates value from a
given investment. But what quantifies how well a company creates
value from its *customers*? For this you need the metric of Return on
Customer^{SM} (ROC^{SM}). The ROC equation has the same form as an ROI
equation. ROC equals a firm's current-period cash flow from its
customers plus any changes in the underlying customer equity, divided
by the total customer equity at the beginning of the period.

THE RETURN ON CUSTOMER EQUATION

Return on Customer can be calculated as follows:

$$ROC = \frac{\pi_i + \Delta CE_i}{CE_{i-1}}$$

Where π_i = Cash flow from customers during period i,

          ΔCE_i = change in customer equity during period i, and

          CE_{i-1} = customer equity at the beginning of period i.

ROC equals a firm's current-period cash flow from its customers plus any changes in the underlying customer equity, divided by the total customer equity at the beginning of the period.

Before going further, let's define customer equity more precisely. The most useful definition of an individual customer's value is lifetime value, or LTV – the net present value of the future stream of cash flows a company expects to generate from the customer. If we add together all the lifetime values of a firm's current and future customers, the result is "customer equity," representing the net value, discounted back to the present, of all the future cash flows a firm expects its customers to generate.[2]

Customer equity, made up of customer LTV (Lifetime Value), is a scarce economic resource with which a company can create more value. What we think of as ROMI, or Return on Marketing Investment, by contrast, might consider the value of customers in evaluating marketing spending, so it can help decision makers choose between, say, a Web improvement or a direct mail campaign, or between closing a call center or cutting the ad budget, but ROMI can't guide a company in making the most of its *scarcest* resource: customers. ROC, however, enables a firm to make decisions based not just on the *capital* needed to create more value, but on the amount of *customer equity* required for it. Because customers are scarcer than capital, ROC is a more efficient metric for maximizing overall value creation, and ultimately, ROC will improve decisions about everything from marketing investments to product development, factory

---

[2] The way in which you add lifetime values together to get the customer equity of a group of customers will depend on the actual lifetime value calculation you use. If you use a "fully allocated" cash flow figure that incorporates all fixed and variable operating costs, then you can simply add lifetime values together to get customer equity. Sometimes you may find it more useful, however, to use marginal contribution when calculating lifetime value, in which case unallocated costs would have to be added in to customer equity as lifetime values are "rolled up" into larger and larger groups of customers. You can find a more complete discussion of this issue in Appendix 2.

improvements, store manager compensation, financial reporting, and even business combinations.

The Return on Customer metric explicitly takes into account the two different ways customers create value for a business – by increasing the company's current-period cash flows, and by increasing its future cash flows. When a customer has a good (or bad) experience with a company, and decides on the basis of that experience to give more future business to it (or less), the firm has gained (or lost) value at that very instant, with the customer's change of mind. It doesn't matter that the extra business a customer might give a company won't happen for a few months or a few years – the customer's intent has changed already, and so the customer's lifetime value (LTV) went up immediately, in the same way a share price would go up immediately if the company were suddenly expecting better profits sometime in the future.

The actions a company takes to achieve either of these outcomes – increases in the customer's current or future cash flows – can have costs and tradeoffs, requiring a balanced approach. For instance, a higher promotion budget might improve customer acquisition. But each new acquisition will be more expensive. It's possible to wind up spending more than an incremental new customer will ever be worth. Or a bigger variety of products might appeal to a wider group of customers, but it could also result in a disproportionately high per piece production or distribution cost. Or an extra service might boost customer satisfaction (and therefore customer loyalty and lifetime value), but its cost still constitutes a drag on current earnings.

Clearly, creating value from customers is an optimization problem, which is something every business manager already knows. Often, however, the tradeoffs occur in terms of increased future cash flows at the expense of reduced current cash flows, or vice versa. This creates a serious problem when a firm is focused exclusively on current-period sales. A short-term focus prevents a firm from making optimum decisions. If a company fires off a truckload of direct mail or email to generate more current sales from its customers, for instance, it might also erode their willingness to buy in the future, or even to pay attention to future solicitations. Similarly, although a cost-cutting effort might not damage current customer cash flows, it could undermine future cash flows. One frustrated manager at a magazine publisher actually confessed to an investor that whenever his company faced a bad quarter, they cut costs by halting their subscriber reactivation campaigns!

Reconciling the conflict between current profit and long-term value is one of the most serious difficulties facing business today. Failing to take a properly balanced approach not only penalizes good management practices but also undermines corporate ethics, by encouraging managers to "steal" from the future to fund the present. Often companies end up destroying value unintentionally – or worse, they know they are destroying value, but feel they have no real choice about it. At the extreme, a firm might even resort to over-promising or tricking customers out of their money, in order to maximize short-term profit. Of course, this almost certainly hampers future sales and destroys customer equity, by eroding the trust that customers have in the firm (more about this in the next chapter).

But there are other extremes to be avoided, as well. For example, a company could invest time and expense lavishing service on its customers to ensure their long-term loyalty, without paying enough attention to current profit or cash flow. While this action might generate higher customer loyalty, if LTV doesn't improve enough to offset increased costs, then value will be destroyed, even as loyalty improves. Or a firm might want to install new call-center or sales force software that is supposed to pay itself off with higher revenue from customers in the future, but not know how much is too much to pay for it.

Balancing between such extremes in order to maximize overall value creation is not a new or revolutionary idea. In an innovative and forward-thinking *Harvard Business Review* article as early as 1996, Bob Blattberg and John Deighton suggested that a firm should apply "the customer equity test" to balance marketing expenditures between customer acquisition and customer retention efforts. They even proposed a mathematical model for fitting exponential curves to find the optimum levels of acquisition and retention spending, based on executives' answers to some level-setting questions.

A 2003 white paper from Mathias and Capon of Columbia Business School considers the implications of managing customers for three "quite different outcomes: Maximizing revenue in the near term, maximizing profitability in the short-to-intermediate term, and optimizing the asset value of customer relationships – customer relationship capital – over the long term." The paper suggests that salespeople have traditionally been held accountable for short-term revenues, but as more organizations have come to emphasize key account management over the last decade, the metric of success has shifted perceptibly from customer revenue to customer profitability. To be successful in the future, say the authors, a firm will have to "take the long view," and "maximize the net present value (NPV) of future profit streams from these customers..."

Clearly, at some point in between the extremes of maximum current-period profit and maximum customer equity growth, there is an optimum level of overall value creation. This optimum point occurs when Return on Customer is at its highest value.

It might be easier to visualize the problem by thinking about the kind of balancing act that farmers must manage, when they try to maximize the overall value of their farming operations. A farmer could plant the richest, most productive cash crop on all his acreage every year and make a great deal of money in the short term, but his land would soon burn out. The more prudent farmer would ensure the long-term productivity of his land by practicing conservation – rotating his crops, fertilizing, aerating the soil, and leaving some land fallow each year. This is a more costly way to farm, and in the first few years the prudent farmer is unlikely to harvest as much profit as he could have. But his land will remain productive for many years.

In farming, land is the scarce resource. For a business, customers are the scarce resource. A business must make the most of its customers in the same way that a farmer must make the most of his land. A prudent farmer must strike the best possible balance, between over-using his land and under-using it. A prudent manager must strike the same type of balance with customers. It is worthwhile remembering that farmers face short-term temptations, just as business executives do. In any given year a prudent farmer can always make more money by fore-going conservation that year. Smart farmers never do that, of course, because it is self-defeating and destructive. It would be stupid, right?

That may be so, but business executives do it all the time. The survey said: *Yes,* three out of four would definitely do it. You've probably been at one of those year-end meetings yourself. Maybe, like the magazine publisher, a company simply suspends its customer win-back efforts temporarily – but in business today, the dilemma between the short term and the long term barely even qualifies as a dilemma.

What if you could hold businesses accountable today for all the future value they had to use up to make today's numbers? You need a workable means to measure the *total* value a business creates or destroys with its actions. Return on Customer is that metric (see "Unintended consequences" on page 20).

UNINTENDED CONSEQUENCES

Many companies have noticed a decline in their overall marketing productivity over the last decade or so. Either they have to spend more marketing money to generate the same sales results, or their response rates to traditionally strong solicitations are falling. The fact is, however, that this general decline in marketing productivity could easily be the result of their own over-solicitation of their customers, over a prolonged period of time. Their overall ROC is probably much lower than their reported profit might indicate, resulting in a steady decline in the productivity of their customer base. Their ROC may even be negative.

To model a very simple example of unintended value destruction, consider a company that has a million customers, each with a 1% likelihood of responding to a direct-mail shot. (In direct marketing, a 1% response rate is not unusual.) Let's assume that each solicitation costs £1 to send out and each positive response generates £125 in cash flow. Thus, with the first campaign the company spends £1 million on solicitations, and generates £1.25 million in cash flow, for a £250,000 profit. The firm can do up to six solicitations a year, and each campaign pulls a 1% response. In this simplified example, every customer has a 1% likelihood of responding to every campaign.

As Table 1.1 illustrates, these customers represent customer equity of £7.5 million for this firm.[3] The firm's Return on Customer remains constant in subsequent years, because it is continuing to generate a steady 1% productivity rate on these customers, year after year.

Table 1.1	Year 1	Year 2	Year 3	Year 4
Total prospects	1,000,000	1,000,000	1,000,000	1,000,000
Response rate	1.0%	1.0%	1.0%	1.0%
Cost per campaign	£1,000,000	£1,000,000	£1,000,000	£1,000,000
Cash flow per campaign	£1,250,000	£1,250,000	£1,250,000	£1,250,000
Profit per campaign	£ 250,000	£ 250,000	£ 250,000	£ 250,000
Profit per year (6 campaigns)	£1,500,000	£1,500,000	£1,500,000	£1,500,000
Year-end customer equity	£7,500,000	£7,500,000	£7,500,000	£7,500,000
Change in customer equity		£ 0	£ 0	£ 0
Total value created	£1,500,000	£1,500,000	£1,500,000	£1,500,000
Return on Customer		20.0%	20.0%	20.0%

[3] Customer equity in this example is obtained using a 20% discount rate to calculate the net present value of a £1.5 million annual future profit. (For a quick review of the principles of net-present-value discounting, see Appendix 1.)

But what if, after six unsuccessful solicitations each year, the customers were to become just slightly less likely to take the company's offer during the next year? Let's build into our model a .05% annual decline in response rate, accounted for by increased annoyance, or just lack of relevance. It's not unrealistic to imagine that customers who begin to see a company's messages as irrelevant will just stop opening them. If the annual decline were only .05%, as is shown in Table 1.2, then every year this firm would actually be *destroying* about a quarter of its customer equity – more customer equity, in fact, than it was harvesting in profit. The result: Its ROC is negative the very first year, and accelerates downward as the company continues to burn out the value of its customer base.

Table 1.2	Year 1	Year 2	Year 3	Year 4
Total customers	1,000,000	1,000,000	1,000,000	1,000,000
Response rate	1.00%	0.95%	0.90%	0.85%
Cost per campaign	£ 1,000,000	£ 1,000,000	£ 1,000,000	£ 1,000,000
Cash flow per campaign	£ 1,250,000	£ 1,187,500	£ 1,125,000	£ 1,062,500
Profit per campaign	£ 250,000	£ 187,500	£ 125,000	£ 62,500
Profit per year (6 campaigns)	£ 1,500,000	£ 1,125,000	£ 750,000	£ 375,000
Year-end customer equity	£ 7,500,000	£ 5,625,000	£ 3,750,000	£ 1,875,000
Change in customer equity		£(1,875,000)	£(1,875,000)	£(1,875,000)
Total value created	£ 1,500,000	£ (750,000)	£(1,125,000)	£(1,500,000)
Return on Customer		–10.0%	–20.0%	–40%

If you look carefully at the example in Table 1.2, you'll see that "profit per year" remains positive, although it decreases as response rates decline. Because of this, the company probably *thinks* it is creating value. But customer equity declines each year by an amount exceeding the year's "profit," with the result that "total value created" each year is actually negative. Because of this, the company's Return on Customer is negative, and while it might think it has a profit to report, it is actually eating its own customer base.

Year 4 is the very last year that the company in Table 1.2 will generate any current-period profit at all, having completely destroyed the productivity of its customer base, at least with respect to this type of campaign. Even though this is a hypothetical model, the fact is that a decline in customer response rates is a leading indicator of a general decline in the value of the customer base. If that is as far as a firm's analysis goes, however – an erosion in marketing efficiency – then it might still choose to continue with its solicitations, as long as the annual profit number is positive at all. Only by calculating Return on Customer will it actually learn that each year it is destroying more value than it is harvesting in profit.[4]

Making the jump from this firm's annual income statement to a calculation of actual value created or destroyed will be difficult. If a firm isn't measuring ROC, then value destruction can easily remain completely invisible, even to a trained accountant. An executive at this company might pat his team on the back for each of these "successful" campaigns, but in fact he should be chastising them! Shouldn't investors want to see the ROC results too?

ROC: Speedometer for organic growth

The most important and overriding financial goal for any management team should be to push the ROC speedometer to its limit, because by doing so they will be maximizing the value being created by their firm. A more ROC-efficient company will not only harvest current profits, but it will tend to conserve and replenish its stock of customer equity, as well, through investments in new-product development, customer service, relationship building, customer prioritization, retention efforts, new-customer acquisition, and so forth.

Return on Customer can be applied to a company's entire customer base, or to any subset of customers and prospective customers within it, all the way down to the molecular level of the individual customer. For whatever group ROC is applied to, a firm is creating the most overall value possible from that group of customers and prospects when ROC is at its maximum. In fact, for an operating business, Return on Customer is equivalent to Total Shareholder Return (see "Return on Customer = Total Shareholder Return" on page 23).

---

[4] This assumes, of course, that there is an alternative course of action – that is, that the firm could take some type of action to stave off the decline in response rates, once it was detected. This won't always be possible, but if the question isn't asked, then it will *never* be possible.

RETURN ON CUSTOMER = TOTAL SHAREHOLDER RETURN

"Total Shareholder Return" is a precisely defined investment term, and refers to the overall return a shareholder earns from owning a company's stock over a period of time. According to one financial authority:

Total Shareholder Return (TSR) represents the change in capital value of a listed/quoted company over a period (typically one year or longer), plus dividends, expressed as a plus or minus percentage of the opening value.

This definition is based on what a shareholder's actual cash flow would be if he were to buy the stock at the beginning of the period and sell it at the end. The shareholder gets cash dividends during the period, and by the end of the period there may also have been some up-or-down change in the capital value of the stock itself. This definition of total shareholder return relies on a retrospective calculation. As a shareholder you can always tally the exact return you experienced during some previous period, provided your share price is set by the market. (You can't use this formula to predict total shareholder return going forward, however, because you don't know what your share price is going to be in the future. Nor can you use the formula to calculate total shareholder return for a privately held firm, because if the company's shares aren't listed or quoted, then there's no easily defined share price.)

In a perfect world, a publicly-traded firm's market-driven "capital value" would equal its discounted cash flow (DCF) value. There's no way to prove or disprove this, because no one really knows what any company's discounted cash flow is going to be in the future. Nevertheless, it is widely accepted that the market price of a public company's stock at any point in time reflects the marginal investor's best guess as to the company's discounted future cash flow value. (You'll find a more extensive discussion of DCF in Appendix 1, in case you enjoy this sort of thing.)

To understand the ROC = TSR argument, all we need to do is start with the premise that all value created by any company's business operation[5] must come from its customers at some point. There are a few exceptions to this, but not many. Asset sales can create value, perhaps, but such gains aren't usually considered part of operating income – and in any case, the asset buyer could often be considered a type of "customer." Rents and royalties could also be considered to come from customers, in many cases.

If the discounted cash flow value of an operating business is created entirely by customers, then its discounted cash flow is composed of a whole lot of individual lifetime values. All the firm's current and future customer lifetime values added together (that is, its customer equity), will equal its total discounted cash flow.

---

[5] In considering a firm's "business operation" we are purposely disregarding capital structure, and thinking only of the firm's actual business, as a business.

Therefore:

Return on Customer (ROC) equals a company's current-period cash flow, plus the change in its discounted cash flow value during the period, expressed as a percentage of its beginning discounted cash flow value.

In other words, Return on Customer is simply a different route to prospective Total Shareholder Return – a method that breaks the economic value of a business down into smaller, customer-specific units, all the way down to specific, individual customers. ROC calculations don't rely on changes in share price, but if your shares are publicly traded then stock price can still provide an important additional reference point for validating your firm's total customer equity.

A final note about shareholder return: All companies have "shareholders." For a publicly traded company, shareholders are the independent and institutional investors who hold the shares. For a small company, it may be a founding entrepreneur and a partner. Whether you calculate your shareholder return in order to flesh out an SEC filing or just to decide how much everybody gets paid this year, and whether your shareholder meetings take place on the 68th floor or around the kitchen table, shareholder return is the most fundamental metric of value creation for any kind of business. Shareholder return and Return on Customer apply to every company that needs a bookkeeper.

Because ROC is a "bottom up" rather than a "top down" calculation, it is *prescriptive.* That is, some groups of customers and prospects will offer more leverage for creating value than others will. The detailed customer insights that underlie a firm's Return on Customer numbers will suggest different actions management should take with respect to creating value with these different groups.

In the final analysis, however, what it boils down to is measuring the extent to which a firm is creating *actual* value for investors with its actions. Which is more valuable – a telecom company that cuts its prices in order to hold on to the customer contracts it has, or one that produces more satisfied customers who trust its recommendations and thus tend to buy more and remain loyal? Which would you rather invest in – a commodity natural gas producer selling into a heavily competitive, deregulated market, or a natural gas producer that collaborates with its largest industrial customers to monitor and maintain their heating environments? Which would you consider to be a better long-term investment – a ferry line operating on a monopoly sea route, but with an abysmal service quality record and a host of highly dissatisfied customers, or a ferry line operating on a competitive route, but with highly satisfied customers who talk about it and frequently recommend it to others?

Using DCF analysis by itself, you'll find it difficult to discriminate among these different types of companies, even with their quite different values. But Return on Customer is a metric that can tell them apart easily.

So the point of this open letter is as follows: In the not too distant future, as you financial analysts meet with the companies you follow, ask them for more than a review of quarterly results and earnings projections for next year. Ask to see figures documenting their Return on Customer. Not only will doing this corroborate and sharpen your own analysis, but it will also directly help the companies themselves, improving their economic performance, their financial stability, and even their management culture. You'll be forcing them to be better companies.

If you're worried about how any firm can take a current measurement of increases or decreases in a customer's lifetime value, or if you're bothered by the possible costs to a company of adopting this perspective in operating its business, or even if you're just not sure what types of new and different management decisions might be made from an ROC perspective – then keep reading this book. We'll address each of these issues, and more. We're going to make the case – *really* – for building long-term, permanent value in a short-term world.

2. Maximizing the Customer Value Proposition: Building Customer Trust

Repeat after us: The only value your company will ever create is the value that comes from customers – the ones you have now, and the ones you will have in the future.

You can maximize the value your firm creates by maximizing your Return on Customer. But to increase the overall return generated by a customer (including long-term value as well as current profit) you must change the customer's behavior, creating more value than was otherwise expected. To create value, you must put yourself in the customer's shoes, understand the customer's needs, and then act accordingly. Ultimately, this requires you to earn your customer's trust.

To see why, consider your value proposition with a customer. You give the customer something of value and in exchange the customer gives you something of value. Over the long term, you can expect to receive the most value from a customer at more or less the same time that your customer is getting the most value from you. But what value does the customer get?

Obviously, product quality, price, and service all factor in to the customer's current purchase decision. But assuming you are roughly on a par with your competitors, there must be other factors as well. To maximize your Return on Customer, you must balance both the current profit from a customer and the long-term change in a customer's value. But doesn't the customer have a similar perspective, as he considers whether to do business with you both now and in the future? The customer, too, must weigh long-term as well as short-term factors, assessing the value he gets from his relationship with you. And for the customer, such a relationship will be of the most value if he feels he can trust you to respect his interests as if they were your own.

The fact is that maximizing your return on a customer and maximizing the customer's trust are quite similar tasks, because what they actually represent are two different views of the customer value proposition – your perspective and the customer's. The more a customer trusts you to act in his interest, the more overall value he will get from you, both in the current transaction, and in potential future transactions, as well.

A firm's Return on Customer is maximized at the point that the customer most trusts the firm. The only caveat to this assertion is that it presumes customers do indeed have memories that will influence their future actions. If they do, then they will balance future benefits and current benefits in a way that companies ought to do, but often don't.

Consider the alternative, however. Imagine a parallel universe in which customers have no memory. In this universe each customer engages in every business transaction in complete isolation from all other transactions. Every customer interaction is a zero-sum game in this universe, which means that you and your customer are adversaries. Your most profitable course for every transaction is to fool or trick your customer into giving you more money for less value, and the customer's most profitable course is to cheat you to the greatest extent possible. This parallel universe doesn't really exist, of course, yet companies focused exclusively on current-period profits behave as if it did. Many of them would be extremely proficient competitors in this parallel universe, if only it existed.

Companies behaving badly

To customers, the trust-eroding actions companies take in pursuit of short-term profits can often appear ridiculous, outrageous, or even hostile. Customers recognize the cynicism of a company that only sees pound signs when it is communicating with them. For instance, when was the last time you actually bought something based on a telemarketing call, even from a company you already do business with? Do you accept telemarketing calls? Do you know anyone who does? The popularity in the United States of the "Do Not Call" list is all the proof needed that this particular type of interruptive marketing is something almost universally detested.

Yet telemarketing campaigns for companies selling things such as credit cards, long-distance service, insurance, and even retailing must make some kind of economic sense on a campaign-by-campaign basis, or legitimate companies and nonprofit fund-raisers wouldn't go to the expense and trouble of making the calls. It might fly in the face of common sense, but it must be the case that a company's calculation of the profit it makes on the services it sells, compared to the cost of making the outbound calls, yields a positive return. Surely, however, the sheer resentment of masses of consumers – including, in many cases, a firm's current customers – must count for something? *Could the company's economic calculations be wrong?* Could it be that the company is focused too much on short-term profits?

The simple fact is that all sorts of companies behave exactly as if they inhabited that parallel universe, where customers have no memories, and transactions have no consequences other than current-period profits. History shows that when a company's obsession with current-period results penetrates into its culture, customer interests usually come in a distant second, and trust recedes beyond the horizon.

In September 2004 Japan's Financial Services Agency ordered Citigroup to close its four private banking offices in that country, following an investigation into problems that included possible money laundering, stock manipulation, and misleading investors. The agency said that Citigroup had exploited their 5,000 well-heeled Japanese private banking clients by suggesting unrealistic returns, urging them to buy complicated derivative products they didn't understand, over-charging, and even pushing second-rate art as an investment. This was in the wake of other problems investigated earlier at the private banking offices, including the unexplained loss of a substantial amount of credit card, banking and investment transaction data. While the effect on Citigroup's earnings is expected to be miniscule – less than 0.5% – Merrill Lynch nevertheless downgraded the firm's stock because "Citigroup might lack something that poses a threat to its future growth: a sense of right and wrong." The bank is reeling from a series of scandals worldwide, including controversial work it did with Enron, WorldCom, and Parmalat, the Italian dairy giant. *The Wall Street Journal* reported that the Japanese investigation "portrayed a culture that tolerated lax practices and suspicious transactions linked to possible criminal activity by clients as long as aggressive business targets were met." And according to the *Japan Times*,

> "As to why Citibank made such repeated abuses, the official said New York headquarters imposed unrealistically high targets for private banking operations in Japan. The bank tied salaries closely to sales performance, giving incentive to managers and employees to break rules if it meant large profits."

Of course, this kind of toxic behavior makes headlines when it surfaces at an otherwise respected, global corporation. But an obsession with short-term results will endanger customer service and destroy value at any business where it's allowed to reign unchecked. A friend recently bought a used DVD for $8 from the chain of video-rental stores where she had shopped frequently for several years, spending perhaps $20 a month on average. The DVD came with a lifetime guarantee against performance failure, and she gave it to her daughter for Christmas. Upon viewing, however, the product had several shifts and jitters in it, so she returned it to the store for a replacement. She was told she had to have the original receipt – a receipt that had also offered a "free rental" coupon, which she had cashed in some weeks earlier. Even after the store manager got involved, pulled up her electronic record, and acknowledged to her face that she had in fact purchased the DVD from his store, she was still refused the exchange without the original receipt.

The result was she left the store angry, vowing never to return. Obviously, this company operated in the parallel universe of isolated transactions, and in this universe they triumphed in this particular transaction. But in the real world, where the company's urge to improve revenues and reduce costs should be balanced against the equally important goal of protecting and increasing the overall value of their customer base, they failed. To make $8.00 in the current period, they lost the business of this $240-per-year customer. Short-term concerns destroy value in a measurable way. If the only thing you're measuring and rewarding is the short term, you and your employees may never know how much value you are destroying.

One American-based Internet service provider heavily advertised a flat $23.99 per month for unlimited access to their network of services. But overcharging is rampant, and this company's customers have learned to count their change when dealing with them. One subscriber was charged several hundred dollars in just three months, because one of his children had subscribed the family to what he thought was a lower cost plan involving a smaller monthly fee. However, it involved a high per-minute usage charge as well, so with a cable modem and several active computers in the house the average monthly bill came to nearly $200. When the subscriber called this to the company's attention, however, he was offered one month "free service" – total value, $23.99. The "service" rep reminded the subscriber that his own family had chosen the plan, disadvantageous as it was for them, and at one point asked him, "What are we, your accountants?" Later, the subscriber ran into a colleague who had had a similar experience and not long after that another and another. Oddly, in each case the company's reps had used nearly identical language. Clearly, this company has had considerable experience dealing with this problem. They like it best when customers don't notice; but even when they do, they still keep the cash.

Operating by "The Goldfish Principle"

It is surprising how often the managers at otherwise competent firms behave as if they operated in a parallel universe of isolated transactions and amnesiac customers. In the real world, however, it is usually the company that retains no memory of its customers.

There is a species of tropical fish with no territorial memory. Perhaps this is because the fish usually inhabits the open sea, where territory is not very important, but the fact is that no matter where this fish swims, it never recognizes it has swum there before. One can imagine such a fish swimming around and around in a goldfish bowl, but never getting bored. There is always something new to see. As ridiculous as it sounds, the Goldfish Principle actually applies to a lot of businesses – companies that fail to recognize their regular customers no matter how often these customers appear. Operating by the Goldfish Principle undermines even the best effort a company makes to cultivate customer trust.

Joe Pine, co-author of *The Experience Economy*, once had a four-day stay booked at a business hotel in Atlanta. As he retired the first evening, he called the front desk to ask for a wake-up call, and was greeted with a "special offer" for the hotel's high-value business guests. He was asked if he would like a complimentary coffee and newspaper brought to his room in the morning. He preferred tea. "No problem," said the desk clerk, "and would he like the *New York Times* or the *Atlanta Journal-Constitution*?" "Well," he asked, "could you bring the *Wall Street Journal*?" "Sure," she said. In the morning everything went well, just as requested. The second night, Mr. Pine called the desk to arrange another wake-up call, and the clerk informed him once more of the "special offer" for high-value business guests. "Would he like a complimentary coffee in the morning?" "No," he said, he'd like tea. "Fine," came the reply, "and would he rather have the *New York Times* or the *Atlanta Journal-Constitution*?" The third and fourth nights it was the same story.

So, from the customer's own point of view, what exactly was "special" about this hotel's "special offer?" This effort was well-intended and designed to provide good "customer service," but absolutely no relationship value. One more company swimming around and around in a goldfish bowl full of apparently new customer opportunities.

On one level, this kind of problem obviously indicates a failure of coordination and execution at a company. But at a deeper level, it also erodes a customer's trust. The message to this customer was that while the hotel might value his patronage each night, it didn't value its relationship with him enough to remember him from one night to the next. There's an advantage to the hotel for the customer to spend all four nights in Atlanta in their hotel. There would be an advantage to the hotel if he came back to that hotel again and again. But there's no advantage to the customer to give the hotel all his business, and he knows it.

The profit snatchers

"Old marketing" is based on the Goldfish Principle. Before computer databases, companies all behaved like the Atlanta hotel, remaining oblivious with respect to their customers as individuals. When a firm has no awareness or memory of individual customers, however, it is not only incapable of delivering any kind of truly personalized service, but it will also be blind to the impact its actions have on a particular customer's future behavior. With no customer memory, each customer transaction appears to be an isolated event, and a firm is incapable of focusing on the overall return it generates on any customer.

Even sophisticated, "new marketing" companies often appear unaware of their customers – the very customers identified in great detail within their own customer databases. Consider America Online, for instance. Anyone who has ever tried to discontinue an AOL subscription can probably tell a good story about how difficult it is. Getting the company on the phone at all is difficult enough, but it frequently then takes a half hour or longer to terminate service. One subscriber complained about having the AOL service rep trying to talk him into continuing his brother's AOL account after he called to report his brother had *died*!

In the short term, perhaps this type of policy generates a bit of extra profit, but it can hardly be healthy for the firm's long-term business prospects. Customer antipathy toward AOL is the stuff of legend. You can easily verify this with a Web search for how many red-faced complainers different Internet firms have. A Yahoo! search for "AOL sucks" generates 26,500 hits – roughly ten times as many hits as there are for "Google sucks" (1,860), or MSN (2,180), or Yahoo! (2,990). AOL is even 50% higher on this scale than "Microsoft sucks" (15,200 hits), even though Microsoft dwarfs AOL in size and is not particularly renowned itself for customer-centricity.

Nevertheless, AOL's attitude towards customers is not unique. Many companies play "finders' keepers" with their customers' money. Some airlines display this attitude when it comes to e-tickets, for instance. Have you ever tried to get an e-refund for an e-ticket you didn't use? It's not easy – most airlines make you show a paper receipt for the charge from your credit card company before they'll issue the credit. A business colleague called a major American carrier to ask for a refund on an e-ticket he hadn't used. His evidence for the fact that it was an unused ticket was that he had boarded a different flight *on that same airline* at the time he was supposed to have used the e-ticket. Amazingly, the carrier demanded $100 to "research" the problem before they would issue a refund. James Schwartz, owner of Windsor Travel in Houston, says the airlines make a lot of money on the expiration of e-tickets that are never used. "You'd be amazed at how much revenue that represents." We had a meeting not too long ago with a top airline executive who told us that his company estimated that unused (and probably forgotten) e-tickets would total an amount roughly equal to 5% of his company's operating profit that year.

Many firms – even firms with vast customer databases that give them a perspective beyond isolated transactions – are intently focused on what they can get from customers today, this minute. Such firms pay little attention to the value they might give to customers, and act as if they were completely unaware of the value these same customers might yield for them tomorrow, or the day after. A 1998 article in *Harvard Business Review* challenged businesses to remember, "There's a balance between giving and getting in a good relationship." According to one of the consumers interviewed for the article, the net effect of all the phone calling, letter writing, and solicitation that companies do is all one way:

> "Sure, they can call me at dinner, but I can't reach them on the phone. They can send me 100 pieces of mail per year, but I can't register one meaningful response with them. You really want to be my friend? Sure you do..."

At a 2004 conference on customer relationship management, more than one presenter acknowledged that while sophisticated customer databases were now making it possible to offer the "next most likely" product to individual customers, the customers themselves were proving increasingly difficult to sell to. Customers just do not want to be solicited every time they call in for some routine action, such as activating a new credit card or inquiring about a bill. Customers call to get their problems solved, but the firms they contact are using their "customer insights" not just to solve problems but to extract more and more revenue, sooner and sooner, more and more aggressively.

Most marketing and customer-relationship professionals analyze customer data primarily in order to quantify individual customer *values*, so they can improve the efficiency of their firms' marketing efforts. For the most part, today's marketers are not very concerned with understanding their customers' needs, or with seeing the value proposition from the customer's perspective. Rather, they want to identify their most valuable customers and "target" them for more intensive marketing efforts.

The problem is that when a firm focuses solely on customer valuations it is taking a highly self-oriented approach; it is analyzing how a customer can provide value to the firm, rather than how the firm can provide value to the customer. This point of view actually encourages the kind of trust-eroding activities that plague businesses desperate to produce short-term revenue gains. Consider an article in London's *Sunday Times* entitled "Are You a Second Class Consumer?"

> "Some of the country's biggest companies are using postcodes to single out customers on the basis of their wealth when they contact call centres. Sophisticated technology automatically 'recognises' consumers when they call, and then diverts their inquiry to specially trained workers authorised to give better deals to wealthier clients. Poorer customers are made to wait in queues and may have their calls answered by automated computer systems."

Businesses are portrayed as manipulative and cynical, exploiting the differences between customers' financial conditions just to sell more stuff and cut their own costs. The article implies that an even more insidious aspect of this practice is the fact that it occurs behind the scenes, without the customer's knowledge.

Firms that flunk the trust test generally do so because they do not have a culture based on taking the customer's point of view – they do not try to see things from the customer's perspective. Sometimes a firm's brand will command the respect of its managers, who will work hard to maintain its credibility. But too many companies cave in to the demand for short-term results, becoming obsessed with current revenues, no matter what the cost is in terms of customer good will or long-term enterprise value. Executives at such companies let the service department worry about complaints. They're busy making money here. In effect, what they are doing is strip-mining their customer bases for quick sales and short-term gains, with little apparent regard for the future value of their customers. Why should they be worried about their customers' future value? By the time the damage shows up in the form of reduced profit, they'll have collected their bonuses and be long gone. No one is holding them accountable *today* for eroding the company's future value.

If a firm were truly aware of the value a customer might actually generate in the future, in addition to the customer's current profit, it would take a different approach altogether. Instead of maximizing short-term sales in a parallel universe of isolated transactions, such a firm would want to maximize the overall value generated by each customer, including not just the customer's current purchases but also his future transactions as well. The overall customer value proposition is at its maximum when the customer actually trusts the firm to respect his interests.

The opposite of self-orientation

Customer trust is easily broken. But it is not easily earned. The secret to earning a customer's trust is to see the situation from the customer's perspective. You will need to treat the customer the way you yourself would want to be treated if you were the customer. This will ensure the customer gets the most possible value from your firm, and that you will therefore get the most value from the customer, over time.

More than this, *everyone* at your company must embrace this mission. Every interaction with a customer – every conceivable point of contact between the customer and the enterprise – should not only maximize Return on Customer, but also reinforce the customer's faith that his or her own interests are being considered first. This requires developing an employee culture focused on watching out for the interests of customers and clients.

Charles Green, co-author of *The Trusted Advisor*, maintains that a customer's likelihood of developing a trusting relationship with a company is a function of four different characteristics of a business – credibility, reliability, intimacy, and self-orientation. Credibility has to do with a company's reputation for telling the truth, or being accurate in its statements to and interactions with the customer. Reliability refers to actions, rather than statements. A reliable company is one that will do what it is supposed to do. Green relates intimacy to safety, security or integrity. An intimate company is one that will keep important personal information secure and private, for instance. The more credible, reliable, and intimate a company is, the more likely a customer will be to trust it.

The most important factor in Green's evaluation of trust, however, has to do with what he calls the firm's "self-orientation." The more self-oriented a firm is, the less likely a customer will be to trust it. A self-oriented firm is one that a consumer is likely to view as greedy, sneaky, or devious. "They are just telling me this because they want me to buy their product…" It is interesting that self-orientation is exactly the attitude one senses in a company that is not paying attention to the long-term value of its customers, but instead is trying to take as much revenue from them as possible, as quickly as it can. Self-orientation is what drives a company to call you during the dinner hour.

In September 1982, a number of bottles of Tylenol pain reliever were tampered with and laced with cyanide, resulting in seven deaths. Johnson & Johnson heard the news and immediately yanked its Tylenol product off store shelves everywhere – approximately 31 million bottles in all. They didn't weigh the loss of profit against the loss of life, making this $100 million decision in a matter of moments. Tylenol's share of the $1.2 billion market for over-the-counter analgesics fell from 37% to 7% following the poisonings, but recovered to 30% within six months, and within a year it had again become the leading pain reliever.

James E. Burke, J&J's CEO during the crisis, put it succinctly: "To me, the old saw is correct, that doing good is good business." Burke recognized the critical role of trust: "The company over 100 years had developed a trusting relationship with the public… Trust is basically what all good trademarks are about."

Trust is hard to establish when a firm is perceived as being highly self-oriented. One could argue that, for corporations as well as for humans, the opposite of self-orientation is simply a concern for others – epitomized by the principle of reciprocity, which is a vital part of every major ethical philosophy and religion. In Christianity the reciprocity principle is popularly known as "the Golden Rule" – treating others the way you yourself would want to be treated.

Robert McDermott, the former CEO of USAA, the direct-writing insurance company with legendary customer service, credits his mutual insurance company's success to what he calls the firm's "Golden Rule" of customer service:

> "Treat the customer the way you would want to be treated if you were the customer."

According to McDermott, this was the mantra for employees that enabled the firm to employ new processes, technologies and training in order to upgrade itself dramatically from the bureaucratic, inefficient and inattentive company that it once was.

More than simply a slogan, this mantra became the basis for an entire employee culture at USAA. No one got fired for taking the customer's point of view in this way. It became *everyone's* job, and the result was not just that earning customer trust was a corporate objective; it became the company culture.

USAA, of course, has now become a virtual icon of good customer service, studied around the world as a best practice. A 2004 Forrester survey of 6,000 North American households found USAA at the top of the list in terms of something they called "customer advocacy," defined by Forrester as "the perception by customers that a firm is doing what's best for them and not just for the firm's bottom line." The research firm maintains that customer advocacy, as they measured it in this survey, is "the best indicator of whether financial services companies are able to achieve cross-sell success to a customer base...Firms that score highest on the customer advocacy scale, such as USAA and Edward Jones, are considered the most for future purchases of products and services."

It is important to recognize that "reciprocity" does not require giving products away at a loss and surrendering self interest. The opposite of self-orientation is not self-destructiveness. Rather, it simply means being fair and honest with the customer, and looking out for the customer's interests in much the same way as you would look out for your own. USAA customers often swap stories of how the company has saved them money by suggesting a less expensive insurance policy or financial product than they had been prepared to commit to. But the company gets more than this value back in the form of increased cross selling, customer loyalty, word-of-mouth referrals, and honest claims (reduced cost to serve), not to mention second- and third-generation customers.

Of course, this doesn't even count the immense benefit USAA must enjoy as a more productive, less stressful place to work, because the customer service reps who answer the phones can concentrate on helping their customers, rather than worrying about how to play "finders' keepers" with their customers' money. Just think about how different it must be to work in the USAA call center, compared to the AOL call center. Which employees feel better about their company and the work they do each day? Which employees take the most delight in a "job well done"? Is it more fun, day in and day out, to say, "Let's see how I can help you," or to have to delay an account cancellation even when it involves the death of a caller's loved one?

Trustworthy executives pay off on the bottom line. Hotels where employees strongly believed their managers followed through on promises and demonstrated the values they preached were substantially more profitable than those whose managers scored average or lower. So strong was the link, in fact, that a one-eighth point improvement in a hotel manager's score on the five-point scale could be expected to increase the hotel's profitability by 2.5% of revenues – representing, in this study, a profit increase of more than $250,000 per year per hotel.

Taking the customer's point of view

Seeing things from the customer's perspective – that is, seeing your own company and its offerings through the eyes of the customer – is a prerequisite for motivating customers to change their behaviors. This is what USAA, J&J, and other highly trustworthy companies have done. Any company that seeks to earn the genuine trust of its customers will focus its employees and partners on this same customer perspective, and it is the most important aspect of a firm's customer "orientation." Earning and keeping the trust of customers is tantamount to taking the customer's point of view.

Such an effort will manifest itself as a constant, unrelenting and pervasive need for you to get into the customer's own head, to see things through the customer's own eyes, to put yourself in the customer's position, and to treat the customer the same way you'd want to be treated. Companies that create lasting, permanent value for their shareholders take this customer-oriented perspective seriously. At Tesco, the highly successful grocery retailer with a sophisticated customer database and detailed shopping records for more than 13 million consumers, "Creating value for customers to earn their lifetime loyalty" is part of the employee mission statement, and every customer-facing employee wears a button that says "No one tries harder for customers." A.G. Edwards' mantra is "We treat our clients the way you want to be treated," and Intel deliberately tried to make its website reflect the company's commitment to trustworthiness, with measurable success.

Companies in a variety of industries are searching for ways to earn their customers' trust by taking customer interests objectively to heart. In 2003 General Motors launched a pilot program to test the feasibility of winning customer trust by providing car shoppers with information and help – not only for GM brands, but for competitive brands as well. One aspect of this pilot program involved creating a new website, AutoChoiceAdvisor.com, designed to give customers objective advice on the type of car that is right for them – from all different brands and makes, not just GM. According to Glen Urban, professor of marketing and director of e-business at MIT, and principal of the MIT/GM customer relationship management project, the website is completely unbiased in its recommendations. It "includes all vehicles and uses an impartial algorithm to look for the best car for you."

One obvious benefit of the site for GM is that it will give the company better insight into customer preferences (including those that sometimes lead customers to choose non-GM brands), enabling GM executives to develop new products and design new cars to address more specific customer needs. The company followed the launch of this website with a car show that allowed more than 100,000 consumers to test drive not just General Motors cars but also BMW, Ford, Volvo, and other brands.

What is the goal of all this activity? According to Urban, it can be summed up in one word: Trust. "Consumers need to trust their vehicles and, by extension, the makers of those vehicles," according to Urban. "GM argues that only honesty and good products will build trust. Customers will find out about non-GM cars regardless of what GM does. The best it can hope for is a fair comparison." This is the practical element in GM's logic. The automaker knows that consumers will explore different brands anyway. So why not facilitate a process that is going to occur anyway, and in effect be "present" for a greater portion of the customer's overall shopping experience, with the opportunity to get smarter? GM is simply acknowledging what should have been obvious all along: Providing good service to customers will, in the end, create good value for the enterprise.

When a company thinks it *isn't* in its own interest to provide such good, objective service, then what is the firm really saying? That it prefers to take revenue from unknowledgeable customers before they acquire enough information to make more intelligent decisions? That its business model depends on customers who don't make smart decisions? Many firms do in fact behave as if the most attractive customers for them would be the same as the most lucrative marketing segment in the Dilbert cartoon strip, the "stupid rich." In the short term, this might be a profitable tactic, but in the long term a company will find it probably uses up more value from its customers than it creates.

If we want to take our customer's point of view, we must look at the situation from the standpoint of meeting the customer's need, rather than simply expounding on our product's benefits or attributes. The customer will not limit his field of view to our product lineup or brand. If we don't provide service by helping customers to learn not just about our products but also about the whole variety of ways they can address their needs, then we are simply hiding our heads in the sand and hoping our customers will join us there, at least long enough to give us their money. To take the customer's point of view means to look outside our own product offering, because that is how the customer will approach the problem. It's the difference between "selling something" and growing our firm in a sustainable way by maximizing Return on Customer.

It is not as easy as it sounds, however, to treat customers fairly and to be seen as doing so. Sometimes, companies have complicated business models, and their business processes can pose direct challenges to earning customer trust. Consider the airline business, for instance. Most air travelers see airlines as highly self-oriented, partly on account of their complex and hard-to-understand pricing policies. But airlines need pricing flexibility in order to deal rationally with the perishable nature of their inventory (not to mention the perishable nature of their corporate existence). Airlines have an extremely high ratio of fixed-to-variable costs. An airline seat flying empty is revenue lost forever, yet it actually costs very little for a carrier to accommodate one additional passenger in that empty seat.

So over the last couple of decades airlines have honed the science of revenue management to a mathematically fine point. As the reservations clock ticks down for any particular flight, the airline's computers constantly evaluate the ups and downs and ebbs and flows of demand for that and similar flights, comparing new reservations made to the empty seats remaining on the plane. As the flight comes closer to departure, the airline's goal is to eliminate the deepest discount seats first, and then the next level of discounts, and so on, in order to capture gradually higher revenues from last-minute air travelers who are probably flying on business and likely to be schedule dependent. Flights for which a higher demand is predicted are not allotted as many low-fare seats to begin with, so that the heavily advertised low fares typically are just not available at peak times.

The airlines figure that if price is the most important factor for a traveler, then the traveler's schedule will be more flexible. If schedule is more important than price, then they want to charge for it. When this system is combined with tariff rules for discount fares that require Saturday night stays, refund limitations, advance purchase and other restrictions, the overall effect is to fill the plane with passengers who have paid many different fares and who are subject to many different restrictions. There is nothing overtly wrong or even sneaky about this type of pricing, which is all pretty much above board. Revenue management simply allows an airline to optimize the revenue on any given flight.

To passengers, however, airline pricing can often seem so complex that they simply don't understand whether they're being treated fairly or not. When they book their flight they ask for the lowest fare and they accept the refund restrictions and other conditions in order to get it. But sometimes, because a flight is still empty just a week or so prior to departure, the airline's revenue management system will inject a quantity of deep-discount seats to try to stimulate demand, which means that the passenger who booked a non-refundable fare earlier might now be able to get a lower fare, or travel on the flight he originally wanted, if only the airline would let him alter his ticket.

Airlines deal with this problem in a number of ways. The completely self-oriented action is to promote a low-fare offering heavily, sell it to as many customers as will buy it, and then offer an even lower fare closer in to departure, in order to fill the plane. While this appears quite cynical on the airline's part, it is in fact the practice of at least a few airlines. But even if the initial low fare (later to be undercut) is not specifically advertised or promoted, reducing the fare at a later point to fill a plane at the last minute might still seem unfair to many of the early planners, unless the last-minute fares have some significant and rather onerous extra conditions.

A random check of airline reservations policies quoted over the phone will show that some airlines automatically issue travel vouchers (usually valid for one year) to refund the fare difference to you when they lower the fare on a flight you've already booked, while other airlines refund the difference only if you call their attention to it. What is clear, however, is that this type of pricing complexity makes earning the customer's trust more difficult.

Ironically, despite the pricing complexity, most established airlines still seem to have one foot in the bankruptcy court. As one marketing expert put it:

> "This still doesn't make for a profitable airline industry! In other words, the average fare is too low, but at the same time, the customer doesn't feel he's getting good value. An anomaly like this can only occur when computers, not people, are making the decisions."

Low-cost, discount carriers such as Southwest Airlines, JetBlue, and easyJet use capacity controls and revenue management also, but they don't use these tools with nearly the level of complexity that the major carriers employ. Moreover, many of the new entrants get most of their reservations online, where they can display an array of flights at one time, with different pricing for different schedules, depending on the demand they are experiencing. Some step their prices up at regular intervals, as each flight gets closer to departure. Some require customers to purchase their tickets within a few days of making their reservations – not just discount tickets, but all tickets, because these are discount airlines.

The methods vary, but a common thread seems to be that a simpler pricing structure helps customers understand – and trust – the airline more. This accords perfectly with what Forrester's survey found with respect to financial services firms. The best, most successful firms opt for simplicity and straightforwardness in all aspects of their dealings with customers:

> "To broaden their customer relationships, firms need to simplify customers' lives and be transparent about rates and fees…USAA scored highest in our ranking, in part, because of its focus on simplifying customers' lives through efficient call center experiences. Many large banks, on the other hand, are at the bottom of our ranking because many of their customers feel nickel-and-dimed."

Earning customer trust breeds a more ethical organization

So why take the customer's point of view? Because trust is more than a fine and wonderful thing. You can measure the ways customer trust creates value for your business, in terms of revenue, cost, production, logistics, payroll and all the rest of it. Yes, the good guys *can* win in the end.

When you create a culture in which employees constantly try to see things from the customer's perspective, putting themselves in the customer's shoes, treating customers the way they themselves would prefer to be treated if they were customers – this is the kind of culture that will maximize your value to customers, which is the best way to maximize their value to you.

A culture of customer trust is also more satisfying to employees. In a 2004 magazine interview, Jeffrey Immelt, the Chairman and CEO of General Electric, said four things would keep GE on top: execution, growth, great people, and virtue. Virtue is not the type of thing most CEO's would place in a checklist of corporate success criteria, but Immelt says the people who work for GE do so because:

> "…they want to be about something that is bigger than themselves. People want to work hard, they want to get promoted, they want stock options. But they also want to work for a company that makes a difference, a company that's doing great things in the world."

People want to work for a virtuous company – a company that can be trusted. Employees don't want to be ashamed of what they do at work. They don't want to have to justify their own business-oriented actions in some kind of complicated moral calculus. Return on Customer, as a metric of success, can bridge the gap between achieving financial success and keeping the trust of customers.

Over and above the economics of Return on Customer, however, this kind of corporate culture will help your firm deal with the most difficult corporate governance issues a company can face. Suppose your senior management were to become corrupted in some way, even though it presided over a corporate culture based on earning customer trust. Suppose, for instance, that a new senior manager got nervous about the stock price and tried to deceive investors by creating a series of fictitiously "independent" financial entities. Or suppose someone at your firm were to devise a scheme for driving up profits by rigging the market with fictitious buying and selling transactions. These are not far-fetched possibilities. History has shown that obsessing on current results can result in, well, criminal behavior.

But if your employee culture were based on earning the trust of customers, then even the CEO and his direct reports would have difficulty implementing such a deception. If everyone's success depends on building customer value, and building customer value depends on operating in a trustworthy way and being straight with customers, it would be hard to scrape out the lining of the retirement fund or pollute the environment, either. Your own corporate culture would produce antibodies to resist this type of cancer. So focusing on building customer value can serve the best interests of the company even as it serves the best interests of the customers, the shareholders, and the employees.

In an article that attempted to analyze the Enron betrayal of trust, Charles Green explains the economics of trust, and betrayal, this way:

> "For the last five decades, most thinkers have described business success in terms of competition. We talk about market share and competitive advantage, we use dozens of sports metaphors – all about winning and losing. The other line of thought – serving customers – has never had the intellectual cachet or hot press of the competition model.... But the truth is, the customer service model is more profoundly right than the competitive model. For economists, the role of competition is to improve value to the customer. For business people, the only guaranteed way to win against competitors is to do a better job serving customers. In both views, customer acceptance is the cause; competitive success is the second-order effect."

The contrast in attitude between a customer-oriented firm and a noncustomer-oriented firm is in most cases obvious and easily recognizable. It does not depend on a company motto or slogan or advertising pitch. Customer orientation is either central to a firm's cultural DNA, or it isn't. A customer orientation manifests itself in the desire, on the part of everyone in an organization, to take the customer's own perspective – to see things through the customer's eyes, and to earn and deserve the customer's trust. In the next chapter, we'll show you how to build your company's value by putting customers first.

3. Building the Firm's Value by Taking the Customer's Perspective

Understanding what customers need from you – figuring out what motivates your customers – is a boardroom issue, because it is vital to your firm's long-term success. If you want to change the customer's behavior take the customer's perspective. It's why your customer will trust you, and it's how you will increase your Return on Customer.

Taking the customer's perspective creates shareholder value

In many industries, customer-oriented firms are seen to secure a competitive advantage, especially in service businesses, and this competitive advantage can easily translate not only into higher earnings, but into a higher price/earnings ratio for a company's stock as well.

A recent *Fortune* article pointed out that customer-centric firms such as Dell, Royal Bank of Canada, and Best Buy concentrate on raising their "returns on specific customer segments." The article went on to say that this results in a "re-rating" of a company's P/E ratio, as the financial community "decides that the company can sustain [its] profit growth for years into the future." The combination of increased earnings and increased stock rating can catapult such firms' stock prices upwards. This isn't about "marketing." It's about your company's ability to succeed and grow.

We've written extensively about both Dell and Royal Bank of Canada before, but Best Buy's more recently launched "customer centricity" effort is worth a quick summary. Among other things, Best Buy trained its store-level employees to recognize and think about the different needs of five types of highly valuable customers, encouraging all store personnel to be proactive in their efforts to satisfy them:

- affluent professionals, who want the best technology and entertainment experience and who demand excellent service
- focused, active, younger males who want the latest technology and entertainment
- family men who want technology to improve their lives – practical adopters of technology and entertainment
- busy suburban moms who want to enrich their children's lives with technology and entertainment
- small-business customers who can use Best Buy's product solutions and services to enhance the profitability of their businesses.

After a successful pilot project involving 32 stores, the company began rolling its customer-centricity initiative out to an additional 110 stores, leading Best Buy to forecast an earnings increase for the following year in the 15% to 20% range.

A UBS analyst's report praising Best Buy's initiative suggests that it should provide the firm with "stronger financial results" as the company refines and improves its program; a "better defense against competitors" in the category; and "less cyclical results," as more stable relationships with high-value customers counteract shifts in general consumer spending and demand for consumer electronics.

The UBS report also notes that employee empowerment is crucial to the success of Best Buy's program:

> "Best Buy empowers its store level employees, those individuals closest to its customers, to tweak merchandising, store signage, store layout, etc., to best appeal to [particular customers]."

For example, the analyst reports that a Pasadena store employee explained how store-level associates had suggested a reconfiguration of the store to better appeal to suburban moms, moving small appliances down onto a low rack along the store's main walkway, rather than leaving them stocked on higher shelves among the major appliances. According to the report, "sales of small appliances skyrocketed to well into double-digit gains from moderately negative." The report continues:

> "The employees in the appliance department...next plan to create displays that showcase items such as refrigerators, stoves, and washers and dryers in home-like settings along the perimeter of the appliance department [and] to develop a child play area...so that customers have a way to entertain their kids..."

Best Buy's customer-centricity initiative is based on seeing its business from the customer's perspective, understanding customer needs, and then taking the initiative to meet those needs. The reason Wall Street analysts like the initiative is that it has shown remarkable power when it comes to driving the company's financial results. The company says the stores included in the pilot project have seen a gain in comparable-store sales more than twice that of other American Best Buy stores and a gross profit rate higher by about 0.5% of revenue.

According to Brad Anderson, vice chairman and CEO of Best Buy, customer centricity is now viewed as a core competency that the company wants to develop, and not "an end in itself." Commenting on the firm's quarterly results, Anderson said "The beauty of our customer-centricity work is how it enhances our operational excellence, our ability to turn talent into performance, and our strength in building brands. We believe that if we succeed in linking those capabilities, we will clearly differentiate Best Buy from our competitors." Key to Best Buy's financial success, in other words, is its ability to see things from the customer's perspective. At least that seems to be the CEO's view, as well as Wall Street's view.

Ready, fire, aim

Still, it is extremely difficult for most companies to see their value proposition from the customer's perspective, rather than from their own. Usually, when companies launch initiatives or undertake major programs designed to put customers first, or to increase customer service levels, or to cultivate long-term customer relationships, they fall short because they focus first on the customer's value to the enterprise, rather than the enterprise's value to the customer. But this is looking at the value proposition from your own point of view, not your customer's. It is a "ready, fire, aim" approach to customer centricity.

No matter how accurately you discern the nuances of a customer's value to you, you can only influence the customer's behavior by understanding your value to the customer. Trying to figure out how to generate economic results by analyzing the customer's value is simply looking through the wrong end of the telescope. Customers rarely know or care what their value is to you.[1] They just want to have their problems solved and their needs met, and every customer will have a slightly different twist on what he or she needs, how your product or service can satisfy that need, and how important it is to do so.

The problem is that customer needs are difficult to understand and complicated to deal with. Moreover, customer needs are dynamic, rather than fixed. Consumers are changeable creatures. Lives evolve from one stage to another; they move from place to place, they change their fickle minds. Business customers also evolve, adopting new strategies, switching out managers, and facing new competitive situations. And a customer's needs at a particular point may be based on a situation or mode of purchase. For example, even the most frequent business traveler will occasionally be traveling for leisure, and will have different needs than when traveling for business.

As a starting premise, it's important to distinguish between your customer's need and your product's attribute or feature. Companies create products and services with different features specifically designed to satisfy particular customer needs, but the features themselves are not equivalent to needs. In fact, different customers often want the same attribute or feature in order to satisfy very different individual needs. One person might buy a high-performance car, for instance, because he wants to drive fast, while another might buy the same high-performance car because he wants people to think he drives fast.

In addition, you have to constantly remind yourself that because customers are different, understanding what the average customer needs is not the same as figuring out what a *particular* customer needs.

---

[1] Exceptions to this general rule include very powerful customers, such as Wal-Mart or GM or Microsoft, and consumers involved in loyalty programs, such as airline frequent flyers.

When you focus on products and brands, you're concerned with identifying the needs that your most valuable customers have in common. But today's market segmentation analyses have become so sophisticated, you can easily be lulled into thinking you understand your "customers," when what you really want is to understand *each* customer. Yes, in a practical sense you will end up doing the same thing for a lot of different customers, but never forget that changing an individual customer's behavior requires appealing to *that* customer's motivation, which may or may not be the same as the "typical" customer. (We'll discuss customer differentiation in greater detail in Chapter 5.)

Customer motivations are much more complex – much harder to dissect – than customer valuations. Customer value is complicated enough. You run tens of millions of data points through your analytics program, or you subject your sales staff to a ten-page questionnaire to assess each and every current and prospective account, and you come up with a gradually improving set of ever-more-accurately-weighted variables to quantify your customers' lifetime values. But at least you are dealing in economic terms: pounds and pence, dollars and cents, euros or yen. Customer value is essentially a one-dimensional variable.

Customer needs, on the other hand, are a completely different and more complex variable altogether. There are as many varieties of customer motivations as there are observers to catalogue them. For consumers, there are deeply held beliefs, psychological predispositions, life stages, moods and modes, aspirations and fears. Consumers will know some of their needs, and be unaware of others. For business customers there are differences in business objectives and competitive strategy, collegial versus hierarchical decision-making styles, cultural and organizational differences, and a variety of planning horizons. Then we also have to consider the individual roles and motivations of the players within a business customer's organization, including decision makers, approvers, specifiers, reviewers, end users and others involved in shaping the customer's behavior.

Of course, each of these business-to-business actors may also be a consumer, outside of his business role. The VP Finance who approves a corporate energy-use contract may also buy her household's electricity from the same energy firm. The CIO who specifies the servers to be bought may have a PC at home from one of the computer companies competing for the contract. In dual roles, the same person will have a unique set of experiences, expectations and unconscious preferences in his relationship with your company, as well as in his relationships with your competitors.

Nevertheless, as complex as it can be, taking your customer's perspective is the true secret to changing his future behavior. Linking customer lifetime values with the needs-based drivers of those lifetime values is critical. Motivations and needs are key to behavior change, and so they are key to value creation. There are many factors at work in creating enterprise value but, all other things being equal, the more insight you have with respect to your customers' needs, the higher return you should be able to generate from them.

What business are you in...*really?*

It's also possible, however, that taking the customer's perspective will actually call into question some of the most basic elements of your company's mission, at least as you conceived it before. It could actually lead you to rethink the nature of your whole business.

If customers are your scarcest resource, then the more value you can create from each one, the more your business will be worth. Adding a service or product to an existing configuration, in order to meet the customer's need more completely, is one way to increase the return on that customer. The only caveat is that any new offering should be made in a way that reinforces your basic competitive strategy and doesn't undercut whatever structural advantage you may enjoy (more about this in Chapter 7).

Consider the Dutch natural gas utility Eneco Energie, for example. In a deregulated market this company sells a commodity product subject to brutal price competition – a truly bleak business, with low margins and little opportunity to create value. If a new entrant, unhampered by fixed infrastructure costs and union contracts, were to appear on the scene, an incumbent like Eneco would be facing a natural exodus of its biggest customers, all looking simply for the lowest cost per cubic meter. Rather than settling for this bleak scenario, however, Eneco has backed up from the product they are selling (natural gas), in order to get a better view of the need they are meeting for the customer, from the customer's own perspective.

Different customers, of course, have different needs. It turns out that some of Eneco's largest customers operate commercial greenhouses. For such a customer, Eneco will install remote monitoring equipment to track each greenhouse's temperature, humidity and carbon dioxide content. Their proposition with the customer is no longer limited to selling natural gas at the lowest price, but subscribing the customer to the correct environment for each greenhouse being operated.

So what business is this Dutch utility firm *really* in? At least for one group of customers Eneco is in the "environment management" business, rather than the "natural gas" business. This allows them to cement relationships with valuable customers whose equity grows with their mutual entanglement with Eneco. Because Eneco's product is so intimately involved in solving a greenhouse operator's broader problem – as it is seen from the operator's own perspective – Eneco ensures that the customer has an incentive to continue the relationship. How much cheaper would a competitor's natural gas have to be for a big greenhouse customer to "uninstall" Eneco and start over?

Seeing things through your customer's eyes has the potential to point you in a number of different directions for increasing your Return on Customer. Eneco is a case in point, but it's not hard to think of similar opportunities in other businesses:

- For a computer manufacturer selling PCs, servers, and other equipment to businesses, how might Return on Customer increase if the company were to provide an online resource for managing each business customer's inventory of PCs, properly configuring and upgrading them for different departments, and controlling the purchase-order process so as to conform to the customer's own budget restrictions? (This is exactly what Dell does for its enterprise customers, using the Dell Premier Pages service.)
- A home insurance company that puts its own customers into direct contact with local repair people can increase its Return on Customer with respect to homeowners.
- A pharmaceutical company can increase its ROC by providing better, more comprehensive advice to its physician-customers about treating a whole therapeutic range of conditions, rather than just the specific symptoms related to the pharma company's own drug.
- A cable television company can increase its ROC by offering on-demand movie packages and broadband Internet access. Many

cable companies do this already. But since they already have a wired connection into the home, how about monitoring and managing household thermostats, providing voicemail or answering services, setting up home security packages, and the like?

- A petrochemical firm can increase its ROC if, in addition to the chemicals it delivers to customers, it also provides an online resource for tracking the inventories and dispositions of these chemical purchases, and for securing the required government permits for transporting and disposing of chemical inventories.

The ultimate drivers of customer behavior are needs and motivations. So, in addition to good old-fashioned market research, you should try to make sense of whatever transaction and other data you have, in order to understand these needs as deeply as possible. However you accomplish it, your goal is to figure out what the real levers of value creation are among your customers, *whether or not* your firm actually produces and sells things designed to pull those levers.

Customer needs should drive your business direction

As you acquire more insight into your customers' needs you will identify latent, unmet needs and opportunities to sell completely new services or products. All *you* have to do, really, is put yourself in your customer's position and imagine you are trying to solve his problem yourself. What more does the customer need, in order to solve his problem, which he can't already buy from his vendor (you)?

Degussa AG, for example, is a German-based multinational with €11.4 billion of sales in the "specialty chemistry" business. In America, its Degussa Admixtures division sells a number of specialty chemicals for improving the performance characteristics of concrete. Most of Degussa Admixture's customers are construction firms and concrete producers with multiple, independently-managed locations. At each location where concrete is mixed, chemical tanks for the additives are maintained by the site manager, who is responsible for ordering new chemicals when needed. Degussa developed a remote tank-monitoring system that uses wireless sensors to relay inventory information to a website that both Degussa and the customer can access. Now the company can anticipate when replenishment is needed by each of its customers in real time, ensuring that their chemicals are always in stock. Customers like this system, not only because they no longer have to pay so much attention to inventory management, but also because they save money with just-in-time replenishment. Degussa likes it because it reduces their own delivery costs, ensures that customers always have their chemicals in inventory, and gives customers a good reason to stay loyal. In short, their Return on Customer has increased.

Cisco Systems uses electronic post-transaction surveys to generate feedback from customers while the transaction is fresh in their minds. With technology from Walker Information, Cisco sent 385,000 surveys through different channels (such as the sales team and partners) and received 65,000 responses, or nearly a 17% response. Customer-facing employees and partners send the surveys whenever they choose. The "by invitation" process prompts people to open them, helping to keep the flow of data steady. Customers typically respond within 18 to 24 hours, according to Steve Cunningham, Cisco's "Director of Customer Listening."

The company's system is centralized and available to employees and partners across the global enterprise. "We wanted to build tools where anybody at Cisco could just click and out would go the invitation to a particular customer," Cunningham said. "That was very important to us, because it allowed us to become part of the DNA of all the people in the field. It would become something they could do any time they wanted, on their schedule." Any employee wishing to communicate with customers or partners has immediate access to the survey tool. In-depth responses, which are tabulated by the electronic system in real time, help Cisco improve service on all levels of the business and give the firm specific action items to work on. For instance, at one point, surveys gave low scores to system engineers on their technical skills and their availability to customers. Cisco responded by launching advanced training and Internet-based labs. Now, Cunningham said, the engineering skill level is one of the company's strongest areas.

Getting insight into customer needs through real-time feedback is an increasingly useful tool for all organizations, including governments –

allowing them to make more immediate adjustments to their services, in order to better accommodate the demands of citizens and constituents. In 2001, the City of Baltimore took steps to transform its five-year-old 311 non-emergency phone line into a one-stop-shop for government services delivered to its citizens. The vision was for a centralized customer service center for all service requests and inquiries. Elliot Schlanger, the city's CIO, says that prior to 311, people often made four or more phone calls to reach the appropriate agency.

"When people called for a complaint, often times there wasn't a record that there was a complaint in the first place," Schlanger says. "Customers had a terrible experience." The city's organization had no accountability built into it – no way at all to judge how its city workers performed. So, working with every city department to prepare for the 311 rollout, Schlanger's team developed 300 "standard" service requests (removing graffiti, filling a pothole, fixing a street light). Today, when a resident calls to report, say, a water leak in front of his house, the 311 customer service operator dispatches the request directly to the appropriate facility, and the system logs the inquiry to track its disposition. As each crew completes its step, they log it electronically and note the materials used. Not only does this information improve internal processes, but it also provides detailed status information about work in progress. With 311, the average time to fulfill a citizen's request has shrunk from seven months to 30 days, not only improving service to taxpayers but greatly reducing overall costs as well.

Schlanger says the combined savings and revenue brought in by the 311 system can be broken out in terms of things like increased productivity, reduction in overtime, more people showing up for work, elimination of unproductive programs, and newly recognized revenue streams. But cities across the country that have implemented 311 "one stop" services are also finding that the requests citizens make of them often point to completely new services, products, or configurations that would not have been considered before. For instance, New York's 311 system, involving 300 agents and an astonishing 171 languages, logged 12,000 pothole complaints in a short period, so the city launched a city-wide pothole-filling initiative. Thousands of calls complaining about swimming pool hours led the Parks Department to change the open-and-close policy. New York's Mayor Bloomberg now reads a weekly report of 311 calls that, among other things, details the number of people who oppose or approve of new programs or regulations. Bloomberg's oft-repeated phrase: "Who ya gonna call? 311."

To identify unmet needs within your customer base it's important not only to do the right research, but also to choose the right customers for it – the "lead users" of your product or service. These are your heaviest and most involved customers, and many will have already pushed your product to its limits as a result. Some may actually have their own communities, with message boards or informal meetings to exchange information and assistance with other lead users. Prof. Eric Von Hippel, of the Sloan School of Management at MIT, says lead users are the ones who "try to make a product perform better than the bulk of the market and prepare it for the future. They're working for themselves, not for you."

Von Hippel has explored the impact of lead users with a number of firms, including 3M, Verizon, and Pitney Bowes. Pitney Bowes, for instance, has taken a proactive approach to find people who have intense needs, and then get them involved in a brainstorming process designed to identify new product and service features. Early in the dot-com era, the company looked at people shipping more than a hundred packages a year as a result of electronic transactions. These power-users' needs fueled the development of new shipping and tracking policies. And in response to anthrax attacks delivered through the mail, Pitney Bowes identified clients with a relatively greater need for security, explored the way they dealt with this need, and eventually created a device that can detect chemicals and then isolate and quarantine suspected mail items.

Walk a mile in their shoes: Anticipating customer needs

The more we understand our customers' needs, the better able we will be to *anticipate* them. We want to know what motivates each different customer's behavior, so we can appeal to that motivation, or satisfy that need, in a more effective and relevant way. What we really want is to understand the customer's own perspective as accurately as possible –

we want to *be* that customer, to think what that customer is thinking, and to feel what that customer is feeling. When we do a good job of taking the customer's perspective, we might even know what the customer wants before the customer has to tell us.

Several benefits come from anticipating your customer's needs. First, you are more likely to influence the customer's future behavior, improving the customer's value to your firm, since you can design offerings and services, position your message, and pitch your business in such a way as to meet their need. But in addition, the customer's perception of their relationship with you will improve, because they can see you have taken their interests truly to heart. Moreover, by anticipating what a customer wants, you can reduce the frictional cost of requiring them to select a product or service from the variety that we offer. This means you will get your customer served more efficiently, with less time and effort going into the act of choice. You save money. The customer saves aggravation.

For example, consider St. George Bank, Australia's fifth largest. The bank has a reputation for excellent customer service, and was named "Best Bank" in 2003 by Australian Banking and Finance Magazine. In addition to such features as color-choice credit cards and cost-efficient wealth management advice, the bank's ATMs "remember" customers individually and prompt them for their usual transactions. When you insert your card into a St. George Bank ATM, the on-screen message might ask you whether you'd like your usual $100 cash, no receipt. If that's what you want you simply press "yes," then take your cash and leave. If you press "no" then of course you get the menu of all the other services and transactions available via ATM. By anticipating its customers' needs at the ATM, not only does St. George Bank satisfy its customers better with faster, more personalized service, but the ATMs themselves are able to handle an increased number of transactions in any given time period.

Compare this to what it feels like, from your own perspective as a customer, when your bank's ATM reads your debit card, looks you in the eye with that big screen and then, for the umpteenth time, asks you to "Choose a language for this transaction."

The logic behind anticipating a customer's need is compelling. If you know what they need, then you can be better at figuring out what they'll want next, and when. You can become more relevant – maybe even essential – and they'll keep doing business with you. Data-rich firms today can adjust their understanding of individual customer needs in real time, on the fly, as and when they interact with a customer and develop a richer transaction history. Sophisticated credit card firms and telcos can now anticipate, in advance, the next most likely product or service that a particular customer will probably want. Again, the effect is not only that your customer is more likely to get the most appropriate products, but also that *you* waste less time and resource trying to sell other, less relevant, products to that customer.

Three basic types of insight can help you anticipate what your customer needs: memory, editorial inference, and comparisons with other customers. Your memory of a customer's past choices or preferences is the simplest and most direct method of anticipating their future needs. When they rent a car and don't have to specify the car model, credit card, or insurance options, the car rental firm is using its memory of their past transactions or the profile they specified in order to anticipate them. If a florist's customer sends flowers to their mother on her birthday, the florist can remember the date and anticipate their need for flowers the next year. However a customer communicates their need or preference, all you have to do, as a business, is to rely on your memory of these specifications to anticipate the next event.

A second way to anticipate a customer's need is to use your memory of the customer, as above, but to couple it with some type of content or "editorial" categorization. The fact that a customer celebrates their mother's birthday with flowers means they might want to celebrate Mothers' Day, too, or perhaps other relatives' birthdays. Because a customer buys music CDs they might be interested in CD cleaning solutions or CD players. If a customer buys Italian suits, they might be interested in Italian loafers. The fact that a customer has bought books on business strategy and relationship management might mean they are interested in buying *Return on Customer*.

Third, you can anticipate a customer's needs by comparing this customer with other customers. Every customer is unique and individual, and our next topic will explore how different customers have different needs. But customers have similarities, as well. Almost everyone who has rented Movie A has also liked Movie B. People who like books by this author also tend to like books by that one. People who wear this type of clothing also tend to drive that type of car.

Your goal in making such comparisons is simply to do a better and better job of anticipating what it is that any particular customer needs.

You want to be there first, ready to serve the customer by addressing that customer's need and activating their motivation, in order to change their behavior.

But even though customers are likely to have similarities that can help you to understand them better, the fact is they are all individual customers, and at some level their needs will be unique and different.

The role of brand

As technology continues to improve, and more products and services are mass-customized to meet individual customers' needs, the brand itself will increasingly be used by brand owners to represent, not the physical product being sold or the actual service rendered, but the problem being solved for a customer – that is, the actual need being met. Instead of the features and attributes of a product, the brand will likely soon come to stand for the *functionality* of the product or service – that is, what it can do for the customer, how it can solve a customer's problem, or how it can enhance an individual consumer's identity.

There is no question that a strong brand preference greatly increases a firm's customer equity, by predisposing both current and future customers to do business with the firm. Amazon's excellent brand reputation came originally from the high volume of favorable publicity the firm received during the first few years of its existence. Then, as millions of customers flocked to the business on the basis of this reputation, the firm's quality of service and attention to customer satisfaction reinforced the brand's promise in ways that the vast majority of these customers found acceptable. Both steps were important to Amazon's success – publicizing a brand promise (Amazon did very little advertising, but received a great deal of press attention), and then satisfying that promise through the customer's actual experience.

In many cases a strong brand can command a price premium completely unrelated to any actual differences in product features or quality. Toyota makes its Corolla model on the same exact assembly line in California where General Motors assembles its car, the Prizm. They are virtually identical vehicles, produced with the same parts and assembly, but the strength of the Toyota brand allows the firm to charge more for its Corolla than GM can charge for its Prizm.

The ability of a strong brand to attract customers or to command a price premium can be thought of in terms of "brand equity," an idea that easily comes to mind when we discuss the concept of customer equity. It's not unreasonable to ask whether brand equity and customer equity might simply be different aspects of the same basic financial benefit, derived by quantifying the future intentions of customers. As tempting as this idea is, however, the two terms are actually quite different. First, brand equity is used most often to describe or quantify the financial benefit of consumers' preference for a brand, relative to its competitors. The preference that many car-buyers have for the Toyota brand, relative to the GM brand, is what makes the Corolla-Prizm comparison interesting. But both companies – GM as well as Toyota – have their own customer equity. If anything, we might visualize Toyota's brand equity as being analogous to the difference between its own customer equity and GM's.

In addition, surely brand equity requires at least the existence of a brand, but even an unbranded firm could have customer equity, simply by selling products or services that customers experience once and then have some intention of experiencing again. Think about the customer equity represented in generic grocery products, for instance. While it's certainly possible to stretch the concept of "brand" to encompass this kind of product offering, it's quite a stretch.

The greatest difficulty with the comparison, however, is that brand equity is inherently product-specific rather than customer-specific. A brand is the same for every customer, but each individual customer will have their own unique relationship with a company or its brand, and each relationship will represent a different lifetime value, and could be based on satisfying a completely different need. In the Toyota-GM example, each firm's brand equity is related to its product, but the products themselves are not actually producing value for the company. The real units of value production are still the customers who intend to buy those products, each of whom has a different level of interest in the brand. Yet "brand equity" only captures the values of these customers in the aggregate, by inference.

It would be better to think of brand equity and customer equity simply as two different financial lenses, each of which can provide different insights into how a company creates value. Other financial lenses might lead a company to quantify the value of its patents or its intellectual property, or its talent contracts, or its oil fields, or its equipment leases. For the reasons we are expounding throughout this book, we think customer equity – which can be broken into customer-specific units of lifetime value – is an inherently more useful lens than brand equity, particularly when it comes to the kind of day-to-day decision-making that characterizes the competitive activities at most firms. There is absolutely no reason, however, not to draw on several different lenses, in order to gain an even better view of your business.

The brand umbrella:
Looking for ROC in all the right places

In addition, for any firm trying to make its customers more valuable, one of the most important roles for a good brand is to provide an umbrella under which the firm can offer a wider array of products or services to solve a broader portion of its customers' problems, within the strategic capability of the firm (see Chapter 7). A brand gives its owner permission, in the eyes of the customers or prospects familiar with it, to engage in the different kinds of activities associated with a customer's more broadly-defined need. Conversely, when a company solves a greater portion of its customers' problems, or meets a greater proportion of the customers' needs, not only will it generate a greater Return on Customer, but its brand will become stronger, as well.

Tesco, for instance, has used its powerful brand name to gain per-mission to sell a wide variety of products and services to customers. Both in its physical stores and through its relationships with online consumers, Tesco has succeeded in categories far removed from "grocery retailing."

Renowned for its frequent-shopper program, Tesco is certainly one of the world's most sophisticated retailers when it comes to managing customer relationships. It has been interacting with customers at the point of sale and tracking those interactions since 1995. When a customer presents her card to ensure that she gets whatever discounts she's entitled to, the company can link her current shopping visit with all her previous shopping, compiling a comprehensive transaction history, and assembling a "picture" of the customer, based on the things she's bought. The customer might fit neatly into one of several lifestyle segments that Tesco has created as a way of categorizing its different customers by their grocery needs – from "convenience" to "finer foods" to "cost conscious."

Tesco didn't start by trying to design the largest data store it could, but instead focused on designing the smallest store of data that would give it useful information. Using this data, Tesco customizes its discounts and other offers to the individual needs of each customer. Ten million customers each quarter are mailed some four million variations of coupon offer, based on each individual customer's history and profile. The program generates £100 million of incremental sales annually for the retailer.

At the individual store level, Tesco's data can show the firm which products must be priced at or below competitors' prices, which products have fewer price-sensitive customers, which products need to be "every day low price" to be successful, and which have different levels of price elasticity for different types of customers. This kind of data gives Tesco the insight necessary to generate store-specific prices, whenever it chooses.

In 2000, Tesco began offering online grocery shopping, coupled with home delivery, and now 500,000 Tesco customers, accounting for some 10% of the company's overall sales, shop regularly online. Moreover, nearly 40% of Tesco's customers have given the company their email address, which makes email communication one of the most cost effective – and important – channels available to the firm. Tesco's ongoing, interactive relationships with its customers are buttressed by the trust that it constantly seeks to earn, as we discussed briefly in Chapter 2.

Today, based first on the strength of its brand, and second, its increasingly detailed relationships with its individual customers, Tesco has expanded its offering far beyond groceries. Either in its stores or at its website the company now sells nearly any type of product or service that a regular consumer might consider ordering from a well-known, reputable brand name like Tesco. On Tesco's website you can buy books, computer games, CDs and DVDs, consumer electronics products, flowers, and wine; you can take out a loan or a mortgage, procure a credit card, open a savings or retirement account, or book a trip; you can buy insurance for your car, your life, your home, your pet, or your vacation; you can arrange for low-cost gas or electricity services, Internet access service, and cellphone or home phone service. In addition to all this, you can get advice on health and diet issues, babies, families, or Christmas gift ideas.

More than ten years after launching its original customer relationship program, Tesco's brand now stands for a great deal more than groceries. It is a brand that consumers have come to trust, based on the company's own culture. In a trusting relationship, the customer is more willing to consult the brand with respect to additional products and services that may appear to be outside the scope of the brand's original offering.

Over just the last few years, by using technology to expand its relationships with customers under the shelter of a powerful brand, Tesco has *dramatically* increased its growth potential, and as a result its publicly traded share price has grown commensurately. Which is worth more? Tesco the chain of retail grocery stores, or Tesco the multichannel solutions provider? (Chapter 3 – What business are you in?) A customer with growth potential represents a bigger opportunity for creating value than one without growth potential. When Tesco only sold groceries, its growth potential was limited entirely to that category. But now that the company sells so many other things, its customers' growth potential is much greater – that is, the same customer base can create a great deal more value than would have been possible just a few years ago (more about customers' "potential value" in Chapter 5 and more details about Tesco in the Endnotes).

It was insight into customer needs, at the customer-specific level, that gave Tesco the knowledge to carry out this expansion of its business, and it was a powerful brand, built on customer trust, that enabled them to do it.

To increase shareholder value, think like a customer

All the value your business is ever going to have, all the money it will ever make, has to come from customers at some point. To increase your value as a business, you either have to get more customers or you have to change the behaviors of the ones you already have, or both. In each case we're talking about influencing individual human beings to change what they were going to do, and then to do something else – individuals who have their own lives, their own families, their own jobs, roles, and responsibilities, their own moods, their own favorite desserts.

And let's face it; your customers are not just sitting around dreaming up ways to increase your shareholder value. If they were, you wouldn't be reading this book.

You can only create lasting value for your business by first creating value for customers, and you can only do that by understanding what it is that customers themselves actually *value*.

Think like a customer, and you'll see that quality, convenience, time-liness, price, and satisfaction all count. Think like a customer, and trust and fairness will suddenly become indispensable considerations; their absence will be a deal-breaker. Surprise: *Customers and trust are board-room issues.*

Because customers are your scarcest resource, the surest route to increased shareholder value is to understand what your customers need, and to offer products or services that meet those needs as completely and relevantly as possible. This is what Best Buy, Tesco, Cisco Systems, Pitney Bowes, Eneco Energie, and Degussa AG, for instance, all found.

Because customers are your scarcest resource, *every* decision you make should be evaluated in terms of the return it generates on this resource. Your company should be making its decisions on the basis of Return on Customer.

4. ROC Around the Clock

Please hold the line for this important message: Your phone company stock is not likely to recover any time soon. You may now kiss a portion of your retirement savings goodbye.

Telecommunications companies are in a terrible mess. Their long-distance margins are in the tank already, and will soon face even more difficult competition from Internet-based calling services. Their land-line businesses are under increasing threat from cable companies and wireless carriers alike. Cable operators are having their own margins undermined by increasingly aggressive satellite companies. The cell-phone category has already reached commodity-like maturity in most Western countries as well as in many developing economies, and technology improvements seem to have outstripped customer demand in a number of areas.

This number is no longer in service

Even in the face of this tidal wave of economic threat, telecom firms continue to make value-destructive decisions every day, undermining whatever small chance they have for a brighter future. This is because managers at these firms are locked onto the wrong metric of success. They are focused on the short-term problem: earnings difficulties, attributable to falling margins. Nearly every initiative they take to correct this problem, however, ends up exacerbating their longer-term predicament. Just as surely as a bank that rewards its managers solely on the basis of quarterly sales and profit, a telecom company focused solely on current-period earnings will end up destroying its own value.

What telecom managers need is a better understanding of the role that customer lifetime values play in their daily business activities. Especially in a market characterized by such commoditization and oversupply, it is important to know which customers are worth more than others to acquire and retain – not just in the form of immediate profitability, but long-term value, as well.

Of course, tracking Return on Customer and customer lifetime value (LTV) will not allow you to escape from a product category character-ized by increasing commoditization, as this one is. It's not unreasonable to think that lifetime values might be declining in general in a number of telecommunications segments, as technology renders products and services ever more interchangeable, and as increasingly experienced customers become more aggressive with their comparison shopping. Averages, however, mask the fact that within every telecommunications company's customer base there almost certainly are some customers whose usage is increasing, or whose appetite for telecom services is expanding, or who will simply be more likely to stay with a company that treats them well. Within every prospect pool there are some who are more likely to stay longer, buy more, and cost less to serve. The problem is that with little expertise in using lifetime value as a decision-making tool, most telecom companies are simply flying blind.

Learning to use the LTV tool all day, every day to make ROC decisions

As a manager, you are constantly creating and destroying value for your company with routine, everyday, tactical decisions. This is the nature of "management." You deploy more resources to sell Product A and less to sell Product B; you strengthen a service or cancel it; you advocate a price cut or a price increase; you treat Customer X one way, but Customer Y another way; you hire Stacey, but not Trent. Some of these decisions create value for your business, and some probably do not.

Every decision you make has an economic consequence for your firm, and part of your job as a manager is to calculate a decision's long-term impact as well as its immediate costs or benefits. To do this, you make projections of likely income streams or costs. You might even put a spreadsheet together to try to visualize the potential outcomes of complicated decisions and quantify the results.

Making decisions requires you to predict the future, as best you can. Return on Customer is simply a lens through which you might be able to see the future a little more clearly. It is based on the common-sense principle that *all value comes from customers, but not all value created by current decisions necessarily comes in the current period.* Your job is to balance current-period profits from a customer against the profit you expect from the customer during future periods (that is, increases or decreases in LTV).[1]

Even though only a minority of firms try to calculate their customers' lifetime values today, more will undoubtedly do so as customer data-bases and analytics applications continue to improve rapidly. There is, in fact, a whole new aspect of marketing analysis today called "predictive analytics" or "prescriptive analytics." Neither term is precisely defined, although the central idea involves forecasting the likely changes in future customer behavior based on current analysis. Suffice to say that the more customers and data you have available, the more confidence you can have, both in your lifetime value calculations, and in your ability to predict your customers' future behavior.

As you commit time and resources to measuring and analyzing customer lifetime values, your firm will acquire more and more insight into how different factors affect lifetime value – factors such as acquisition cost, retention, service cost, operating margin, customer attitudes, cross-selling ratios, account penetration, and so forth. Pioneering firms in this discipline have already begun to acquire significant practice in using customer lifetime value as a "tool" with which to create value.

However, as a decision-making aid, occasional measures of lifetime value will only go so far. *It is the expected <u>change</u> in a customer's LTV that should drive your business decisions.* A customer's lifetime value is, in essence, value that you have already "earned" through your past actions – you just haven't collected the cash yet. Your actions today, on

---

[1] We are using the term "profits" here, but in most cases it makes more sense to base your ROC calculation on cash flow, rather than profit, per se. A more detailed discussion of this issue can be found in Appendix 2.

the other hand, could change a customer's lifetime value, moving it higher or lower, and this change represents an important part of the overall value you are generating with your decisions.

Once you are practiced enough with the lifetime value tool to begin monitoring how changes in LTV are caused, you can begin to apply the ROC metric to manage your business more productively, focusing on the most important factors in your own customers' lifetime values. (In Chapter 6, "Predicting the Future," we'll talk more specifically about the "leading indicators" of lifetime value change you'll need to identify and measure *today* in order to make ROC into a more useful metric.) If customer retention is the dominant factor in your equation, then improving customer loyalty will be key to success. If service profit is the dominant variable, then services should be emphasized. Making the right business decision depends on the current performance of your lifetime value parameters, and on the effort required to influence the value of these parameters. Improving on a metric where performance is already high is generally more difficult (and costly) than focusing on an area with more room for improvement.

The irrational economics of self-defeating decisions

Tracking LTV allows you to calculate Return on Customer in a variety of situations, sometimes in order to decide what the best course of action is, and sometimes simply to avoid self-defeating business decisions that generate unanticipated (or unmeasured) costs. At many firms, acquisition programs are evaluated on the basis of the *quantity* of new customers acquired, rather than their *quality* (that is, their expected LTVs and growth potential). Profit optimization programs often look at cost savings without considering customer retention issues. And retention programs designed to reduce churn might do so by maintaining marginally profitable customers, or even unprofitable ones.

These are, in fact, the self-defeating criteria by which many telecom companies evaluate their own actions. Because they don't track changes in customer lifetime values, they have no real understanding of the overall value they are creating or not creating with their everyday tactical decisions. For the most part, telecommunications firms seem to have an indiscriminate hunger simply to win any new customers at all, as well as to avoid losing their current ones, no matter what the LTV economics are. These firms are making decisions designed to maximize their current-period earnings, and it's possible that they are actually doing so. The problem, however, is that this undermines their companies' long-term viability. They may actually be destroying more value than they are creating.

According to one group of industry experts, many if not most telecom firms have seen the average LTV within their customer bases decline quite significantly in recent years:

> *Some [telecom companies], for example, have tried to reduce churn by offering discount plans and other incentives – but ended up retaining customers they would have been better off losing, and making formerly marginal customers unprofitable. Others have tried to contain the surge in unpaid bills by tightening credit limits on new applicants but are now turning away many customers who would have been profitable.*

In essence, according to this authority, telecom companies are strip-mining their base of customers and prospects in order to feed current-period results. As they continue with these policies, it becomes harder and harder to pump up the current period, while at the same time the customer environment is becoming increasingly polluted with uneconomic offers and unprofitable programs. It is anyone's guess as to whether telecom firms are actually *willing* to sacrifice the future in their increasingly desperate effort to prop up the present, or they are simply *unaware* of what they are really doing because, they don't have the right metrics in place (that is, ROC).

Rather than trying to sell their products to as many customers as possible during the current quarter, what telecommunications companies should be thinking about is the *types* of customers who are more likely to contribute to their overall success. They need to maximize their Return on Customer, by optimizing the mix of short-term profit and long-term value creation.

But it's difficult for these firms to think in such terms because they simply aren't organized to do so. The way they are organized and their managers compensated is designed to generate quarterly revenues and to acquire new customers – any customers. If your primary gauge of success is new-customer acquisition, then you can tally your results immediately after each campaign. But the loyalty, spending patterns, and lifetime values of the customers acquired don't figure in the calculation. They are irrelevant to your metric, and so they will be irrelevant to your company's decisions and actions.

Moreover, this will hold true even though your managers and employees might know better, because chances are your firm's whole metrics and compensation system is aligned with producing current results, without balancing any quantifiable estimate of the long-term value being created (or destroyed) at the same time. One young graduate student we ran into described to us the "moral dilemma" he faced, as a lowly call center representative at a phone company. He knew that most of the customers his firm was "winning back" would cost the company considerably more than they were worth, but each win-back added to his own personal bonus. What to do? The answer, predictably: Win back as many as you can. Value-destruction while-u-wait.

WHAT ABOUT THE SHORT TERM?

Lifetime value improvements don't pay salaries. It takes cash to run your business in the short term, and if there's no short term, there's not going to be any long term, right? How do you pay today's bills with Return on Customer?

The Return on Customer argument does not imply that increases in lifetime values are any more important than cash. Far from it. Lifetime value, by its very nature, is already a diminished version of cash. LTV is calculated based on *discounted* future cash flows, and even if you have no short-term cash worries at all, you are still going to prefer having a dollar today over having it next year (see Appendix 1 for more on the nature of discounted cash flows and the rationale behind them).

Obviously, short-term results are important to any business. The more cash you can generate with a business right now, today, the less financing you need and the more growth and investment you can fund. And short-term results are more important to some businesses than to others. The degree to which you prefer immediate cash versus future cash – the *intensity* of your preference for the short term – is captured by the amount of your discount rate. The more important the short term is, or the more risky it is to wait for long-term results, then the higher your discount rate should be.

When the short term is a real worry, common sense and economic principle suggest using a higher discount rate. If cash is extremely tight and you have no borrowing or financing resources, for instance, then you might prefer having one dollar today rather than two dollars next year. That would be a discount rate of 100%, implying that if someone were willing to lend you money today, you'd be willing to pay 100% interest on the loan. If your actual business survival is at stake, your discount rate might even be more, implying that future cash has very little value at all to you, compared to short-term cash.

The problem is that when companies don't consciously try to quantify the benefits of long term versus short term, they usually end up making decisions based almost exclusively on the short term, with destructive overall results. That is, even though their survival is not threatened, they behave as if they were using a discount rate of 100% or more, and as a result their decisions are not economically rational.

As Return on Customer becomes a more widely accepted and respected metric, having reliable ROC calculations might actually help you finance your short-term cash requirements. Showing a lender or investor how much discounted-cash-flow value you can create from particular groups of customers should be a persuasive argument. If you can prove you are building equity, you can nearly always get your bills paid today.

Telecom companies are just one of the most obvious examples of the phenomenon of eroding marketing effectiveness. Many different industries are afflicted with this disease; it's just that in most categories it isn't so painfully obvious. To deal with the problem, you have to know which customers are worth acquiring, and which are not worth keeping. You have to know which customers offer the most growth potential, and which present the most risk. Then you have to organize your firm to deal with these facts. You have to be able to treat different customers differently, holding managers within your organization accountable for the enterprise value that is either created or destroyed by their various actions.

Using ROC to acquire *profitable* customers

It is not just current customers who provide value to a firm, but future customers, as well. Every company can be expected to acquire a fairly steady stream of new customers in the routine course of business.

A rapidly expanding company, in a new or growing category, has a great deal of customer equity in the form of the lifetime values of customers it does not yet have but reasonably expects to have in the future. Applying the ROC metric to customer acquisition is important for calculating the genuine cost and benefit of your acquisition program. ROC is the metric you should use in order to choose which particular types of customers to try to acquire, given the expected acquisition cost, and the immediate and future profit expected from them, because ROC measures the rate at which *overall* value is being created – considering both the current costs of your acquisition program and the changes in overall customer equity generated for your firm.

As companies acquire more experience with the LTV tool, increasing numbers of them are calculating not just the amount of current-period revenue gained from new customers, but also things like whether the acquired customers dilute or enhance the average LTV in the portfolio, whether they merely shifted their future spending to today, or whether they just came for the discount and will leave as soon as the firm tries to turn a profit on them. By paying attention to LTV you can decide if your actions are creating genuine incremental value or merely cannibalizing your own customer equity. Consider, for instance, the problem of deciding whether customer acquisition is or is not the most bene-ficial objective with respect to any particular type of customer or prospect. The easiest way to understand this issue is to visualize it as a question of opti-mizing the right mix of customer acquisition activities, when compared to retention and growth activities. If you have a group of customers with a relatively poor retention rate and poor lifetime values, you might suspect that more value can be created by raising the retention rate (and thereby increasing their lifetime values), rather than by trying to acquire more of the same type of customer. Over time, however, as your reten-tion rate increases, customer acquisition programs will become more attractive, not only because new customers entering the franchise will be retained longer and therefore have higher lifetime values to begin with, but also because as retention improves it will likely become harder to gain further improvements in it. ROC can help you identify this *inflection point* in order to prioritize your growth investment.

Company K is a hypothetical high-end specialty retailer with customers generating an average of £1,000 in annual margin. From experience, Company K knows that some 30% of its customers leave the franchise each year. Accounting for this attrition, and using a discount rate of 15%, it has calculated its average customer's lifetime value to be about £2,500. Company K has pursued more and more aggressive customer acquisition efforts in the past, in a futile race to replace the many customers it loses each year. But now the most recent figures show that acquisition costs are running to £3,700 per new customer, far in excess of the average customer's lifetime value.

Based on some tests it conducted in the past, Company K believes that with an investment of £1,200 per customer it can reduce the probability that a customer will leave by about 50%. But this is an activity with diminishing returns. That is, whatever the cost of reducing overall attrition from 30% to 25%, it will cost more to reduce it from 25% to 20%, and so forth. Moreover, as customer retention improves, lifetime value will increase as well, and customer acquisition campaigns will look more promising again.

The question for Company K is at what point will it have reduced attrition sufficiently to justify launching a renewed customer acquisition effort? This decision can be pictured graphically in Figure 4.1, which shows how Company K's Return on Customer varies for both customer acquisition and customer retention, as the customer attrition rate is driven steadily downward. The lines cross once attrition drops below about 14% (at which point customer acquisition will become a better investment than customer retention).

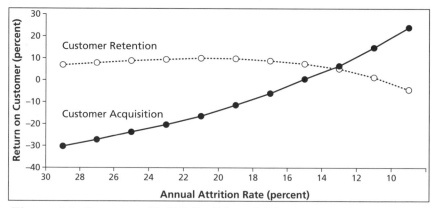

Figure 4.1: **Company K: ROC of Acquisition versus Retention**

This is, of course a highly simplified example, with simplified assumptions regarding the cost of customer acquisition and retention. As a practical matter, you will want to balance your firm's customer initiatives, such as retention and acquisition in different ways for different groups of customers simultaneously, as appropriate. Different types of customers will have different lifetime values, different likely retention or repurchase rates, and different levels of responsiveness to acquisition and retention efforts. But Return on Customer is the metric you should use to determine the true value of each of your initiatives.

ROC AND TACTICAL DECISION-MAKING

Consider one department store retailer with a lifetime value equation based on limited customer transaction data, mostly revolving around the recentness and amount of a customer's purchases with the firm, and the amount of cross-department shopping the customer has done.

By careful examination of its transactional records over several years, the retailer has derived this algorithm for predicting the lifetime values of its customers:

LTV = £2500 + (£500 if female) + (£250 if between ages 35 to 54)
    + (2.5 × total amount spent during last 12 months)
    − (£3 × number of days since last purchase)
    + (£300 × number of departments spent in during last 6 months).

Obviously, this LTV algorithm is not the same thing as a mathematical definition of a customer's lifetime value, per se – that is, it isn't a formula for discounted future cash flows. Rather, this algorithm is derived by correlating the retailer's currently available customer data, such as gender, spending level, or days since last purchase, with customer spending patterns over the last several years. (For more on how to derive such an algorithm, see Appendix 3.) The variables in this lifetime value algorithm are leading indicators of lifetime value change. When one of these LTV drivers changes for a customer, past experience indicates that the customer's future behavior (lifetime value) is also likely to change. Therefore, by affecting one or more of these drivers the retailer should be able to influence its customers' lifetime values. The real question is how to decide among different types of marketing initiatives and other activities for different types of customers within the customer base.

Let's assume that at the end of a particular time period a sample of this retailer's customers has the profile shown in Table 4.1. Now the retailer wants to generate current profits from these customers, of course, but the company also wants to increase their lifetime values – by increasing the annual amount they spend, their frequency of purchasing, or their cross-department purchases. (Gender will not be affected, obviously, and we have no impact on the aging process!) To determine which particular lifetime value drivers offer the most growth potential, we need to examine the profile of each different type of customer.

Customer	M/F	Aged 35-54	Last 12 months spending	Days since last purchase	Depts shopped last 6 months	LTV
A	1	0	£500	60	1	£4,370
B	1	0	£500	60	3	£4,970
C	0	1	£750	10	1	£4,895
D	0	0	£0	550	0	£850
E	0	1	£200	300	0	£2,350
F	1	1	£2,000	2	4	£9,444
G	1	1	£0	400	0	£2,050
H	1	0	£0	900	0	£300
I	0	1	£100	15	1	£3,255
J	1	1	£50	200	0	£2,775
K	1	1	£900	12	1	£5,764
L	1	0	£1,000	30	2	£6,010
						£47,033

Table 4.1

Table 4.1 shows, for instance, that there is a set of customers (represented by Customers A, C, and K) who have spent £500 or more during the last six months, but only in a single department. These three customers' lifetime values total approximately £15,000 in all, but the retailer suspects they could be made much more loyal and valuable (that is, their lifetime values would go up substantially) if they could be encouraged somehow to shop in more than just the one department. (Note that Customer I spent money in only one department also, but it was a much smaller amount. In addition, customers who spent no money at all in the last six months show up as a zero in the "departments shopped" column, but the retailer considers them to be a different type of customer.)

The retailer knows that when a customer spends in more than one department, her lifetime value increases. You can easily see this from the table by comparing Customers A and B. These two customers have the same profile, in terms of age, gender, and recent spending, but B has spent in three different departments, compared to A's single department, so B's lifetime value is significantly higher.

Let's consider what the retailer's options might be for creating more value from this group of single-department customers (A, C and K). The company's marketing department has devised two new "shopping the shop" customer treatments, each of which it plans to test on a representative sample of customers from this A-C-K group.

Treatment 1 is a £10 restaurant voucher, offered to these customers when they shop in the furniture department. The voucher is effective at increasing the number of departments these customers shop in, from just a single department to two, with about £50 in incremental spending. In addition, the redeemed voucher itself generates an average profit of £20 per customer, over and above its costs, so the marketing department initially sees Treatment 1 as a completely self-liquidating offer. The more people redeem it, the more profit the firm will earn.

Treatment 2 is a prize vacation sweepstakes and coupon combination given to customers spending in two departments on any given day. Rather than a profit, this promotion costs an average of £20 per customer – so it depletes the promotion budget. However, it does a much better job at increasing the multi-department spending of these customers (three departments rather than just two, with £100 of incremental spending).

The question to ask is whether Treatment 1 is *better* than Treatment 2 because the restaurant voucher generates a profit while the vacation sweepstakes costs the firm money. But this question can only be answered by calculating the Return on Customer for each alternative. When you make this calculation, it turns out that Treatment 2 generates twice as much improvement in lifetime value as Treatment 1, more than offsetting the difference in current-period cost. As shown in Table 4.2, Treatment 2's Return on Customer is 18%, compared to just 10% for Treatment 1.

Customers A, C and K	Depts shopped last 6 months (avg)	LTV, all customers	Treatment cost or profit, all customers	Total change in LTV, all customers	Total value created	Return on customers
Currently	1	£15,029				
Treatment 1	2	£16,532	£60	£1,503	£1,563	10%
Treatment 2	3	£17,807	–£60	£2,778	£2,718	18%

Table 4.2

What the ROC figures show is that Treatment 2 is the right course of action for this company, as long as customers are limited in number. It's important to note that if there were an unlimited number of single-department customers (profile A, C and K), then the retailer could create an infinite amount of value, incurring no current-period cost, simply by running Treatment 1 over and over and over again. But like every other business, this retailer has only a finite number of customers, and must decide which treatment is the most appropriate for creating the most value from this scarce resource.

Two points of caution: First, this is an intentionally simple example, but LTV algorithms like this one are never completely accurate, no matter how much detailed transactional and other data go into them. In the end they are nothing more than statistically-compiled approximations, and you must always remember to apply your own common sense and judgment. And second, don't assume that whenever two events are statistically correlated, one must cause the other. Proving causality requires a bit more statistical sophistication. See Appendix 3 for more on both of these points.

Thinking (cleverly) about customer retention

In your own business, customer retention may or may not be the most appropriate variable to try to evaluate. Customer values can change in many ways. Customer attrition or retention is like an "on-off" switch, but in most categories customers should be thought of more in terms of volume dials. Increasing the amount of business your customer does, or at least avoiding a reduction in the business they do, could be much more useful objectives in many cases. A recent survey of more than 1,000 American households' behaviors across a variety of industries concludes that, while reducing defection definitely represents an opportunity for most businesses, there is far more financial leverage in simply increasing the amount of business done by customers, or avoiding reductions in the volume of business done.

Moreover, customer loyalty itself is not always easy to define. If a consumer who is loyal to a particular retail brand of fuel were to stop at a different brand's fuel station because it is more convenient at a given time, have they become less loyal than they were? When a business that buys all its office furniture from a particular contractor decides to put the next set of furniture purchases out to bid, is that "defection"?

Most companies end up creating a practical definition of retention for their customers that includes two features. Unless the customer has a single, subscriber-like relationship with your company and clearly "leaves," retention is rarely considered an all-or-nothing variable. Thus, at a first level, retention tends to be defined progressively – from "downgrading" behavior, to "inactive" status, to "no longer a customer." For some firms, a downgrading pattern itself is an indicator of increased risk of loss. A cable customer with many premium channels and pay-per-views each month may downgrade to just basic cable, or even to local-broadcast-only, before completely defecting to satellite.

At a second level, any definition of retention must also recognize the multiple relationships that a customer may have with a firm in terms of products that span business units. A customer who terminates a relationship in one area – paying off their home mortgage with a bank, for instance – may or may not retain a strong and active relationship in other areas, such as retail banking, investments, and credit. You won't be able to understand this phenomenon unless you take an enterprise-wide view of your customer.

While any lost customer is a real loss, understanding the nature of the loss will help to manage the costs of trying to reactivate customers, or even to win them back. You need to distinguish between customer attrition and customer defection. Attrition almost always results from a circumstance outside your direct control – an elite business traveler retires, an office supplies buyer declares bankruptcy, a retail customer moves to another territory. Defection, by contrast, is a customer loss you might have been able to mitigate, because the customer is clearly choosing to move part or all of their business to the competition – for example, a landline customer chooses to drop her service in order to go "only mobile", a video-renting family decides to use an online movie service, and so forth. By distinguishing defection from attrition, you can isolate the drivers of each behavior and invest where you can earn the highest Return on Customer.

There is also the question of tenure. In any population of customers, the most likely to defect will be the first to do so. Thus, the longer any particular group of customers has remained loyal, the less likely any of them are to defect in any given time period. Stated another way, the average annual retention rate among any population of customers will tend to increase with time. So when we talk in general about "improving retention" we have to be quite careful, because the easiest way to improve *average* retention is simply to stop acquiring new customers altogether. Again, resolving this problem requires a metric that can balance the benefits of immediate profit against the benefits of long-term value being created or destroyed.

In the final analysis, regardless of whatever behavior changes you effect in your customers, whether it is an increase in purchasing, or a reduced likelihood of attrition, all of the financial results are captured in the customer's lifetime value. The only questions are how accurately you have constructed your lifetime value equation, for this particular customer, and how well the equation will be fed with the leading-indicator data available.

To maximize ROC you have to gain some practice in using lifetime value as a tool, and in tracking changes in LTV over time. You'll probably never know exactly how much an investment in acquisition will yield, or how to measure retention precisely over an extended period, or how much additional business will actually be stimulated by a particular offer. Yet from empirical observations you will eventually deduce how lifetime value is likely to be influenced by its various drivers, and by the attitudes of your customers. The big challenge will be to fashion your company's strategies not just to maximize this quarter's sales, or "new customers added," but rather to maximize the rate at which your company is creating overall economic value, in the long term as well as the short term.

WHAT IS THE VALUE *today* OF A CUSTOMER YOU DON'T YET HAVE?
A current customer has a lifetime value, but does a prospective customer have a lifetime value too, even though you aren't yet doing business with them, and you may *never* do business with them? As strange as it may sound, the answer to this question is "yes," a prospect does have a lifetime value to you, today – even if you don't really know whether they'll ever become a customer. As long as there is some probability that the prospect will become a customer, then the prospect has a value to you, today.

The lifetime value of a prospective customer is equal to their lifetime value if they were to become a customer, multiplied by the likelihood of their becoming a customer.

To take one highly simplified example, suppose you expect a 4% conversion rate from your entire prospect pool each year. If you have a 20% market share and lose 16% of your current customers each year, then a 4% annual acquisition rate from non-customers exactly offsets that attrition rate (20% × 16% = 80% × 4%). In other words, your business is in a steady state, neither growing nor shrinking. Let's suppose new customers added from your prospect pool have an average lifetime value of £120 when they come into the franchise (after accounting for the attrition rate once they become customers). You use a discount rate of 20% when valuing future cash flows (see Appendix 1).

Thus, 4% of your prospects will convert each year, and when they do come in, each one will have a lifetime value of £120 *at that time*. So this year, the average prospect is worth 4% × £120, or £4.80. Using a 20% discount rate means that next year's prospects are worth 20% less, or £4.00. The following year's prospects are discounted by a further 20%, and so forth. Every individual prospect's current value, today, is therefore a probability-weighted calculation based on the 4% likelihood they will come into the franchise in any given year at the present value of £120 that year.[2]

To calculate the total current value of a single prospective customer, you just add together all these probability-weighted present values for all future years. The result in this case would be £24.[3]

In this example, if your market share is 20% of one million total customers and prospects, then your total customer equity is approximately £43 million, because you have 200,000 current customers at £120 lifetime value each (£24 million), and you have 800,000 prospects, with £24 lifetime value each (£19.2 million).

Note that because prospects have probability-weighted lifetime values, you can generate a higher Return on Customer not just by targeting your customer acquisition campaigns at higher-LTV prospects, but also by taking actions to increase the *likelihood* that prospects will become customers. If your business-to-business firm conducts a free seminar for prospective customers, the prospects who elect to attend have almost certainly increased their likelihood of becoming customers. When your consumer marketing firm offers free samples, the prospects who respond to the offer are more likely to become customers. Because you need to know whether it makes economic sense to run a seminar for prospects or to give samples away, you must consider the current values of these customers you do not yet have. Increasing the value of prospective customers is a legitimate and time-honored business activity.

But what about when a prospect becomes a customer? In our example above, a customer has a lifetime value of £120, so when you convert a prospect to a customer, doesn't that mean you've increased your customer equity by £120?

No. If the prospect was already worth £24 to you, then the net increase in value to your firm, in making that prospect into a customer was only £96. You could think of it in terms of a new customer being activated at a £120 LTV, while a prospect is being "de-activated" with a £24 LTV. Another way to think about it is that the prospect had a probability-weighted LTV, and the probability changed. When the prospect became a customer the probability of their becoming a customer increased to 100%, from what it used to be, which was 4% each year.

---

[2] Purists note: The exact calculation would adjust the 4% probability down slightly each year, because the probability of a prospect becoming a customer in Year 2 is 4% times the 96% probability that he didn't already become a customer in Year 1, and so forth. This more precise calculation is not justified, however, for our highly simplified example.
[3] If you remember "infinite series" from school, at a 20% discount rate £24 = £4.80 ÷ 20%.

Technically, a prospect has an "actual value" to your firm of £24, and an additional, "unrealized potential value" of £96. You could easily think of a prospective customer as a customer with a great deal of growth potential. Your mission, as a business, is to realize some of that potential, by changing the customer's otherwise expected future behavior. We'll be talking about this in the next chapter.

ROC is qualitative, not just quantitative

ROC will never replace traditional financial measures as a gauge of business success. But it will inevitably become the driver for more and more of a firm's tactical decisions and actions in the future. One of the biggest advantages for Return on Customer, as a metric, is that it can help you accurately evaluate your firm's day-to-day competitive actions. Because you can break ROC down into its individual elements – customer lifetime values – you can use it to evaluate the real value created by your company's actions with respect to selected groups of customers, or even individual customers.

This is not all just a numbers game – far from it. Increasing a customer's value requires you to take the customer's own point of view, to put yourself in the customer's shoes, and to try to earn the customer's trust. Nevertheless, *without Return on Customer as a metric of success, cultivating the trust of customers will always seem an unnatural act.* It will require large investments in education and training, and never quite escape the need to be rejustified with every downturn in short-term sales or profits.

But there is still a great deal you can do even if you aren't measuring the right financial quantities – even if you aren't formally calculating Return on Customer. *Any* company, no matter how unsophisticated its financial systems are, is capable of turning its own organization into more of a service-oriented, customer-sensitive culture. *Any* company, with or without financial tracking mechanisms, can encourage smiles and active listening at the point of purchase and the call center, better complaint-recovery processes, more customer-oriented (and less product-oriented) sales messages, zero-tolerance quality assurance programs, no-questions-asked product or service guarantees, and similar initiatives. *Any* company can build a culture of trust.

The vast majority of employees at a company will *want* to treat customers better, if they're given the license to do so. Nearly all employees will find it more rewarding to say "That makes good sense, sir, let me help you." rather than "I'm sorry, but that's our policy" or "What are we, your accountants?" It's usually just a matter of releasing these pent-up desires and directing employees' energy in the right way. Most companies are understandably hesitant to let employees have at it, though, fearing that without discipline, the costs of serving customers better will quickly eat up profits. By using a metric like ROC to take account of current profits and customer equity at the same time, management will have a disciplined overlay to keep costs and returns in balance, and to provide guidance for prioritizing in the face of limited resources.

In short, the argument in favor of using ROC to gauge and report enterprise success, and to make daily managerial decisions, is partly based on financial and quantitative factors, but it is also a qualitative argument for a more customer-oriented approach to business – an approach that we all know, intuitively, to be better. The very best examples of such service come from companies that understand the common-sense, non-quantitative argument that maximizing the value proposition they have with their customers requires them to give as well as to get – companies that have made it their central mission to cultivate the trust of their customers.

So ROC as a metric, is a quantitative way to assess how much actual enterprise value you are creating. But ROC is not the mission. Delivering more value to customers *is* your mission, because that will ensure that you get more value from them. Return on Customer is just the lens for viewing your results more accurately, and for managing and reporting these results more responsibly and effectively. It is a metric that can help ensure that everyone's daily decisions not only serve customers well, but also create the optimum balance of short-term and long-term value for the business.

Because the ROC metric is based on customers, you can use it to analyze the value created by a single customer or by any group of customers. This is fortunate, because customers are all different, and they create value at different rates, for different reasons. Certainly one benefit of taking a Return-on-Customer perspective is that you can quantify the actual shareholder value you are creating with the kind of decisions you need to make all the time, around the clock, no matter how many (or how few) customers are involved in them.

But a second benefit of Return on Customer is that it will help you understand and use the *differences* among your customers to maximize the overall value your firm creates. It's certainly no news that customers are different, unique, and individual – but until ROC, companies had no unifying metric that could actually quantify the real benefits of treating different customers differently. This is the subject of our next chapter.

5. Building Enterprise Value, One ROC at a Time

Because all value comes ultimately from your customers, creating maximum overall value for your business requires that you generate the maximum possible value from each individual customer – not just in the short term, but over the lifetime of the customer. This is exactly how you would maximize your ROI on an investment portfolio, too – by maximizing the return on each individual security.

If there is a single phrase that best captures the nature of the business revolution that has been set in motion by computers and interactive technologies, it is this:

Treating different customers differently.

This phrase also captures perfectly the nature of your task if you want to maximize Return on Customer.

Businesses of all sizes and shapes are now technologically capable of treating different customers differently. They can interact with them individually, and they can configure different products and services for different customers, based not just on what the businesses themselves want to sell, but also on what they perceive their individual customers need. Because of these new technologies, businesses today can make customer-specific decisions and take customer-specific actions in a cost-efficient way, and predict the consequences of those actions with a reasonable amount of confidence.

The problem is that treating different customers differently is a highly subversive idea, undermining many of the tried and true premises of traditional marketing and business competition. Rather than looking for a single "unique selling proposition" that appeals in some way to the largest possible group of customers, you must now find the proposition that appeals most to particular, individual customers. Instead of focusing on one product or service at a time, in order to sell that product to as many customers as possible, you must focus on one customer at a time, and try to sell that customer as many products and services as possible – over the entire lifetime of the customer's patronage. Rather than trying to figure out what *all* your customers need, in other words, you now have to figure out what *each* of your customers needs, one customer at a time.

Taking customer-specific action – treating different customers differently – also requires a firm to track its ongoing relationships with individual customers. Relationships are driven by interaction,[1] and as interactions accumulate, a relationship develops an increasingly rich "context" that makes it difficult to replicate, so the customer is more likely to remain loyal for sheer convenience and reassurance. When an online merchant remembers your address and credit card from your previous interaction, for instance, you can order the next product simply by clicking on it, which is something you would not be able to do right away with a different merchant. A successful relationship provides an ongoing benefit to each party, so both sides have an incentive to recover from mistakes.

You can improve ROC for an individual customer by taking that customer's perspective and understanding their needs. However, when you also involve the customer in an interactive, mutual relationship, you can improve ROC even more. For both the buyer and the seller involved in an ongoing relationship, the problem or cost of a single *transaction* is far outweighed by the value of the *relationship*.

One of the most important and transformative outputs of a successful customer relationship is *trust*. When a customer is engaged with you in an ongoing relationship, they will tend to trust you, more and more, to act in their own interest. Trust, affection, and satisfaction are all related feelings on the part of either a consumer or business customer. They constitute the more emotional elements of a relationship, but we already know how important it is to earn the customer's trust if you want to maximize Return on Customer. If your customers don't trust you, then they will see your database and analytics technologies as nothing more than exploitative tools.

---

[1] This is, if you think about it, one of the key differences between a "relationship" and a "brand." Brands don't interact with customers, and don't remember anything about them. In a relationship, you must.

Keep in mind, also, that the customer has their own self-interest at heart. The only way to change the customer's behavior is to appeal to that self-interest, and the only way for you to truly understand that self-interest is to *think like* the customer. In the end, genuine customer understanding will only come from treating the customer like you would want to be treated if you were the customer. This means seeing your company from your customer's perspective, and it will drive you to earn the customer's trust.

Finding jewels in the rough

Understanding how your customers are individually different, in terms of both their needs and their values, is key to maximizing Return on Customer. This kind of understanding can also help you prosper in difficult economic climates, or in difficult market situations. Even in a declining economy, for instance, there are *some* customers who are willing to trade, eager to buy, and in need of your product or service. Unemployment may soar to 10% or more, but *some* consumers will still be making money and spending it freely. Business investment could plummet to a third of its former level, but *some* firms will still be investing. The worse an economic downturn becomes, the more important it is to know which customers are which.

Conversely, even in the best of times, not every customer is going to be profitable. But if you have no insight into your customers' differences then you'll have to settle for the average growth in your sector, rather than exceptional growth. You'll rise with all the other boats on a good economic tide, but no faster.

Whether the challenge involves a faltering economy or a rapidly expanding one, a product flaw or a technical innovation, if you understand the *differences* among your customers, you are more likely to triumph. You can come to grips with the fact that different objectives are appropriate for different types of customers, and different strategies are going to be required to achieve those objectives. Customers with the highest value offer the most financial leverage, but you must understand the economics of all your customers if you want to align your resources efficiently.

Yes, but what *could* this customer be worth?

Up to this point, we have talked about customer values in terms of life-time value, but what about a customer's growth prospects? Whether you define lifetime value by cash flow or by income, and whether you calculate it on a fully allocated basis or on a marginal basis, LTV represents your quantified expectation of the future benefits of dealing with the customer. In addition to the future value you *expect*, however, there is at least the possibility that you can create additional value from this customer, if you adopt just the right strategy, or if you appeal to the customer's motivation in just the right way. After all, this is the reason for trying to understand customer needs in the first place – to *change* the customer's future behavior.

Different customers have different potentials for growth – some have a lot of upside, while others do not. To come to grips with this issue, we will define a customer's "potential value" as the maximum LTV we *could* realize from a customer, *if* we were to employ the best possible strategy to increase his LTV from what we currently expect. Our task is to try to realize as much of this potential value as possible – that is, to convert each customer's unrealized potential value to actual value, by influencing the customer's future behavior with our own communications, offers, and actions.

Estimating a customer's potential value can provide insight into the kind of value-creating leverage you have with that customer, or with particular groups of customers. Lifetime value equations help explain the mechanics of value creation, in terms of both long-term and short-term value, but potential value goes to the heart of the issue on the top of every business agenda: old-fashioned, organically sound business growth. As difficult as LTV may be to model, potential value is an even more elusive quantity, involving not just predicting a customer's future behavior, but also deciphering the customer's options for future behavior.

Nevertheless, it isn't impossible to estimate the customer-growth potentials of individual customers, especially if you begin with a set of customers who have already been assigned lifetime values. Probably the most straightforward way to estimate a customer's potential value is to look at the range of lifetime values for similar customers, and then to make the arbitrary assumption that in an ideal world it should at least be possible to turn lower-LTV customers into higher-LTV customers. In the consumer business this means examining the LTVs for customers who are perhaps at the same income level, or have the same family size, or live in the same neighborhoods. For B2B customers, it would mean comparing the LTVs of corporate customers in the same vertical industries, with the same sales or profit or employment levels, and so forth. A company selling sales-force automation software, for instance, might reasonably expect that two companies in the same industry with the same size sales forces could be worth roughly similar amounts. So if, say, Customer A has bought twice as many software licenses as Customer B, and also requires less maintenance and support, then Customer B probably has the potential to do business at this increased level of profitability, too.

The problem at many companies is that a customer's value to the firm is confused with the customer's current profitability. Measuring customer profitability at all, even in the short term, is often an achievement for a firm. But when a customer's lifetime value is taken into account, the results will be more revealing. Making an explicit estimate of customer potential values will yield still more insight.

SHARE OF GARAGE, LIFETIME VALUE, AND GROWTH POTENTIAL

Table 5.1 shows hypothetical profiles and profitabilities for three different consumers, as seen by a car company. The figures are shown on both a current-period and a 12-year basis. Mr. Higham owns the most expensive model. If the company limited its analysis to the figures available to it on quarterly and annual sales, he would be counted as the most valuable customer among this set.

However, Mr. Jefferies buys a new car from the company more frequently than Mr. Higham (every two years, rather than every three). In addition, Jefferies buys more expensive accessories. He also uses the company's in-house financing, and his family owns an additional car made by the company. As a result, an analysis of the expected 12-year profit from each customer (this company's proxy for lifetime value) reveals that Jefferies' value is more than 50% higher than Higham's.

Mrs. Thompson is clearly the least valuable of the three customers, in terms of both current and 12-year profitability. However, the company has a great deal of potential to improve her value, by finding ways to encourage her to shorten the amount of time between purchases, selling her a financing package, and persuading her to replace the other car in her garage with one of theirs. The result: She has more *growth* potential than the other two customers combined. The point of doing an exercise like this is to become familiar with the idea that customer valuations can hold a great many surprises. If you haven't thought through the many elements that make up lifetime value, as well as growth potential, then you may not fully appreciate the degree to which your firm can actually create more value by maximizing the value of each customer.

	Mr Jefferies	Mrs Thompson	Mr Higham
Current Model	ABC	JKL	XYZ
Profit from Current Model	£6,483	£4,545	£9,124
Purchase Cycle (years)	2	4	3
Retention Probability	80%	60%	50%
Accessories	Alloy wheels, Leather seats	None	CD changer
Profit from Accessories	£625	£0	£200
Finance	£10k / 24m / 10% APR	Other credit provider	None
Profit from Financing	£514	£0	£0
After Sales Average Invoice	£285	£335	£520
Profit from After Sales	£155	£190	£270
Additional Family Vehicles	FGH	Competitive brand	None
Profit from Additional Vehicles	£569	£0	£0
Current Annual Profitability	£4251	£1326	£3378
12-year Expected Profitability	£31,363	£10,398	£19,001
Estimated 12-Year Potential Value	£37,636	£26,385	£25,271
	Most valuable	Most growable	

Table 5.1

Shareholder value at the molecular level

It is easier to think about the dynamics of customer equity at the level of the individual customer if we start by assigning actual and potential values to all current and likely future customers. Doing this might generate a scattergram similar to that shown in Figure 5.1, which portrays how Company D, a business-to-business firm, arrayed its customers by both their actual value (that is, their currently expected lifetime values) and their unrealized potential. Arraying its customers in this scattergram enabled Company D to visualize the nature of its customer base, and to categorize customers into "value tiers" based on their current and potential worth to the firm.

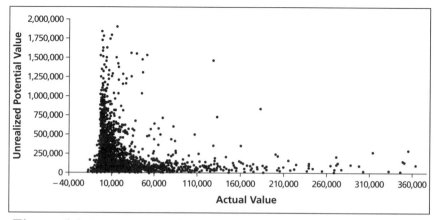

Figure 5.1: **Unrealized Potential at Company D**

To evaluate individual customers' actual and potential values, the company used quantitative metrics derived from several sales periods, overlaid with proxy variables that came from sales force estimates and business judgments. Some of the judgment-based variables that Company D quantified included the sales representative's best guess as to a customer's potential, the current degree of account penetration at the customer, and the willingness of the customer to engage in strategic discussions.

Customers lying along the lower right side of this scattergram have high actual value but little unrealized potential, which means the firm is getting just about all the value it can from them. Company D called these customers its "MVCs" – for "most valuable customers." Although they are highly valuable, they are not likely to grow significantly, so the company's primary goal for this value tier is simply to keep their business through retention strategies and tactics.

On the left side of the graph is a tall spike of what Company D called its "MGCs," for "most growable customers." These customers have little actual value but a great deal of unrealized potential (note the difference in scale between the horizontal and vertical axes). They represent growth opportunities, because most are in fact the most valuable customers of Company D's primary competitors. More investment is warranted for such customers and prospective customers, because this is where a great deal of leverage exists for increasing the firm's overall customer equity – and its shareholder value. While none of these customers are most valuable customers for Company D today, with the right initiative any one of them could become one.

At the lower left of the graph are a few customers with less-than-zero actual value, and relatively little unrealized potential. These customers, which Company D nicknamed "BZs," for "below zero" customers, are the type who sap a company's resources. They are likely to cost more than they are worth, no matter what the company does. Most companies have a number of such customers in their customer base. It's not uncommon for a retail bank, for instance, to find itself losing money on a quarter or more of its customers. One authority cited a wireless telecom company that discovered some 15% to 20% of its customers to be costing it more money than they could ever be worth. Losing money on customers can occur whenever a company has no formal mechanism for assigning potential values to them. When you don't make explicit assumptions regarding customer potential it's easy to deceive yourself into believing that all customers hold at least some prospect of profitability. (If you can't name any below zero customers in your own customer base, seek out a sales person and ask. They'll be able to point out a few.)[2]

By arraying its customers in terms of both their actual lifetime values as well as their estimated growth potential, Company D was able to set different objectives for different customers, and plan distinct strategies for them. It could easily get a picture of where the key opportunities for increasing its own value were to be found, from within its customer base.

---

[2] In some situations, BZs might actually serve a broader purpose for a firm. For instance, a regulated monopoly, such as an electric utility or a phone company, might be required to serve all customers, regardless of economics. Or perhaps a business simply can't operate at all unless its scale encompasses a larger number of customers, including unprofitable ones. The important questions to ask are these:
• Do you know which customers are profitable? Do you know how to make them more profitable?
• Do you know which customers are unprofitable? Do you know whether you can ever make them profitable, over the period of the relationship?
• If the answer to that is "no," then do you have an exit strategy that works for the customer and for your firm?

Growth factors for customer value

In the fields of medicine and cell biology, a "growth factor" is a protein that attaches to a receptor on a cell and then changes that cell's behavior, usually leading to proliferation of the cell culture. Growth factors are a useful concept for thinking about customers, as well. There are many different variables that figure into calculating the growth rate of a customer or group of customers, but two of the most important growth factors are customer loyalty and revenue stimulation.

Research supports the generally accepted wisdom that loyal customers buy more, cost less to serve, and generate higher margins. However, in the last few years a question has been raised as to the intrinsic value of "loyalty" as a customer characteristic. One academic study of a large catalogue retailer concluded that some customers remain loyal simply because they have negotiated the lowest prices. Such customers return little profit to the enterprise; some one-time-buyers generate higher margins and are more valuable, either because they are concerned primarily with seeking out particular products, with less regard for price paid, or because they don't have enough knowledge of the enterprise's costs to engage in effective price negotiations.

Just because a customer is predisposed to be loyal does not necessarily mean that the customer will not also be a tough price negotiator or a frequent service problem. Whether or not customers who are predisposed to be loyal are more or less profitable than other customers will probably depend on the reasons behind their attitudes and the structure of the business itself. The trick is to ensure that your retention efforts are focused on the most profitable customers, and to quantify the value created by an increase in retention. Remember that lifetime value is your goal – not just customer loyalty, per se. (You could easily generate increased customer loyalty by selling your products below cost!)

There is a more useful way to articulate the role of customer loyalty in creating value, however. In addition to thinking about loyalty as a characteristic that can be ascribed to a particular type of customer, think of it as a *growth factor* that can be used to increase a customer's lifetime value beyond what was otherwise expected. By definition, lifetime value will increase for any profitable customer who continues with your company for a longer period than previously expected. Loyalty, in other words, can help you capture more of a customer's unrealized potential.

In some businesses, customer retention is a more important element of potential value than in others. Consider the graph in Figure 5.2, which shows how a life insurance company's customers have been ranked by their lifetime profit contribution and then parsed into deciles accordingly. (These figures have been "actuarially normalized" – that is, none of the customers lost any credit for dying prematurely!) While you might think the size of a policy would be the primary determinant of lifetime value for a life insurance customer, the U-shaped curve in the chart shows clearly that a policy's face value actually correlates with two types of customers – those with high positive value as well as those with high negative value. Why is this? Because the more important factor in determining lifetime value in this category is the customer's renewal longevity. If a life-insurance purchaser does not remain a customer for at least a few years, the company may not earn enough from the premiums to recover the sales commission paid. And the bigger the policy, the more value is lost by the firm if the customer leaves the franchise early.

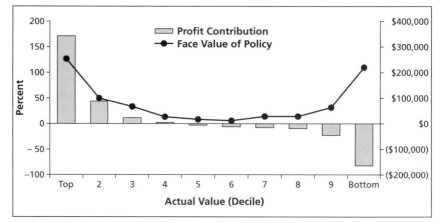

Figure 5.2: **Customer Profit Contribution at a Life Insurance Company**

The second important "growth factor" to consider in improving a customer's value is revenue stimulation – selling additional products or services to customers, in addition to whatever the customer is expected to buy right now. It's only logical that the more products and services you have available to sell to a customer, the greater his potential value is, and you should try to realize as much of that potential value as possible. Moreover, in many industries there is a strong correlation between the number of different products or services bought by a customer, and the customer's loyalty. In retail banking, for instance, it's accepted wisdom that customers with three or more products from the same bank were more likely to remain loyal during the year than people with only one or two products.

But even without considering its impact on customer loyalty, selling more things to current customers will almost always improve lifetime values. If an automotive manufacturing company sells the customer a car, then it should also want to sell accessories for the car, the financing of it, a warranty and service extension, and perhaps even an insurance policy. If an advertising agency sells its corporate client a television and radio broadcast campaign, then it should also want to sell print advertising, media planning, direct marketing, sales promotion, and a number of other services that are usually planned and executed in conjunction with broadcast advertising. Homebuilders are buying mortgage companies and leasing homeowners their monthly security and landscaping services.

In each case, the number of additional products and services available for sale to a customer provides an important indicator of that customer's potential value. By this criterion, the total unrealized potential of a company's customer base is closely related to the company's overall growth potential. One reason for Tesco's relatively high market valuation is investors' perception that the retail chain now has a good deal more growth potential, which derives from its highly successful online and home delivery business – a business that sells a lot more products than you could find in a typical grocery store.

In trying to assess a particular customer's potential value, some of the questions you want to answer include:
How much of the customer's business currently goes to your competition, but might be pried away with the right approach or relationship?

- How much more of a customer's business could you capture if you modify your treatment?
- How many more product lines might the customer buy from you? What other services or products could you sell the customer, if you had the products available?
- What additional value would you capture if you could prevent the customer's defection?
- The customer has needs you know about. How can you identify the needs you don't yet know about?

- How much could you reduce the cost of serving this customer, while maintaining their satisfaction?
- How much could this customer be worth in terms of referrals and other non-monetary contributions?

Your opportunity for organic growth is directly related to the unrealized potential values of your current and future customers. But that is just your perspective. From the customer's perspective, potential value has to do with *need.* This is important: *The outside limit of any customer's value is defined by the customer's need, not by your current product or service offering.*

If your goal is to grow the value of a customer, then you want to meet a greater and greater portion of that need, creating more value as you do so. Additions to your own offering may or may not be required.

Therefore, after examining all the different cross-sell, up-sell, retention, and other immediate opportunities, you should always take a step back from the product or service you're actually selling, and ask yourself – for this customer and other similar ones – what is the actual problem the customer is trying to solve? Seeing your value proposition from the perspective of the customer, putting yourself in the customer's shoes, trying to visualize what is involved in solving the customer's problem with or without your product – all these activities are essential to understanding customer needs. And they are essential to capturing more of your customers' potential. When your customer buys from you, what else do they need to solve their problem? What specific part of that problem are you helping to solve? Are there products or services you *could* sell as an additional part of the overall solution? As we first saw in Chapter 3, you have to ask yourself again and again, *what business are you really in?*

In the end, increasing the return on any particular customer requires the customer to change their otherwise expected future behavior, in such a way as to yield more value. With better insights into what a customer needs, you should be able to make your value proposition more compelling, timelier, and just more relevant to the customer, and with any luck you'll influence their behavior.

Grouping customers by their needs

Getting a handle on what any particular customer really needs can be difficult. Categorizing them into groups will help you to (1) understand their differences more easily, (2) communicate customer insight to others, and (3) devise and execute different strategies for different types of customers in a straightforward, cost-effective way.

There's no single best way to group customers by needs, but market research can provide an initial framework. You may already have on hand one or two good market-research studies categorizing customers by attitudes, needs, or preferences, and this is not a bad place to start, in terms of planning strategies to change the future behaviors of different types of individuals.

When thinking about customer needs, it's important not to focus too much on your product or service, because this will put "blinders" on your analysis. Your thinking must distinguish clearly between a customer's need and your product's attribute or feature. Companies create products and services with different features specifically designed to satisfy different customer needs, but the products and features themselves are not equivalent to needs. If you work for a credit card company, for example, don't define your research in terms of gaining a better understanding of, say, platinum card holders. Define your research in terms of gaining better insight into the needs of high-end consumers, *some* of whom hold, or would consider holding, platinum cards. One such consumer might value status and position, while another might want convenience and practical benefits, and still another might look for good deals and consider the total financial value of the relationship.

Seeing things from the customer's perspective requires you to visualize at least some of the many different perspectives your individual customers will have. Best Buy's highly successful customer-centricity initiative (Chapter 3) is based on meeting the different needs of five different types of customers. A package shipping company selling to business customers might categorize them as urgent shippers, efficient freight users, or up-and-coming direct marketing firms. A financial services firm might categorize customers as secure borrowers, advice-and-consent decision-makers, or dealmakers.

One American hotel operator asks its family vacation prospects a few questions in order to be able to map each prospective customer into one of five different categories, including: "variety seekers," "family tradition builders," and "security blanket" customers. Each type of customer goes on vacation, but they vacation for entirely different reasons – that is, to fulfill different needs. These needs are characteristics of the customer, not of the vacation service or product. Each type of customer has different requirements for various ancillary services that contribute to the vacationing experience, and different "hot buttons" that provoke their interest and desire.

Golden Questions

Defining the right categories for your customers is important, but once you've devised the categories it's also important to be able to classify individual customers accurately. You can get this insight from a variety of sources – perhaps from the customer's transactional records, or from a third-party database, or from survey-and-projection research. However, the most effective way to classify an individual is to use interactions with the customer.

At most firms, existing market research into customer needs has probably relied on lengthy questionnaires administered to samples of a few hundred customers, with the results being projected to the broader population. But if your goal is to influence an individual customer's behavior, then your very first task is to decide what type of customer this particular one is – which of your 3, or 5, or 20, or 200 different needs-based categories most accurately describes this specific customer? You must be able to place the customer into one category or another based either on what you already know or on what you can find out quickly, in just a few simple interactions.

If the customer first appears on your website, then you may be able to deduce their needs by following their click stream. Online merchants are becoming expert at categorizing customers into different needs-based types, in order to speed the service provided to them. In a complex category in which customer tastes or preferences vary immensely – books, music, or videos, for instance – customer needs might be analyzed by a statistical technique that has become known as "collaborative filtering," which predicts a customer's needs by making mathematical comparisons with large numbers of other customers. Amazon predicts you will like a certain book because, of the several million customers they serve, a few thousand have bought more or less the same books you have bought from Amazon in the past, and most of them liked this other title, as well. You may never have heard of this particular book, but based on such statistical results, chances are you'll like it. CDNow offers videos and CDs using the same type of analytics. The needs-based categories produced by collaborative filtering software are not mapped out in advance, and do not depend on survey-and-projection research. Collaborative filtering categories are instead constantly changing, "real-time communities" of customers likely to have similar tastes or interests.

If, rather than the website, your customer calls in to the call center or shows up at the sales counter, or if he sits down with your sales rep, then you need a simple interaction to generate the right feedback directly from the customer. We call an interaction like this a "Golden Question." It should be designed to elicit the most possible insight while requiring the least possible effort from the customer. A research subject might have been willing to sit still for a 100-question interview in return for a £25-coupon or maybe a sandwich. But you need a quick-and-easy way to categorize *each* of your customers, when you encounter them.

A vacation time-share company, for instance, wanted to be able to distinguish between two primary types of buyers – "vacationers" and "traders." Vacationers tend to buy a time-share at a particular resort they like, and then vacation there regularly, allowing the company to rent their property out in the meantime to defray the ownership cost. Traders, on the other hand, like to exchange their time-share property for other owners' properties at a variety of different resorts, and usually vacation in different places each year. The company wanted to be able to tailor its investment offer to address the different needs of these very different prospective customers. But how could it decide which category any particular prospect belonged to? The demographics were, in many cases, the same, and residence postcode was irrelevant.

It turned out that the most useful and predictive characteristic of a trading family is that they have no under-age children. So, during any discussion with prospective new customers, the sales rep asks whether there are children at home under 18. If the answer is "yes," it's almost a certainty that the family will not be trading their property much, at least not until the children grow older. Armed with this knowledge, the firm could design more appropriate offers, communications and treatments for its customers.

In 2002 a large American health-care insurance firm selling to employers began providing different treatments to different types of employer, based on what each type wanted from the insurer. The insurer hoped to provide a greater level of service, improve each employer's satisfaction with the relationship, and increase customer retention. But before it could carry out this ROC strategy, the insurer needed (a) insight into how it might categorize these employers, based on what they each needed from the firm, and (b) a mechanism (i.e. Golden Questions) for mapping different employers into the correct needs-based categories.

The company sold to three different types of employer customers: small businesses, large businesses, and public sector employers.

For small businesses, the company first identified the most valuable and growable of these accounts, and then conducted interviews among a research sample of them to identify their needs. They were able to categorize some small business employers as "engaged customers," who are highly involved in the health insurance process and constantly solicit feedback from their own employees on the process. "Engaged customers," they discovered, want a high level of information regarding cost-saving options, different health-care plan configurations, and new product and service offerings. They also expect a close interaction with the health insurance company, especially when it comes to keeping their employees informed about the specifics of the health-care plan.

In contrast, "bare bones" small-business customers are basically not interested in the health-care insurance process, with all its complications and intricacies. These customers just want the system to run on autopilot, and are unlikely to spend much time trying to figure out their bills or cost summaries from the insurance company. They rely on their broker to handle this kind of detail.

Large-business employers were categorized as either "Don't Rock the Boat" or "Lend me a Hand" types, based largely on the fact that companies have very different answers to the question of whether the insurer should be "more proactive in its relationship with my company – for example, reviewing my claims history and making cost-saving suggestions, or contacting me on a regular basis about changes in the industry." The "Lend Me a Hand" customers rated this almost twice as important as the "Don't Rock the Boat" customers.

Finally, the insurance firm found that there were many needs that Public Sector employers have in common with one another simply because they *are* "public sector" organizations. These employers could be categorized as either "fulfilled" or "unsatisfied" customers, depending on whether they thought their needs were actually being addressed properly.

The insurer's research enabled it to identify the Golden Questions necessary to categorize different types of customers into the appropriate needs-based groups. To take just one example, below is the decision tree of questions to be asked of the firm's most valuable and growable small business employers. These questions could be asked when the customer calls in to the call center, or on the website, or during a face-to-face sales call. (The first question, for example, was "how important is it for you to understand the specifics of the healthcare process?" and the second question was "do you prefer to have your primary relationship with the insurance company or the broker?")

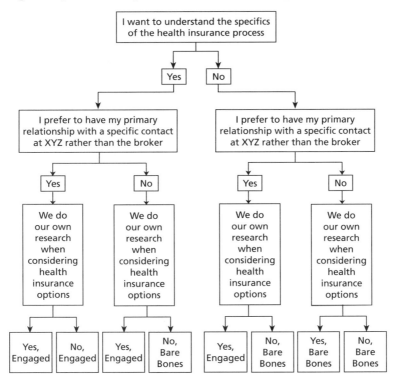

Figure 5.3: **Decision Tree for Small Business Customers**

Does all this mean "customer dialogue" is a boardroom issue?

It should be obvious by now that managing customer dialogue is way too important and valuable to be thought of as merely a "marketing" activity, or as something you can outsource to a web firm or an email ad agency. Customer interactions are how you get your customers' perspectives, so that you can meet their needs accurately, and increase their value to your firm, which ends up increasing the value of your firm.

Managing customer interactions is the most direct way to understand customer differences. And understanding their differences is how you can grow your company's value, no matter what, in good times and bad. It's how you figure out the different things that different customers need most, so you can have the biggest influence on each individual customer's future behavior.

But in addition to knowing what motivates individual customers, you have to have a mechanism for quantifying the results of these behavior changes. You need to know, in advance, whether a customer's lifetime value will go up or down – and by how much – based on your current actions. Stay tuned, because that's the subject of our next chapter.

6. Predicting the Future

Making money in the stock market is easy. Just find a stock. Buy it.
When it goes up, sell it. If it don't go up, don't buy it.
Will Rogers, 1935

Making money in business is easy. Just find a customer. Do something
to increase his lifetime value. If it don't go up, then don't do it.
Don Peppers and Martha Rogers, 2005

Yes, we know what you're thinking. Return on Customer requires you
to track changes in customer lifetime values, even though they represent changes in customer behavior that will happen months or maybe
years into the future. Heck, the lifetime values themselves are just
predictions, too.

But you don't have to depend on clairvoyance. While it's by
no means a trivial exercise, more than half of medium and large
businesses are already ranking their customers by some measurement
of value, and nearly a quarter of the time it involves explicit lifetime
value calculations. Return on Customer, based on *changes* in lifetime
value, is within the grasp of virtually any firm that maintains a com-
puterized record of customer transactions. Obviously, what we're
suggesting will entail some forecasting. It won't be easy at first, but
your forecasts will grow more reliable with experience.

Whether you are dealing with a large, statistically stable population
of consumers and sophisticated predictive modeling, or spreadsheets
describing smaller numbers of business-to-business relationships, lifetime value still requires prediction. This makes some people nervous,
because no one can know for sure how accurate a forecast is until the
future actually arrives. But don't forget that many different aspects of
your business already depend quite heavily on accurate predictions.

You predict market prices, distribution logjams, employee hiring rates, currency fluctuations, R&D results, investment returns, customer demand, inventory losses, delivery timetables, and competitive actions. You plan for alternatives using the best information available, seasoned with a good dose of plain judgment. That's what they pay you to do, right?

Well, what we're going to be talking about in this chapter is no different. In fact, as we'll see, in many ways the predictions that go into ROC calculations will involve more accuracy, and more stability, than the predictions that go into other areas of your business.

Leading indicators of LTV change

ROC requires you to predict future customer behavior changes, using currently available information. In essence, you must identify and track the "leading indicators" of lifetime value changes. The question is, what data is *available today* to forecast up or down movements in a customer's lifetime value?

The predictive modeling process involves two basic steps. First, devise an equation for lifetime value that includes whatever transactional records or other data are available on your customers' actual past spending (and other measurable behaviors, such as visits to the website, and trackable referrals). It's best if you have several years' worth of transactions, but often you'll have to make some assumptions based on business judgment or sampling. Such records might include, for instance, each customer's purchases every year, the margin on those purchases, and the number of years the customer did business with you. Essentially, you'll use the computer to go back through historical customer records and make the actual calculations of lifetime value for as many individual customers as possible.

The second step is to identify the most predictive currently available variables with respect to the lifetime values (LTVs) you calculated in the first step. You started by calculating LTVs for individual customers using historical records, and now you comb back through all the information you have about these individual customers in order to pick out correlations and relationships with their individual lifetime values. The data you use will include purchase transactions, but might also include complaint and service records, demographic or firmographic information, needs-based research, or even attitudinal information on customer attitudes – essentially, any information at all that you can obtain in a customer-specific form, with respect to the customers whose lifetime values you have already calculated.

In the end, you're going to generate a second equation for lifetime value, but this will be an equation that uses currently available data to *predict* an individual customer's lifetime value, rather than using transaction data to *calculate* it retrospectively. For example, the LTV equation devised by the British department store in Chapter 4 included variables such as the customer's age and gender, along with the number of days since the customer's last purchase, the amount spent in the last twelve months, and the number of different departments shopped in during the last six months. Each of these variables can be measured currently, and changes in their value will drive changes in lifetime value.

A large consumer-service business devised a predictive model for lifetime value based on ten years of customer transaction records. Because the likelihood of returning seemed to be the most important single factor in determining lifetime value, the company first ran a statistical analysis to see what independent variables most affected a customer's likelihood of returning. Using the findings from this analysis, they created an equation for predicting the future revenue from each customer. This formula was not limited to transactional records, but included "outside" variables as well, such as the general level of consumer confidence in the economy at large. Each customer's future contribution was estimated by applying historical margin to their predicted future revenue. In the end, in addition to demographic data, the company's lifetime value model used such variables as the first type of service purchased, the average rate paid, and how recently the last service was purchased.

The variables driving your lifetime value model can be thought of as the leading indicators of lifetime value change. It won't ever be perfect, because predictions never are. You'll also probably face problems having to do with the availability of data, analytical issues, and other obstacles. But reliability will improve with experience, as you learn to collect, monitor and weight the information more and more accurately. The leading indicators of lifetime value change fall into four general categories:

1 *Lifetime value drivers.* These are the elements of the LTV equation itself – the actual components that determine how much value the customer creates for the company, over time.
2 *Lifestyle changes.* When a customer takes a new job, or gets pregnant, or retires, or gets married or divorced – when their lifestyle or personal situation undergoes a substantial change, their LTV may also be affected.
3 *Behavioral cues.* The number of contacts initiated, the services or products contracted, or the number of complaints or comments submitted, and payments made or not made – are all examples of behavioral cues.
4 *Customer attitudes.* These include such things as satisfaction level, willingness to recommend your company or products, and likelihood of buying from you again. A customer's attitudes have a strong influence on their future behavior.

Lifetime value drivers:
Supersize your firm's worth

Academicians as well as businesses are paying more attention to the issue of customer lifetime values, and customer equity. One study that calculated customer equity from publicly available information for five companies – Ameritrade, E*TRADE, eBay, Amazon, and Capital One – found a close relationship between customer equity and market capitalization for three of the firms. Only Amazon and eBay seemed to be over-valued by the market, relative to the average customer lifetime values the study inferred for each company. On the other hand, these were the two most rapidly growing companies in the study and, while the authors attempted to use a sophisticated forecasting tool to model the future growth of each one's customer base, it's possible the tool needs further development. It's also quite possible that these companies' rapid growth as high-profile Internet companies created its own, self-fulfilling stock-market valuation.

This study found that a 1% improvement in the customer retention rate would increase customer equity by 3% to 7%, depending on the individual company being analyzed. The researchers also found that a 1% increase in sales margin would generate about a 1% increase in customer equity, while a 1% reduction in acquisition cost would generate an increase in customer equity of just 0.3% or so. In other words, at least for these companies, customer retention has more impact on customer equity than sales margin or customer acquisition cost. This shouldn't be surprising, because all five firms in the study have frequent and direct interactions with their customers.

As customer lifestyles change, so do their lifetime values to your company

Demographic information and vital statistics can be useful tools to help model a customer's lifetime value. A major advantage of using this kind of data is that you can often obtain it from third-party databases, independent of your own records. Because it's available independently, you can frequently use demographic and other data to predict the lifetime values of prospective customers with whom you may have had little or no past contact, by comparing them demographically to similar current customers. (However, many databases don't contain an individual customer's demographic information; instead they use a combination of census data and overlaid projections based on address or postcode.)

A lot of demographic information won't change much in the short term, and won't be much help in predicting lifetime value changes. It's highly unlikely, for example, that a person's race or gender will change (although it's not unlikely you'll have to revise an incorrectly keyed data entry for one of these items from time to time). The demographic information that will change, however, is the kind of data we generally associate with a person's lifestyle or personal situation. Categorizing customers by their lifestyles is one of the most frequently found elements of any customer-management program. It's logical to think that a customer's lifetime value will change with their age, albeit gradually. But more sudden changes in a person's lifestyle are even more important, such as professional or career moves, household address changes, and changes in marital status, education level, or health.

For some businesses, lifestyle changes are extremely important indicators of lifetime value. When people get married, move, or get divorced, for instance, it precipitates all sorts of buying activity, from appliances to cars. It's important to have some mechanism to learn about your customers' lifestyle changes, whether through an online profile update, or perhaps special offers for special occasions.

Business customers, too, go through stages, and "lifestyle changes." When a business becomes less profitable, or more profitable, its buying behavior is likely to change. When a privately held business goes public, or when a company acquires another firm, its behavior will change. Pharmaceutical companies, for example, watch for changes in the professional lifestyles of the doctors who write prescriptions, such as taking in new partners or employees, adopting new medical practices, relocating offices, or acquiring new medical technologies. Similar changes occur within clinics and hospitals. Technology firms watch for lifestyle changes among companies that are heavy technology users, including changes in the size or makeup of a firm's internal IT staff, and increased (or decreased) interest in outsourcing or offshoring.

Behavioral cues: Watch what they're doing

Suppose you have a satisfied customer spending £100 a month, with an estimated lifetime value of £1000. Now suppose this customer calls in to complain about a faulty product or an episode of bad service. Your call-center rep handles the complaint professionally, and as a result the customer not only remains satisfied, but actually writes a complimentary letter to the firm. Your customer's lifetime value increased dramatically with that transaction. That transaction *created actual value for your company right then*, even though you haven't yet collected any cash as a result of the customer's increased propensity to buy from you, or to recommend you to friends. The fact is, you might actually have incurred a current-period cost to satisfy the complaint.

That transaction was a very big and obvious behavioral cue. There are many other such cues, not always as big and obvious, but just as predictive. If you're in a business like telecom, or financial services, or retail, you have an abundance of behavioral cues within the millions of data points in your customer transaction database. Your credit card customer begins to use their card less (or more). Your mobile phone user signs up for a different plan. A customer buys a second product upgrade in just two months. One of your frequent business travelers begins flying in fully paid first-class seats. This is equally true if you're a B2B firm selling to corporate clients. You may detect an increase in the number or quality of the people at the customer who are involved in your business, or an early contract renewal, or a reduction in the service agreements in force at a customer's business site. Perhaps one client agrees to a more comprehensive service contract while another puts part of your business out for bid.

Behavioral cues have always been important to high-volume financial services businesses, primarily as an aid to managing credit risk. A credit card firm is likely to review its database of cardholder transactions closely in order to spot any anomalies that might indicate either that a card has been stolen, or that a cardholder is getting into debt over their head. You might remember a call from your credit card company when you first used it in another country, or when you bought that larger-than-usual piece of jewelry, or when you ordered some expensive products online. Typically, the card company will call you just to verify that it is really you engaging in these unprecedented activities, and to reassure itself that your card is still actually in your possession and hasn't been lost or stolen.

Behavioral cues are not hard to identify, and some of them can be easily understood on their face:

- When a husband and wife each carry a credit card using the same account, the couple is much less vulnerable to competitive offers from other cards than either would have been as an individual cardholder.
- When a new customer buys a car on the recommendation of a friend, he is more likely to be satisfied for a longer period, and to consume additional branded services from the car company, such as financing and warranty extensions.
- Retail consumer-electronics customers who enlist for an email newsletter have a significantly higher probability of returning for additional purchases in the future.

Obviously, you should track transactions involving purchase and consideration, but you should also remember that not all interactions involve purchases. In addition to purchasing events, you should keep track of web pages visited, sales calls received, surveys completed, and call center inquiries, for instance. It's not necessarily the wisest policy to pester your customers themselves for data, but it's always smart to capture whatever interactions and transactions occur naturally during the course of business. The more transactional data points you have with respect to your customers, the more opportunity you have for using the data to deduce the future behavior of particular customers or groups of customers within your base.

Remember the large consumer service business we mentioned earlier? The company's lifetime value model was useful as far as it went, for example, but executives lamented that it would have been far more useful had the company been able to access additional records. They would have liked to account for each customer's supplementary spending, because this is a key element of the company's profit. But their systems couldn't make the connection. They also send out a regular satisfaction survey to recent customers, and while they use its results to improve their overall service, this data might have proven even more useful in predicting individual lifetime values – not to mention improving a particular customer's value by meeting the needs they indicated in the satisfaction survey, perhaps generating additional business as a result.

Royal Bank of Canada has been focused on customer relationships in its retail banking business for more than a decade now, and became a "best practice" case study in this area years ago. One of the secrets of the bank's success is the fact that it constantly monitors the behavioral cues in its customer database, in order to optimize current income results against likely changes in lifetime value for individual customers. It has a great deal of data, but it must also do the right analysis, in order to spot the cues. For instance, until recently the bank's "Behavioural Based Modeling" system calculated the effects its various products and services had on customer lifetime values by using customer-specific revenues, but using the average (non-customer-specific) cost-to-serve figure. The problem is that banking customers don't all cost the same to serve. Different customers incur different costs. One might prefer dealing with the bank online, for instance, while another might prefer the more expensive teller window.

Customers will generate different levels of credit risk, processing charges, and other expenses. After upgrading their software, Royal Bank of Canada began tracking customer-specific costs as well as revenues, and the result was that the accuracy of their lifetime value figures improved immensely, with more than 75% of their consumer customers moving two or more deciles in rank as a result.

In evaluating its actions for different customers, Royal Bank of Canada optimizes "overall efficiencies," a term the bank uses to include both current income and LTV changes in the calculation. One example of a policy change based on maximizing overall efficiencies has to do with "courtesy overdraft limits." This product is now provided for the vast majority of consumer customers, rather than just its heavy-hitters. Each customer's overdraft limit is set based on that particular customer's overall relationship with the bank. Anyone who has been a customer for at least 90 days, has a low-risk credit score, and has made at least one deposit in the last month will have some level of overdraft protection. Not only does this enhance each customer's experience with the bank, but it actually increases the bank's efficiency during the check clearing process, reducing the number of write-offs and allowing account managers to focus on sales activities. Overall, since 1997 the bank has increased the profitability of its average client by 13%, and increased the number of high-value clients by 20%.

The metrics of attitude

Other leading indicators of lifetime value change come not from customer behaviors, but attitudes. Attitudes influence behavior, so to the extent a firm tracks such attitudes (either through surveys or via regular interactions with individual customers) it should be able to make informed judgments about changes in its customer equity. Although it's certainly not a linear relationship, in general a customer who is highly satisfied with a firm's product or service is more likely to remain loyal to that firm, more likely to refer other customers to it, and more likely to buy additional products or services from it, than is a customer who is not highly satisfied. Some authorities have even tried to correlate customer satisfaction levels with market value, with moderate success. According to the University of Michigan's National Quality Research Center, for instance, increasing a company's customer satisfaction by 1% correlates with a 3% increase in market capitalization. Just as important, any decrease in customer satisfaction, or willingness to recommend the company, would almost certainly indicate a decline in a company's value.

The degree to which a firm is perceived to pay attention to its customers also affects customer attitudes and willingness to do business with it in the future. One study, jointly led by Roper Starch Worldwide and Peppers & Rogers Group, showed that among bank customers who rated their banks as providing good customer service, an ability to treat a customer as a distinct individual (such as providing a personal contact, sending only relevant messages, and anticipating the customer's needs) made a significant difference in that customer's future intentions. Twenty-six per cent of those who rated their banks high on customer service, but low on such "relationship capabilities," stated that they were likely to switch away at least one product in the next year. However, among those who rated their banks high on customer service and relationship capabilities, just 1% stated any intention to switch products! This astounding contrast is a strong endorsement for a customer relationship's benefits in retaining customers, at least when it comes to retail banking, and we've seen similar findings in the telecommunications industry, too.

The key to using customer attitudes as a useful tool in tracking real-time lifetime value changes is to identify the correlation between a customer's current attitude – or change in attitude – and their actual behavior in the future (as seen through new purchases, customer loyalty, share of wallet, and so forth). Measuring a customer's change in attitude would be particularly helpful for businesses that don't have the advantage of a sizeable volume of customer transactions.

One survey tool that measures customer attitudes, RSx, uses data from customers, employees, and channel members to assess the strength of their relationship with the company, and then correlates various elements of that relationship with particular customer behaviors or stated intentions, such as their intent to buy from the company again, to calculate financial outcomes. Designed by Carlson Marketing Group with the assistance of Prof. Robert M. Morgan of the University of Alabama, the RSx framework also helps organizations identify the important drivers of stronger relationships as well.

RSx was applied to one retailer's situation, for example, and showed that customers who had a strong relationship with the company (defined in terms of trust, commitment, and mutual benefit and alignment) delivered 48% more sales than customers who had a "medium" or "low" relationship with the company. The retailer found that strong relationships were driven by customers' perceptions of the store's personal service, convenience, shared values, and communication. For the retailer, the RSx model showed that strong relationships with customers resulted in:

- 34% higher stated intent to purchase
- 50% higher positive word of mouth
- 16% greater share of wallet.

These outcomes enabled the retailer to quantify the projected impact of its relationship-building efforts on business outcomes.

Stats and the single customer

In the final analysis, all lifetime value calculations are predictive, because no one can know the future for certain. But statistical analysis has its limits. In a group of a million consumers a statistical model can predict aggregate behavior, such as a likely response rate or attrition rate, with reasonable accuracy. Such models can detect behavior patterns that tend to indicate some future actions, such as defection, providing the manager with an ability to intervene. They can also be used as benchmarks. But reduce the size of the overall group being analyzed, and the stability of these statistical calculations begins to break down. At the level of the individual customer, even the most sophisticated statistical models are subject to a great deal of randomness and noise.

On the other hand, once you do get all the way down to the level of the individual, you can make direct, one-to-one contact, and this kind of interaction will always trump statistical models! If you have really good, up to date, reliable data about an individual customer, and that data is based on direct interaction with the customer, then you should be able to predict the customer's behavior much more precisely than you could if he or she were simply one customer in some statistical cluster. For this reason, direct interaction with your customers will provide you with the most useful and reliable leading indicators of their future behavior.

For a company serving just a few hundred B2B customers, statistical models are rarely as useful as the objective judgments of the sales and account managers closest to the customers. These judgments, too, are just educated forecasts, but they can be made more reliable and accurate by adhering to a standardized set of criteria. Has a contract been proposed? Is there a standing purchase order? Do we provide the back-end maintenance as well as product installation? Is the relationship characterized by partnership and collaboration? Can this customer refer other customers to us? Have they done so in the past? Judgments made on the basis of such objective but non-quantitative criteria are critical to making educated decisions about customer lifetime values. They help get a firm as close as possible, in as objective a manner as possible, to understanding the actual values of individual customers.

AN EARLY WARNING SYSTEM FOR INCREASING OR DECREASING RETURN ON CUSTOMER

The sooner you see indications that some of your customers' lifetime values are changing, the more prepared you'll be to take advantage of those changes, either by intervening to delay losses, or by trying to hasten or facilitate gains.

Consider, for example, how British Airways used "leading indicator" data about incoming Executive Club frequent flyers to increase its customer equity. As is the case with other airlines, British Airways' distribution of revenue in North America was highly skewed, with a small minority of frequent flyers producing the majority of the revenue tracked through Executive Club.

British Airways knew that if it could identify these high-value members as they joined the program, then it could take steps to ensure their early activation and to increase the likelihood of longer-term retention. Using data from the Executive Club program, the airline developed and implemented a set of predictive models to classify new Executive Club enrollees into groups based on their estimated future value. Analysis showed that valuable members could be identified as early as one week after enrollment, allowing the airline to adjust its marketing and management actions with respect to these high-value customers early on.

To make use of this information, the company sent different communications to different customers, depending on members' expected future value. The most valuable members received enhanced enrollment kits, communications encouraging them to fly in premium cabins, and access to the most experienced Member Services agents – all with the objective of enhancing their experience and strengthening their relationship with British Airways. The less valuable members received less expensive communications focused on economy travel.

As a result of its initiative, British Airways was able to increase the customer equity represented by its high-value Executive Club members, essentially by adding value from them earlier than would have otherwise been the case, with more predictability and dependability. It also saved money on marketing and service for low-value members, without decreasing its member satisfaction scores.

The fact that ROC analysis can apply to individual customers, one customer at a time, also provides some interesting opportunities for a firm to create value that is truly lasting. Consider that the longer a customer relationship endures, the less likely any single positive experience is to improve it. A customer's expectations of being served well will go up, over time, as dependable service continues and a relationship prospers. But, even though a relationship may have lasted a long time, a single bad experience can substantially harm it – unless, during the course of the relationship, the customer has invested time and effort in teaching you how to better serve them. In this case, the more the customer has invested in structuring the service you are providing, the more likely they will be to try to work out any problems that spring up along the way. A greenhouse operator whose greenhouse environments are being managed by Eneco, for instance, is less likely to flip to a competitive natural gas supplier on account of a glitch in one month's service. Rather, such a customer has a strong self-interest in working out problems in order to continue the service it has helped architect.

What's on the ROC dashboard?
Leading indicators

Return on Customer may well be the speedometer for organic growth, but the rest of the dashboard is filled with leading indicators of lifetime value change.

Most firms will find it helpful to mix their methods – a snippet of behavioral cues, a few lifetime value drivers, and maybe a jot of attitudinal metrics. A financial analysis of the costs and benefits associated with particular customer activities or transactions can be mixed with and weighted against an assortment of variables to account for all the nuances of customer value that can't be easily quantified.

One academic study maintains that companies should begin focusing on measuring customer satisfaction, brand equity, customer loyalty and share of customer, because these metrics…

> "…can enhance the value of the customer base in the same way that an investment in technology enhances manufacturing capability. Such metrics are leading indicators of how the firm will perform in the future."

The first step may be to identify and track these leading indicators. But the payoff comes when you use these metrics to calculate the changes in lifetime value and customer equity they imply. Suppose, for instance, that through research and historical analysis you were to determine that an increase in a customer's "willingness to recommend" your company or product or service implied a predictable increase in your customer retention rate. This, in turn, would imply a fairly precise and foreseeable increase in lifetime value (and customer equity).

Let's say we calculate that a 1% retention improvement increases customer equity by 4%. Comparing historical survey responses to transactional records, we discover that first-year customers who rate themselves 5 out of 5 on a "willingness to recommend" scale are 20% more likely to remain loyal through the second year, compared to other customers. Thus, if we could increase the proportion of 5/5 ratings within the population of first-year customers from, say, 30% to 40% (ten percentage points), we would be generating a 2% increase in average first-year customer retention. That in turn would imply an 8% increase in the customer equity attributed to first-year customers.

OPTIMIZING RETURN ON CUSTOMER

We've already discussed the fact that the actions you take to acquire more customers, or to stimulate more business today, can have negative effects on your customers' future value to you. Maximizing ROC requires you to balance your actions. The most common and obvious marketing strategy that can reduce a customer's future value is over-solicitation. All of us, as consumers, can intuitively feel the negative effect of excessively being bombarded with marketing.

A colleague of ours, for instance, banks with one of the new, Internet-only financial services firms. From its beginning, this particular firm enjoyed a good consumer reputation, and became one of the most recommended financial institutions. At first, our colleague was impressed with them, and recommended them to all his friends. But after a while, they started in with the "campaigns," sending him repeated solicitations to entice him to borrow money. Our colleague never borrows, and hates the very idea of being in debt. The bank's solicitations were completely irrelevant to him. Their latest offer is a cash reward to any customer of the bank who refers a friend. He still banks with them, but he has stopped recommending them to his friends. The moral of the story: Now the bank can't buy from this customer what he used to give them for free. Today's revenue sometimes becomes tomorrow's cost.

This poses a problem for marketers, however. Research by advertising and direct marketing agencies, as well as by academic investigators, has shown that it often does require more than one "hit" to communicate a message to, or elicit a response from, a consumer. A television ad, for instance, might require three to five exposures before most consumers absorb it and can "play back" its central message for a researcher. So clearly, in most situations, it makes sense to repeat your solicitation, at least up to a point.

On the other hand, every customer's "optimum" level of communication or messaging is different. Each customer has their own tolerance for marketing messages and information. In addition, the difference between reinforcement and annoyance depends on the relevance and helpfulness, to a particular customer, of the message. Once you exceed an individual's tolerance level, the ROC on that customer will turn negative with increased messaging. More messages will not only fail to create value from that customer – they will actually *destroy* value. The customer will simply become less and less likely to respond to future offers (or even consider them!), less willing to pay attention to your various entreaties, less positive in their attitude toward your firm, and less interested in your advice or information. You may add new customers with

your efforts, pushing your overall customer equity up, but this positive effect
will be offset by an erosion of value among some of your existing customers.
This is the dilemma that marketers face.

You can visualize the ROC optimization problem by tracking the leading indicators of lifetime value change. Figure 6.1 illustrates the results of a survey of
some 200 British companies to quantify the RSX metric of customer attitudes.
The graph shows how customers' attitudes toward a relationship improve,
reach an optimum, and then degrade, as communication frequency increases.

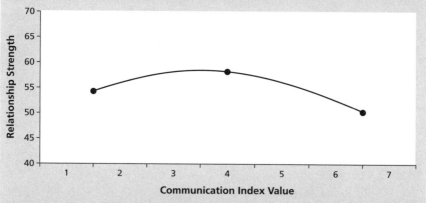

Figure 6.1: **Optimization curve, RSX**

Marketing in the pharmaceutical business is often characterized as an
"arms race," as rival companies compete to make increasing numbers of sales
calls on doctors. The drug companies deploy legions of representatives
charged with visiting doctors and providing them with more details about their
drugs. A big problem, of course, is that doctors are very busy people themselves, and they don't have a lot of time to meet with sales reps, even when
those reps bring free samples with them. IMS Health, a Connecticut-based
company that collects and disseminates healthcare and pharmaceutical information in more than 100 countries, plotted the percentage increase in
prescriptions written for particular drugs against the frequency of "detailing"
calls made by the drug company's sales representative on those doctors.
The optimization curve shown in Figure 6.2 illustrates how this behavioral cue
– increased prescribing volume – changes as the frequency of contact
increases over a one-year period, based on nearly 20,000 British doctors
writing prescriptions for a market-dominant drug.

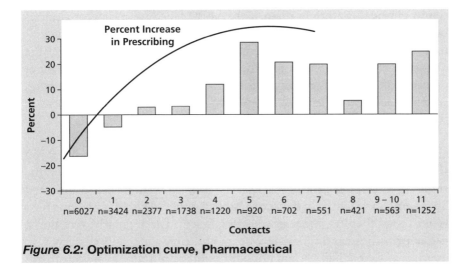

Figure 6.2: **Optimization curve, Pharmaceutical**

In the end, a company's leading-indicator variables will resemble, in many ways, some of the non-financial metrics espoused by a number of management thinkers today, including the "Customer Perspective" of the Balanced Scorecard method pioneered by Harvard Business School's Robert Kaplan and David Norton. The purpose for all these nonfinancial metrics is similar, as well. According to Kaplan and Norton.

> "...financial measures tell the story of past events, an adequate story for industrial age companies for which investments in long-term capabilities and customer relationships were not critical for success. These financial measures are inadequate, however, for guiding and evaluating the journey that information age companies must make to create future value through investment in customers, suppliers, employees, processes, technology, and innovation."

The primary difference between an ROC approach and most existing nonfinancial metrics models, such as Balanced Scorecard, is that ROC is a financial metric. When you track leading indicators, even though some of them may be "nonfinancial," what you will be doing is linking them quantitatively to specific corporate value creation (or destruction).

It might be tempting to dismiss this sort of leading-indicator analysis because it doesn't seem rigorous enough to yield a meaningful calculation, but a firm's other projections of market growth or profit over the next several years (and not just the next quarter) are certainly no more precise. All we are suggesting is that *companies should pay more rigorous, quantitative attention to the actual impact that their current actions have on their customers' future behavior.*

By all means, you should continue to do whatever other financial analysis your firm has always done. But in addition to that analysis you should also try to measure the impact your current actions have on the value of your most productive asset – your customer base – and then hold someone at your firm accountable for the results. If your business is like most, then your managers will come and go regularly, remaining in their positions only for a few years at a time. ROC will allow you to measure *now* the likely impact of your managers' actions on your firm's future value. Think of it this way: ROC is the measure that will *drive better decisions every day,* and *traditional measures* will be the *result.*

Tracking your ROC should give you a leg up competitively, as well. But you can't just install the speedometer on your dashboard and expect to max it out. You have to anticipate the actions of your competitors, as well. In other words, you need more than a plan for measuring ROC: You need a *strategy* for succeeding with it.

7. Strategy: ROC in a Hostile Environment

Shhh! Sit perfectly still, please. Listen carefully, now...there! Do you hear it?

That sound is the soft, steady drumbeat of your competitors coming for your best customers. Your competitors are not sitting perfectly still. They are not being nice to you at all.

It doesn't matter how good you are. Your Return on Customer will be affected by your competitors' actions. Whenever one of your competitors improves the quality of its product or service, or lowers its price, or invests in better relationships, or offers some compelling benefit, your customer equity will be affected. Even if you sit perfectly still and do nothing at all, the return you generate from your own customers will decline.

Strategy – to borrow the military definition – is a plan for succeeding in a hostile environment. You may have a plan for maximizing your ROC, but you still need a strategy for succeeding with this plan, given that your competitive environment is hostile, very hostile.

In this chapter we're going to think through the strategic implications of Return on Customer. For instance, how will an ROC perspective change your business strategy? Can you use ROC to gain an advantage over your competitors? Are there structural factors that might allow you to apply ROC in a way different from how your competitors do it?

ROC offers you competitive leverage for your business

If Archimedes had the right ROC, could he move the world?

You can use your own structural characteristics as a lever to deliver added value to your customers – providing customer benefits on account of such things as your geographic scale or the scope of information you have available, for instance. By doing this, you will increase your Return on Customer, and generate a higher shareholder return.

ABB is a $20 billion Zurich-based industrial conglomerate with diversified operations selling more than a hundred different types of products, from arc welding equipment to wind turbines, and with offices in dozens of countries around the world. Among its many products, ABB sells oil-drilling pipe and equipment for both onshore and offshore drilling operations. An oilrig might cost upwards of £80,000 per day to maintain on location, and so ABB's drilling customers all want to avoid any unanticipated delays in receiving pipe from ABB. The problem is that even if ABB is perfectly on time in its production of pipe, after a drilling company takes possession of its shipment at ABB's factory it must then get the pipe through the frequently complex customs barriers at the country of destination. Oil wells are often located in far-flung locations, from Africa to Vietnam to Chile. A common cause of delay is the customer's own inability to clear importation and customs on time.

While ABB could easily take the position that its customer's import problem is not its problem (it's the customer's pipe now, not ABB's), instead the company has figured out how to meet its customers' need in a more comprehensive manner. ABB operates many different businesses in multiple locations on six continents. For a few of its key customers, the firm has begun offering drilling pipe contracts that are priced for delivery to the rig, taking on the risk of customs delays itself. The company charges for these deliveries at cost, and this service is not designed to be a profit center. But ABB is offering great added value to its key customers using its own global structure, and this gives the firm a *competitive* advantage, relative to other, less global drilling-pipe suppliers.

Using the unique characteristics of your firm to provide added value to your customers, relative to your competitors, not only generates increased shareholder return from your customers, but does so in a way that gives you a *strategic advantage*. It's an advantage that anticipates a hostile competitive environment.

Consider Orica, a publicly held Australian company that sells chemicals, paints, fertilizers, and explosives. In the commercial explosives business, Orica is a global company serving a large number of mining companies and quarry operators. Quarry operators want their blasts to break rocks up into optimally sized pieces. An ineffective blast might leave the rock in chunks too large to be processed in an economically viable way. But as many as 20 different variables have to be considered when calibrating an explosive blast, and each quarry's ability to experiment with these parameters is limited. Because of its size, and the many different mines and quarries Orica deals with, the company can collect a great deal of information from around the world, cataloguing input parameters and blast results for a wide variety of situations.

As a result, Orica has developed a sound understanding of blasting techniques, and now offers to take charge of the entire blasting process for a customer, selling a service contract for broken rocks of a specific size. This service has two advantages for Orica's customers. First, they minimize the risk of poorly executed blasts. With an Orica contract, they basically establish a "floor price" for correctly broken up rock. Second, many of a customer's fixed costs, such as equipment for drilling, and employees to manage the process, now become variable costs, which makes it that much easier for the customer to manage each separate blasting project, for their own customers. So, what business is Orica really in? Commercial explosives are commodities bought mostly on price, but by solving an additional part of the customer's problem Orica has established a sustainable model for escaping from the limitations of a commodity business.

What makes the whole idea possible, however, is the fact that Orica is one of the largest global providers of commercial explosives. Because of its ubiquitous customer base, the firm is uniquely positioned to compile information on blast techniques and parameters. It would be difficult for one of its smaller competitors to match this offering. While maximizing the return it earns on each customer, Orica also leverages its unique structural characteristics to advance its business. It has utilized the qualities that are unique to its structure to increase shareholder return.

If you look closely at the nature of your own business – your distribution structure, geographic footprint, scale of operation, and so forth – you should be able to see ways to use your insights into your customers to magnify any strategic advantages you have, and sometimes diminish your disadvantages, as well. If you concentrate on maximizing your return on each customer, you may be able to create a sustainable advantage for your business that your competitors will have difficulty matching.

But inevitably, you will have to decide what your limits are. You can't be all things to all people – or even all things to your most valuable customers. Like farmers, you will need to optimize what you do – to see things from your customer's perspective and match their needs with the realities of running your business in a way that works.

Just say "no"

An effective competitive strategy requires you to decide what you want your firm to do. In many cases, you may decide to expand your capability to meet your customers' needs. But it may be even more important to decide what you will *not* do – what types of products you will *not* sell, what services you will *not* offer, and even what types of customers or clients you will *not* serve.

Narrowing your focus is the essence of strategy. That necessarily means deciding which opportunities to give up, as a business. It is one of the most difficult decisions any firm can make. Any company that succeeds with its competitive strategy usually does so by structuring its entire business around the strategy, from supply chain and distribution issues, to hiring, production, intellectual property, and even financial reporting. Often the resulting business structure itself will make it difficult, if not impossible, to do everything. The structure of the business, designed as it is around a strategy, in effect makes the choice for the company.

Southwest Airlines, for instance, is well known for its superb, easily articulated strategy that involves low-cost air service. This strategy is supported by the airline's decision to offer point-to-point service only, with no interline connections, and by labor work rules that permit employees to perform multiple tasks. It is supported by the airline's decision not to offer meals on board its flights, not to offer any first-class seating, and not even to sell tickets through traditional corporate travel agency channels. Southwest's low-cost strategy is the reason behind the airline's remarkably efficient airport and gate operations, enabling flights to get into an airport and out again in a mere 15 minutes, far less than the minimum 30- to 45-minute turn time that other American airlines require in domestic service. Southwest could probably attract more high-value corporate air travelers if it were to offer a first-class section, agency commissions, and interline baggage transfers. The problem is that this action would undercut its overall competitive strategy, which is integrated into the very structure of its business. Turn times would have to be longer, travel agency policies would be more costly, baggage handling would be more difficult, and so forth. Similarly, while the airline could undoubtedly increase customer satisfaction by serving meals onboard – at least on its longer flights – this, too, would undermine its overall strategy. This is the nature of an effective strategy – giving things up, and refusing to engage in activities that do not further the strategy.

FedEx began its life competing with traditional freight carriers such as Airborne and Emery. These firms collected freight packages of varying size and weight, and then used airplanes to ship them. Rather than offering to carry freight packages of any size, however, FedEx restricted its service to small, airborne packages, which it shipped en masse on its own hub-and-spoke air transportation system, delivering them to their destinations using its own trucks. While FedEx out-performed its competitors in delivering small, urgent packages, it had to forego opportunities to ship other kinds of packages.

Firms with clear strategies find it necessary to make such choices. They just say "no" to what might otherwise seem like lucrative business opportunities – not because they don't want to make money, but because they do, and every business activity must promote their competitive strategy if they are to be successful. This is at least one good reason why McDonald's is unlikely to offer white-tablecloth restaurant service as an add-on in any of its establishments, and why German software maker SAP is unlikely to offer desktop operating systems in addition to its enterprise software. Even diverse financial conglomerates with multiple-business units must still ensure that each individual unit has a clear strategy for succeeding among its own group of competitors.

To decide whether your own firm has a clear competitive strategy, you need only ask yourself what types of products you would choose not to make, what services you wouldn't offer, and what customers you wouldn't serve. If you and the other executives at your company answer these questions the same way, then you have a clear strategy that everyone understands. If not, you may be vulnerable to a competitor who has a clearer, more effective strategy than yours.

Maximizing Return on Customer does require you to make choices; you must say "no" to some activities that you might otherwise find attractive. Certainly, a key aspect of this strategy is the principle of customer selectivity. (And as we learned in Chapter 5, saying "no" to doing business with "Below Zero" customers can increase your Return on Customer.)

Perhaps a more difficult choice, however, is involved simply in the act of treating different customers differently. When your offering anticipates an individual customer's needs you are by definition refraining from offering that customer all you could offer – and this flies in the face of traditional marketing practices. Traditional marketing is based on maximizing product sales. Each of your product managers wants to expose as many customers and prospects as possible to his product. For you to choose *not* to communicate an offer to a customer simply because it may not be quite as relevant for that particular customer – well, that can be difficult, because you are, in effect, forgoing a product-selling opportunity.

But ROC has a lot more to tell us about strategy. When you focus on the overall value your customers create, you can change the very nature of the competitive process.

How ROC can strengthen your competitive approach

Why do your customers choose to buy from you rather than from your competition? This is the question two Canadian marketing professors asked more than 2000 senior executives from around the world, in interviews and group discussions that stretched over more than four years. The industries represented in their study cover an extremely wide range, including consumer packaged goods, utilities, construction, e-commerce, software, telecom, financial services, cars, chemicals, packaging, airlines, and retailing. But according to their study, the answers to this question were remarkably similar, and tended to focus on the company's interactions and relationships with its customers. The executives said they thought the most important drivers of customer choice were things like "trust, confidence and strength of relationships, as well as...convenience, ease of doing business and support..."

However, despite the fact that customer relationships and interactions are clearly the most powerful competitive tools in management's hands, these executives spend much more time and energy trying to improve and perfect their products and technologies, rather than their customer relationships. Customer-based innovations, the professors claim, would be a better subject of executive attention because they "are less easily replicated by competitors, and thus offer a more certain basis of sustainable competitive advantage."

Are they right? *Does* a Return on Customer strategy yield a truly sustainable advantage? There is no doubt that customer-oriented firms are more likely to focus on the most profitable customers, with better, more relevant offers, than their less customer-oriented competitors. Customer-oriented firms will configure their products, their services, and their stores to meet these customers' needs more effectively. Their competitors, at least initially, may not be prepared for the technologies required, or they may not have access to the expertise and analytical capabilities they need. Or they may simply be less aware of the business benefits of thinking all the time about how to increase the return they generate on customers.

This kind of "first-mover advantage" can rarely be maintained indefinitely, at least with respect to most competitive strategies. As the customer revolution progresses, more and more firms will embrace the idea of customer-oriented competition, and competition will undoubtedly intensify. But contrary to what you might expect, a customer-specific approach can actually create a sustainable competitive advantage – perhaps even a permanent one – when you measure this advantage one customer at a time.

The most effective way to protect a customer from competitive predation is to lock him into a "learning relationship" that makes it progressively more attractive for him to stay loyal than to defect. A learning relationship is one that develops a "smarter and smarter" context as you continue to interact with your customer and learn about their individual needs, responding with increasingly relevant products or services. The more you can get a customer to "teach" you about their needs – provided you can actually meet them with an increasing degree of customization or an increasing amount of service – the more loyal that customer will become, because they won't want to have to expend the time or take the risk to reteach some other firm what they have already taught you.

In effect, *a learning relationship* dramatically increases a customer's cost of switching companies or brands. Success depends on learning how to serve this particular customer better than any of your competitors can, because you know more, through direct interaction, than anyone else can know. There is an important distinction to draw between the kind of customer insight gained through third-party databases and market segmentation, and the kind that comes from direct customer interaction. It is direct, one-to-one interaction with your customer that gives a learning relationship its real staying power. Your competitors won't be able to duplicate this kind of customer insight by themselves simply by tapping into the same third-party database or performing the same type of analysis. In order to learn what you know, they would first have to entice the customer to go to the time and effort of interacting with them, in the same way they have already interacted with you.

Creating learning relationships can be an expensive but rewarding tactic, depending on how detailed your customers' needs are, and how difficult it is for your firm to accommodate them. However, there will almost certainly be at least a few, very valuable customers (or very growable ones) who are well worth your investment. These are the customers Eneco found, when it began offering to monitor greenhouse environments, for instance. Moreover, these most desirable customers are exactly the ones you most want to take from your competitors, and the ones your competitors are trying to take from you.

At least on a first level, then, a customer-oriented competitive strategy is in fact just that – a strategy, based on securing a competitive advantage that will withstand competitive response. But this strategy is executed one customer at a time. If you're a smart first-mover in your own category, you'll try to lock in the most desirable customers before your competitors begin copying you.

On a second level, however, ROC can provide additional leverage for your chosen competitive strategy. For instance, against the front bulk-head on most Southwest Airlines planes there is a row of backward-facing seats, sharing a table with a front-facing row. Most of the company's planes have just one cabin (and one bulkhead), so there's only one row of these seats. Rather than assigned seating, the airline boards its passengers by group number (in order of check-in), and the highly desirable back-facing seats are usually among the first taken. But hypothetically, let's suppose the airline were considering whether to install more back-facing seats in its fleet. The company might take this action if, by doing so, it could streamline its boarding process or reduce operating costs somehow. In the absence of any ROC analysis, this is the criterion by which the decision would be made.

But what if the type of passenger who checks in early for Southwest (and therefore gets these seats) tends to cost the airline less to serve, not just by showing up early, but perhaps also by booking online more often, or carrying less baggage, or even complaining less frequently? The cost savings the airline would realize by attracting more passengers of this type would be realized in the future as well as the current period, and the actual amount of cost savings would depend on their lifetime values (in Southwest's case, primarily their frequency of travel). Alternatively, ROC analysis might show that this type of customer tends to cost the airline more to serve, so the cost-reducing benefits would not be as great as the airline originally thought. The point is that by developing a Return on Customer perspective, the airline will be able to make a decision that more accurately advances its fundamental competitive strategy.

Think of it this way: Your competitive strategy is always set at the enterprise level. To provide a sustainable competitive advantage, a strategy must be based on some innate characteristic of your business – your size or cost structure, for instance, or your organizational culture, or your industry position. Whatever your strategy is, however, and regardless of the rationale, Return on Customer can translate it down to its customer-specific implications. Your competitive strategy won't change a bit; ROC simply shows you how to gain more advantage by applying that strategy in different ways for different customers.

Product, price or service

In *The Discipline of Market Leaders*, authors Michael Treacy and Fred Wiersema argue that companies face a structural dilemma in choosing whether to offer customers the best product, the lowest price, or the most comprehensive service. Customers want all three benefits, but it isn't possible for any business to be the best competitor when it comes to delivering all three attributes simultaneously. The disciplines required to produce the best products, lowest prices, or best service, are product innovation, operational efficiency, and customer intimacy, respectively, but these disciplines are structurally incompatible. Product innovation requires creativity and agility, while operational efficiency requires simplicity and scale, and customer intimacy requires neither agility nor simplicity, but rather a scope of different offerings and expertise for different types of customers.[1] As a result, the best *strategy* is to choose one discipline or another, in order to be the most competent competitor in your category when it comes to delivering that particular benefit.

However, the customer insights that come from your efforts to maximize Return on Customer can strengthen *each* of these competitive disciplines, leveraging each one's different structural advantages:

- *If you're a customer-intimate competitor such as* USAA *or Eneco,* the advantages of customer insight are obvious. You can better configure your services, offer broader and more relevant solutions, and concentrate on client acquisition, retention and development, rather than on product innovation or cost control, per se. Your Return on Customer increases as you generate greater customer loyalty, more cross selling, better satisfaction, and word-of-mouth referral business. Nordstrom Department Stores, for instance, is a customer-intimate company whose success is directly related to the high quality of its customer relationships. It relies on personal shoppers and advisers who cater to the individual needs of its higher-value customers – advisers who make recommendations based on each shopper's previous purchases and declared preferences, individually recorded in the firm's customer database.

- *If you're an operationally efficient competitor such as Southwest Airlines or McDonald's,* customer insight helps you keep your costs even lower by aligning your processes with individual customer values and needs, eliminating redundant marketing activities, and trimming the services offered to your lower-value customers even while adding services for higher-value customers. Anticipating your

---

[1] While Company A might choose to be flexible and agile, in order to produce the most innovative products, when Company B chooses to scale its operations up and simplify them so as to drive production costs down, Company A will be unable to match B's low costs and still maintain its agility. Similarly, if Company C adds a series of services and product features to ensure its customers always have the most relevant solution for them, then B may not be able to match the scope of these offerings without giving up its efficiency.

customers' individual needs improves customer loyalty (an important side benefit), but also reduces your costs by simplifying the effort required to fit the right product to the right customer. You can use interactive relationships with customers to encourage less costly behavior from them, so your firm can handle their transactions more efficiently. Dell, for instance, sets up dedicated web pages on its site to help its enterprise customers manage their purchase orders and requisitions for Dell equipment. But by providing cost and efficiency benefits to its customers for ordering online, Dell also holds its own costs to a minimum, in addition to saving its sales reps from having to take time out from selling in order to answer routine inquiries.

- *If you are a product innovator such as Toyota or Cisco Systems*, then your competitive success depends not only on being nimble, but also on staying ahead of market trends, constantly driving down the "cycle time" for bringing your new products from concept to production and rollout. More timely and accurate customer insight, including direct customer interaction, can help you "foresee the future" more effectively in your market. For example, a product-oriented pharmaceutical company wants near-real-time feedback on medical indications, prescription patterns, and market intelligence that doctors have regarding the use of its drugs and the actions of its possible competitors. It uses customer insight to better track and understand the outcomes of new product test panels, in order to shave a few months or even just a few weeks off of the time required for a patented product to be brought to market. The sooner it learns about impending changes or other developments in the medical products landscape, the sooner it can start on its own next round of innovation. Once again, ROC can play an important role. Whenever you bring a new product on stream, you will be generating current-period profits as well as lifetime value improvements for the current and future customers you serve.

Because of the cost-reducing benefits of making things simpler for customers, there is in fact a great deal of overlap in the customer-facing technologies different companies use, even when the underlying competitive goals are quite different. For instance, JetBlue places a heavy reliance on web-based bookings. Their online self-service function not only makes it more convenient for the customer, increasing satisfaction and loyalty, but also allows the airline to operate more efficiently, with lower operating costs. In reality, this kind of technology would fit JetBlue's competitive strategy whether it were pursuing customer intimacy or operational efficiency.

Choosing the right customers

From a Return on Customer perspective, the battle with competitors is not just a battle over products and positioning, but over customers. Maximizing ROC requires a firm to treat different customers differently – to engage in customer-specific activities. But the very first customer-specific question you have to answer is: *Which customers should you concentrate on?*

This much we know: In nearly any category, some customers have a great deal more value than others. However, if everyone simply goes after the most valuable customers, then wouldn't that violate the cardinal rule of strategy? Wouldn't you have more chance of succeeding if you pursued some group of customers not being chased by everyone else?

Your best ROC strategy is to ensure that your own organization is the most structurally appropriate, when it comes to dealing with any particular type of customer. Even if you have enrolled a customer in a learning relationship, when you face a determined competitor who is structurally better suited to handle a particular customer than you are, then you can expect your relationship with that customer to degrade over time, or at least to require a greater investment on your part.

The idea of aligning your customer relationships with your competitive or structural advantages has different implications depending on whether you are selling to consumers or businesses. If you sell to businesses then you should think of yourself as participating in your customer's value chain, and find a role in the customer's ecosystem that fits most closely with your strength. ABB uses its international presence to reduce the risk its customers face with respect to meeting complex and demanding customs requirements. Orica uses the data it has collected on a large number of controlled mining blasts in all sorts of environments. Each firm is adding value for its customers in ways that its competitors will find hard to match.

If you sell to consumers, then the kinds of customers you want are the ones who have needs for things you are better able to provide than your competitors. If you're a solution seller, focus on those customers who find complete solutions more compelling. If you're a low-cost producer, you might actually find it competitively advantageous to focus on the lower margin customers who are not likely to be well served by your competitors. If some companies are sending BZ customers packing, then as a low-cost producer you might actually be able to restructure the value proposition just enough to make a decent profit on these same customers.

Enterprise Rent-A-Car is a well-documented case proving that it is sometimes more important to select the right customers for your competitive structure, rather than simply focusing on the most "valuable" customers in your category. Instead of competing for the highly lucrative frequent traveler car renter, Enterprise caters to the occasional renter – the infrequent renter. Usually, this is a consumer in need of a car for a few days while their other vehicle is being repaired. The company's entire structure is oriented around this competitive strategy, including how it contracts with insurance firms and repair garages, and where its offices are located. On its website, Enterprise boasts it has an office within 15 miles of 90% of the American population, which is critical when it comes to serving the occasional renter. This is a person who is not likely to want to travel out to a Hertz or Avis airport location just to rent a temporary replacement car for their own use at home for a week.

The single most salient characteristic of Enterprise Rent-A-Car's strategy, in fact, has to do with its choice of customers. Everything else flows from this strategic choice. While the customers Enterprise serves are "low value" in the overall car rental category, the company knows that these particular customers have a certain unique and different set of needs that aren't well met by the competition. These are the needs Enterprise has chosen to meet, and they are meeting them better than their competitors can. Why? Because the structure their competitors have set up to deal more efficiently with the most valuable customers in the category makes it difficult for them to deal well with the occasional renter.

As a part of this competitive strategy, Enterprise is a highly customer-focused firm. With nearly $7 billion in revenues, Enterprise says of itself, "it is our goal to be the best and not necessarily the biggest or most profitable" car rental firm. Like Tesco, its mission statement is centered on the goal of creating long-term value from its customers:

> "We will strive to earn our customers' long-term loyalty by working to deliver more than promised, being honest and fair; and 'going the extra mile' to provide exceptional personalized service that creates a pleasing business experience."

Perhaps it is a coincidence, but Enterprise Rent-a-Car is a privately held company, and not publicly traded. It can afford to pay attention not just to short-term results, but to long-term value creation, as well.

Tough customers

Sometimes, because of the structure of your industry or your distribution network, or simply because of the type of market you're dealing with, you will have to cope with very powerful customers – customers who have a great deal of negotiating leverage in their relationship with you. Customers like this can demand and get highly favorable terms, in the form of lower prices, better services, priority delivery, and so forth. Occasionally such customers are so powerful that they may all but require you to lose money just to serve them.

In retailing, the giant mega-stores and category killers, such as Wal-Mart and Toys "R" Us, are very tough customers. In the high-tech field, companies that manufacture components in mature markets, like microchips, must sell to tough customers like Dell, or Hewlett-Packard. In the car category, almost all of the manufacturers are large, difficult to deal with, and obsessively concerned with price.

It's important to keep your perspective when you must serve "oppressive but necessary customers." In the first place, you can only make rational decisions with respect to such relationships if you actually do a good job of tracking your customers' actual and potential values across your entire customer base. This means not just annual customer profitability, but some forecast of customer lifetime value as well, along with an estimate of growth potential – for all your customers, not just the largest, most powerful ones.

But in addition, you should realize that it really is a power struggle, so you must somehow develop more power for yourself in the relationship. (Ironically, given all our discussion about "trust," a tough customer will very likely trust *you*, but you will need to step carefully when dealing with *them*.) Keep in mind that your goal is to serve your customer's best interests, but you won't be able to do this if you have to give up on the relationship because it has become too one-sided.

One former senior executive at Company T, a Fortune 100 technology firm, says that "[Company T] was always looked upon as the must-win account for every supplier – and we knew that well. So we routinely adopted very tough positions and made stringent demands." According to this executive, the company's "typical behavior" with respect to suppliers was to "work closely with that company, study them, and try to extract as much of the process and knowledge as possible, then fire the supplier and do it ourselves. Overall, being self-sufficient was always a key objective. A few companies managed to avoid this ultimate fate by continually innovating faster than we [at Company T] could absorb, so they maintained the ability to deliver new value each year."

This is not unethical behavior – far from it. It's the policy that many firms follow. Indeed, probably most large and powerful firms operate this way, especially in highly competitive environments, or during periods of rapid and potentially disruptive innovation. The problem, if you're selling to such a customer, is that it will be very difficult to increase your Return on Customer, or even to maintain it. It will be nearly impossible to establish any kind of loyalty, or to protect your margins – but that is in fact the purpose behind your customer's behavior in the first place. When dealing with suppliers this kind of customer *wants* to use its power to hammer its costs down, which means hammering down your margins if you're the supplier. And powerful firms have powerful hammers.

Magna International sells parts to all the world's giant car companies. Car companies are renowned for their tight-fistedness, their tough price negotiations, and their buying power. This is a brutal environment for a seller, but Magna is an innovative firm. With 219 manufacturing operations and 49 product-development and engineering centers employing 77,000 people around the world, Magna is a large company – but it is still at a disadvantage when it comes to selling to most of its gigantic customers.

Magna set up its Magna Steyr operation specifically to cater to the most important, unmet needs of these car giants. As the car business has matured, it has seen increased fluctuations in demand for particular models. The car companies themselves are often unable to cope with these demands, and a "hot" model might be sold out for months at a time. Rather than selling parts at arm's length, the Magna Steyr division brings together all the capabilities required to manufacture cars, from parts to engineering, design and production. For example, when demand for the new Mercedes M-Class SUV exceeded the capabilities of Mercedes' Tuscaloosa assembly line in late 1998, Magna Steyr was producing additional M-Class vehicles for Daimler-Chrysler on its own assembly line in Graz, Austria within just nine months. This kind of service can help a firm protect its margins even with the toughest customers. And as a strategic asset, Magna Steyr's capabilities provide the company with a sustainable competitive advantage over its own competitors.

There are a number of tactics that can be used to generate a reasonable return even on tough customers, however, and each of them involves increasing your own company's relative power, uniqueness, or indispensability in the relationship. In our experience, you should concentrate on tactics that fall into any or all of four general categories:

1 *Customization of services or products.* When you build a high-end, customized service around the more commodity-like products or services you are selling, then you can create switching costs that increase the customer's willingness to continue to deal with you rather than bidding out the contract at every opportunity. Ideally, you will lock the customer into a "learning relationship," but most tough customers will be wary of allowing such relationships to develop. The trick here is to ensure that any high-end services you develop can only be duplicated by your competitors with great effort, even if they are instructed in advance (and they will be – by your customer!). This is the strategy behind Magna Steyr, but other examples include Orica's crushed rock business, and Eneco's greenhouse environmental management business.

2 *Perpetual, cost-efficient innovation.* To the extent you can stay ahead of your customer with innovative product or service ideas, you will always have something to sell. Your organizational mission must center on being nimbler, more creative, and cost-efficient – all at the same time. But the value you are really bringing to the customer here is innovation – not the products themselves. Realize that many

tough customers will do their best to absorb your innovation in order to do it themselves, or perhaps even to disseminate it to your competitors. In either case their motive is to regain their negotiating power in dealing with you. So perpetual innovation is just that – perpetual. If you can keep the wheels spinning fast enough, and provided that you don't lose control of your costs, then you can safely deal with very tough buyers.

3 *Personal relationships within the customer organization.* In the end, businesses have no brains and make no decisions. Only people make decisions, and people are both rational and emotional by nature. The individuals in your own organization need to have personal relationships with the individuals within your customer's organization. In the high-tech or car-manufacturing arena, this might mean developing relationships with the design engineers within a customer's organization who are responsible for designing your firm's components into the final product. In the retailing business it could mean developing relationships with the regional merchandising managers who get promoted based on the success of the programs you help organize for them.

4 *Appeals directly to end users.* A highly desirable brand, or a completely unique product in heavy demand by your customer's customers will pull your products through the customer's own organization more easily. The "Intel Inside" advertising campaign is designed to create pull-through for Intel. When Mattel offers Toys "R" Us an exclusive arrangement for particular configurations, or products with brand names such as "Barbie" or "Hot Wheels" or "Harry Potter," it is making itself indispensable to this very tough customer. Similarly, any sort of information system or added service that saves time or effort for the end user can also be expected to put pressure on a tough customer. Dell's web pages for enterprise customers not only save money for the customers, but also give Dell a direct, one-to-one relationship with the executives who actually have the Dell computers on their desks.

Don't forget, however, that selling to a tough customer is a deliberate decision, and it's possible that this decision has been made for the wrong reason. There are almost always choices to be made, when thinking about the types of customers to serve, but often companies focus on the very large, most visible and "strategic" customers (tough customers), in the erroneous belief that simply because of their size they will be the most profitable. According to the ex-technology executive from Company T,

> "Overall, I don't think that we [at Company T] are all that different from most category dominant companies. These guys know they're good and can get away with demanding just about anything. What many suppliers discover sooner or later is that despite the outward allure of serving a company like ours, once you actually win the business, the long-term payoff can be too painful to harvest. It was not unusual for a supplier to 'fire' us as a customer by politely declining to bid on the next program."

Does your customer strategy support your competitive strategy?

By this point it should be clear that ROC should be aligned carefully with your overall competitive strategy. You'll run into problems if your business strategy is not well articulated, or if it doesn't enjoy wide consensus among your company's various operating departments. We regularly encounter problems like this in our consulting practice and, while they are usually couched in terms of poor employee training, cultural obstacles, or inadequate change management, often the root cause of the problem is a disagreement or misunderstanding among senior managers with respect to the central competitive strategy of the firm. Different cadres within an enterprise will have different opinions regarding the firm's primary competitive goal, and when implementing a customer strategy these conflicting ideas will play havoc with the metrics chosen to build the business case. Without a clearly agreed business strategy, a customer strategy may be simultaneously judged a success by one set of metrics and a failure by another.

This is a particularly difficult issue for a multinational firm trying to push its customer-oriented strategy outward from headquarters, to be implemented by operating units in its various countries. Frequently such a multinational will have fixed on a set of supporting technologies

– a Siebel or SAP platform, for instance, or maybe an Oracle database –
and while it provides the support standard and technology platform, it
will leave it up to the regional or country managers to implement the
programs necessary to take advantage of this platform.

The attitude at headquarters is likely to be: "We get it here in
London (or Brussels, or New York), but how do we convince our
various operating countries to commit to the right customer strategy?"
The biggest problem, however, often involves a misalignment of the
company's competitive strategy. It is frequently the case that the HQ
staff and business strategy folks have a vision of their company as a
customer-intimate competitor, and the "selling in" goal of their
message to the operating countries is to use this new platform to
improve customer retention and account penetration, or to protect
margins in the face of the increasing commoditization of their products. But for many such international organizations, the regional or
national operating units are evaluated primarily in terms of cost
containment and operational efficiency. Thus, the country managers
themselves are more likely to want to employ their technologies for
streamlining and cost-reduction purposes.

Remember that your strategy, whatever it is, can be leveraged and
improved with the customer perspective you take to maximize ROC.
But alignment is important throughout your firm, and once you do
have alignment with your competitive strategy, the next step is alignment with your people. Everyone in your organization has to "get it"
with respect to ROC. That's what we'll be discussing in the next chapter.

8. Making It Happen: The Adoption Challenge

We know nothing about motivation. All we can do is write books about it.

Peter F. Drucker

Baseball is 90% mental. The other half is physical.

Yogi Berra

Maximizing Return on Customer is easier said than done. It's a question of motivation, rather than skills and tools alone – a mental game, not just a process or technology change.

To treat different customers differently, you have to bring together people playing different roles in a variety of functions across your whole company. Sales reps, marketing managers, contact-center personnel, service technicians and financial staff – everyone must understand and embrace the task, and they will need access to the appropriate technology. Not only your employees, but also your vendors and partners will need to use the technology, as well as the customers themselves; customer self-service offers compelling benefits to them, not just to you. ROC is not just for "marketing," or "sales." Eventually it will touch everybody who touches your company. It's therefore vital that your processes accommodate all the various roles and responsibilities of these different users and participants.

At most firms, taking the customer's perspective requires a truly sweeping cultural transformation, inculcating a kind of customer sensitivity in every employee. Because it is so radically different, as a business practice, this new type of business competition can have severely disruptive effects on any organization with an already well-established culture or mindset. People within your firm must not only understand what it means to be customer-oriented, but they must also *want* it to happen. They must adopt this new way of thinking as their own. Even if half of it *is* strategy and systems and process and technology, it's still 90% mental.

"We spent a lot of money on CRM but it didn't work"

Customer relationship management (CRM) initiatives fail for many reasons. Often, the information systems just don't connect well enough to provide the right customer data where and when it is needed. In other cases, the customer strategy is not properly aligned with the competitive strategy, as we discussed in the last chapter. By far the biggest single factor behind most CRM failures, however, is a simple lack of adoption. *Everyone* who touches a customer must adopt the objectives behind the program as their own. They must not only embrace the idea of treating different customers differently, but they must enthusiastically pursue it. If they do not, then there is little chance your firm will be able to work out all the problems of implementing CRM you are sure to encounter.

"Company Z" is a large, established telecommunications firm selling local phone connections, long distance, and wireless services to both retail consumers and businesses throughout the United States. It has a number of call centers for inbound and outbound customer and prospect communications. In 2002, as part of a general effort to improve and personalize the services offered to its best consumer customers, the firm undertook a comprehensive and very forward-thinking customer-relationship initiative, focused on its inbound call centers.

The company first assigned each of its retail customers to one of six categories, based primarily on lifestyle attributes, as inferred from a variety of outside data sources as well as the company's own transactional records. While the categories were based on customer needs, these categories also correlated well with customer valuations. Four of the six customer groups were made up of customers who seemed to offer considerably more current value and growth potential, so Company Z set a goal for its customer-relationship effort of generating increased sales and profits from customers in these four groups. It planned to do this by tailoring its treatment of them, offering more individually relevant products and services, and generally increasing these customers' loyalty and propensity to buy.

The program was supported by new software and more sophisticated customer data, made available to call center agents on their screens. An agent who entered a customer's phone number into the customer database would see the customer's pre-assigned classification to a particular customer segment. Classification information was designed to give the agent a hint about each customer's probable lifestyle. Five different "treatment strategies" were devised in advance and made available to the agents, who were then empowered to assign whatever they considered to be the most appropriate strategy to any customer within these four "high opportunity" customer groups. The treatment strategies were designed to emphasize the product and service benefits most relevant to that particular customer's needs.

A separate database was created to store information about each high-opportunity customer, including a variety of "clues" that might be picked up by an agent on an ad hoc basis. As the agent and customer conversed on the phone, Company Z anticipated that the agent might learn additional things about the type of customer, and the customer's motivations for using various services. These clues might arise from direct statements by a customer, or not. If a customer mentioned information found on the web, the agent could jot a clue: "has PC." An agent hearing kids playing in the background could make a note: "children at home." The clues field was designed to capture the agent's free-flowing comments and insights. In this way, when the customer called in again, the next agent handling them would be even more informed, and thus better able to tailor the firm's offer to meet the customer's need.

This initiative represented a big change in the way Company Z would conduct business through its call centers. It was designed to give customers a much higher level of personal attention, but it would also turn the firm's current call-center processes topsy-turvy. So to prepare the agents and encourage their adoption of this new, personalized approach to dealing with customers, the company trained more than 1000 agents over a seven-month period in groups of no more than 20 per class. Unfortunately, the training focused on *what* was to be done, and *how*, but it was light on the reasons – the *why*.

Company Z was surprised to find that its call-center agents strongly resisted their new initiative, despite the training. Some of the call centers actually reported zero percent utilization of the new customer software tools and database, causing nightmares for the firm's management, and requiring a complete reevaluation and relaunch of the program.

The agents' resistance was the result of a number of seemingly unrelated opinions, misconceptions, obstacles, and structural impediments. They questioned the basic fairness of the segmentation scheme, for instance, because it singled out just four of the six segments for personalized treatment (leaving out the other two segments and so creating a kind of "second class" customer). Many agents felt the "clues" field invaded a customer's privacy. In any case, the clues field remained completely empty for most customers. Clues were to be entered by agents, but because there was no data in these fields to start with, agents soon gave up hope of finding useful information on the clues screen. Eventually they stopped opening it altogether. As a result, conversations with customer didn't capture any additional data.

The agents' interest in training was lackluster at best, and this had a historical basis. It had not been unusual for the firm to have trained some agents months in advance of the launch of a new system, while others were scheduled for training long after a system's deployment. The very best sellers didn't want to take time off from their regular work in order to train, as it meant endangering their monthly incentive payment, which was based on sales. Agents were not rewarded for utilization of the new system, nor were they penalized for not using it. From a purely economic standpoint, they had little reason to waste time learning it when they could be earning more pay.

Customer initiatives can't be installed. They must be adopted

Company Z's failure stemmed primarily from a failure of adoption. The call center employees never fully bought into the program. When problems were encountered, as they always are in this kind of initiative, the employees made no real effort to work them out. Everyone did his job, but few felt any responsibility for the success of the company's effort.

What would have made a difference for Company Z? Could the firm have done it differently? Yes. The company could have done several things differently, for instance:

Leadership commitment. While Company Z's CEO expressed support for the program, the firm never tied incentives to the activities surrounding it, and the CEO played no active role in its implementation. Instead, the program was assigned to the company's marketing department. Unfortunately, even though the firm's senior marketing managers realized early on that the obstacles they confronted would likely defeat the program, they didn't have the standing or political muscle required to overcome them. Company Z's initiative died of the nibbling of a thousand ducks. If the CEO or his direct reports had been personally committed to the program, many of the obstacles afflicting it could probably have been overcome.

Metrics and compensation. Company Z should have aligned its measurement of success and its incentives with the goals of its customer initiative. This kind of program generates the most value to the company in the long term, as customers become more loyal, buy more products and services, and cost less to serve. Clearly, the company needed to make at least some attempt to measure the long-term benefits as well as the short-term benefits. Instead it gauged its success entirely on current sales and profits, rewarding reps for monthly sales targets and not compensating them at all for the time invested in learning about the program and its goals.

Remember, the single most important element of your value proposition with any employee, at any level, is compensation. Compensation, alone, buys compliance, and compliance is what you need if you expect your organization's behavior to change. It is a very simple equation:

no compensation = no compliance = no behavior change.

On the other hand, if pure compliance is all you get then you are still in trouble, because problems and difficulties inevitably arise, and no set of metrics can completely capture every possible situation. You want your employees to exercise good judgment with respect to unanticipated issues.

Culture. Good judgment will spring more from your employees' belief system than it will from training, process, and compensation. The sustainability of this kind of initiative will require a genuine culture change – one that alters the mindset at your firm, increasing not only your employees' fluency in customer issues, but also their desire to involve themselves in those issues. And this change in mindset must be sustained over time. It's possible that, if Company Z had had a mission statement similar to, say, USAA's "Golden Rule" of customer service, employees would have put these new technologies and tools to work effectively. The tactical bugs and other problems would have been worked out because the individual employees and managers would have *wanted* to work them out.

Culture shock

True, change is threatening. We all resist change. But think about the alternative. Technology is already enabling companies to individualize their treatment of customers, and customers in fact want to be treated individually. The result is that treating different customers differently is fast becoming a competitive issue – you can't afford *not* to do it. Whether you like changing or not, competition requires you to come to grips with the business implications of this new technology. *This change is already happening. The only question is whether you'll be driving the train or sitting on the tracks in front of it.*

No matter how much you invest in maximizing your Return on Customer, you won't see any economic results unless you build a *culture* of trust – a culture that constantly encourages everyone in your company to see your business from the customer's perspective. Only then can you put the processes, technology, and organizational structure in place to succeed.

Even if the planning and measures are right and the technology and data are airtight, unless everybody in your company accepts the importance of taking the customer's point of view and makes every decision, no matter how small, with an eye to growing a positive Return on Customer, you will fail. Yes, it's possible for you to roll the effort out in a manageable way, but this kind of initiative is not just for marketing or sales departments. Eventually it will touch everybody in your company.

So, while adopting Return on Customer as a metric of success – a metric that properly balances long-term customer value with current-period results – is a good thing, success requires you to *transform your corporate culture*. A culture based on ROC is one in which every employee strives to see things from the customer's own perspective, and to earn their trust by acting in their interests. You want your employees not just to understand and support your efforts to build long-term customer value, but to be genuinely enthusiastic about the prospect.

Geoffrey Colvin, co-author of *Angel Customers and Demon Customers*, says you can't run a company successfully unless employees have something to do every day that inspires them. "Improving share price," says Colvin, "never got anyone out of bed in the morning, except maybe Al Dunlap, and look where he ended up." Enron posted a huge screen in their main lobby with their constantly fluctuating stock price on it, and that inspired people to commit crimes. Instead, give people a unifying mission that has both short-term and long-term consequences – making customers' lives better. By doing this, Colvin says, you're much more likely to create real value for your enterprise.

John Kotter and Dan Cohen, in their book, *Heart of Change*, compare two different types of change – the "analyze/think" kind of change and the "see/feel" kind of change. Rarely, they maintain, is a successful organizational transformation based on analysis and thinking. The success of a change-management effort almost always depends on changing the *feelings* your employees have – on changing their assumptions and emotions. Engaging employees deeply is the "secret sauce" that will propel a company through this change. It's one thing, for instance, to insist that your executives review their units' customer satisfaction scores. It's another thing altogether to have executives sit for a half hour or so to hear audios or see videos of customers using their products or talking about their level of satisfaction. Kotter and Cohen's admonition is doubly important when you're trying to make the kind of sweeping transformation required to treat different customers differently.

Fortunately, it's easy to ask people to treat the customer the way they would like to be treated if they were customers. It is not only a compelling and easily understood mission statement, but has a high "feeling" content, as well. Employees feel good about this type of change, and if they feel good about it they'll want it to succeed.

That's certainly what Tesco is learning with its own award-winning change management effort. Tesco wants to transform its employee culture to one that is service-oriented. They want employees to be able to recognize exceptional service, compared to ordinary service, and to do so, they need to impart the skills necessary for employees to achieve that kind of standard. One interesting approach is to create a team of change agents at the company, dubbed "firelighters," to serve as role models. According to the *Guardian*, Tesco has "created a 26-week Living Service Programme to be deployed by approximately 80 'living service coaches' from across Tesco. A method was created to identify 'early adopters' and incorporate them into the change process. Under the programme, firelighters will eventually number 20,000 and work with 225,000 employees at 800 Tesco stores across the United Kingdom." Employees' responses to the program have been positive so far. Tim Mason, Tesco's marketing director, claims the program is working because it involves participants both emotionally and intellectually.

To make this type of transformation successful, you have to change mindsets, processes, technologies, and in some cases, personnel. You'll have to rethink how your employees interact with customers, how products and services are positioned both externally and internally, and how people are trained and compensated.

Return on Customer is clearly a value that needs to be managed. That is, employees and managers must be evaluated – and compensated – based on their success at achieving ROC values. One study of "value-based management" found that in companies that failed with it, the link between employee bonuses and shareholder value was tenuous, and employees were able to game the system. As a result, the value was not really vital to decision-making at these firms.

Boise Office Solutions transforms its culture

In 1999, managers at Boise Office Solutions (now known as OfficeMax), knew that to be successful their 13,000-employee company would have to be able to compete as a more customer-intimate company. The continued consolidation of industry players and steady commoditization of basic office products were bound to put increasing pressure on shareholder value. And, in a price-sensitive market with profit margins of less than 5%, customer retention was critical. Accordingly, Boise embarked on an effort to understand, increase, and manage customer value.

The office products distribution arm of Boise Cascade, a $3.2 billion business in 1999, had grown largely through corporate acquisition, and was known to its business customers in America variously as Reliable (for mid-sized companies), Boise Express (focused on small companies), or Boise Cascade Office Products (serving its larger corporate customers). This program of acquisition led to customer overlap, inefficiencies in sales and operations, and lost opportunities to sell new and existing products. Additionally, in a service-driven and price-sensitive business, it was not clear to Boise which customers would contribute the greatest business value over time, and how marketing budgets should be allocated among various types of customers and their interactions with the enterprise.

So in 1999, the company began a comprehensive transformation of its business, relying on leading-edge technologies and implementing a complete reconfiguration of its processes, accompanied by a significant amount of staff training. The initiative was called at the time "One Boise," and its goal was to generate a level of customer focus unprecedented for both Boise and the office products industry at large.

At its core, Boise Office Solutions had always been customer-focused. Consequently, "we've always scanned beyond the horizon in search of the best means of satisfying customers," says Matt Parsons, marketing communications manager. For example, he said, "we were the first office products company to adopt EDI as well as the first to migrate those capabilities to the Internet...It's ingrained in our culture to do everything we can to lead the industry in terms of the quality of the customer experience."

But that leadership role gained greater importance as the company began making significant technology investments in enabling technologies, and in training people and modifying its business processes. The company used its new technologies to consolidate all customer interactions, or "touch points," into a single, integrated system. "What that means for customers," says Parsons, "is that no matter where a customer chooses to interface with Boise, that touch point is intimately familiar with all previous interactions." Specifically, "if a customer calls us, the associate also knows what the customer did on the web or via direct mail." The associate can address past orders, current orders, make adjustments, research and reconcile inquiries – the entire relationship "is on the screen right there, and the associate is empowered to handle any request the customer might have," says Parsons.

The new technologies and training meant not only that Boise could take an integrated view of its relationship with each business customer, but also that the firm was now in a position to provide powerful analytical tools for those customers, helping them to manage their office products inventories, minimize their expenses, and anticipate needs. "Say you're a purchasing manager," says Parsons. "We can now show you everything your company is buying from Boise. Any shipments, any returns, literally every piece of business we're conducting with your company at any time, and we can work with you from any point of contact." Using special Program Management Tools, Boise's customers can now benchmark between individual users, review case resolution performance, or designate spending limits and other account control variables. "These are very useful and insightful analytics," says Dave Goudge, Executive Vice President of Marketing.

Additionally, the new tools present a number of unique opportunities. For example, one feature enables customers to use Boise's website to communicate with others in their own organization. As Goudge explains, "Say there's a certain brand of products a customer's vice president of procurement wants to give special preference." In that case, says Goudge, the customer can easily configure pop-up screens to deliver these or any other relevant messages to other users. "It's a unique and very effective means of communication and control," says Goudge.

The individual decision-makers and influencers within Boise's business customers each have a secure PIN (personal identification number), permitting them to "get down to business faster," says

Parsons, "with a customer service rep who knows their name, order history and past interactions." Whether the interaction takes place by web, catalogue or phone, Boise "knows" this individual. In addition, new tools and functionality available on the firm's website enable customers to "research past orders, review billing, delivery, whatever they need, whenever they need it," says Parsons. "That means better service and greater efficiency, resulting in a noticeably superior experience for our customers."

The core concept behind Boise's approach was personalization. "Everyone should be treated uniquely," says CIO Gary Massell. "We wanted to identify the customer, and then be aware of their unique needs and preferences." Boise, by its nature, has relationships with overall companies, but the needs of individual buyers within any company vary greatly. Moreover, even if the "buyer" is centralized, often the delivery of an order is decentralized. (For example, a buyer in Minneapolis might be acquiring office furniture or paper products to be delivered to an office in Peoria.) In all cases, while the overall "corporate" relationship remained vital, "we indicated to the teams that we wanted to be able to respond to the individual needs and preferences of everyone involved in the purchase process," says Massell. "We wanted tremendous ease of use for individuals."

Boise's ultimate ambition for its people was that they would all be able to see the business from the customer's perspective. The company began to include a handful of customer-oriented performance indicators, including such measures as customer retention, relationship growth, share of wallet, customer acquisition, channel migration and cost-to-serve, as a part of compensation planning.

And there was never any question at Boise about the involvement of the company's top management. As part of a comprehensive employee communications and training effort, every employee at the firm saw a video of the CEO introducing One Boise. More than a thousand field representatives at forty-six distribution centers were required to attend a six-hour immersion course on the project, as were executives and managers. Some 1,500 customer services reps also got thirty hours of training on the technology they would be using. Boise even created a video to show customers how the new program would benefit them.

The net result was that in 2001, Boise Office Solutions won Gartner Group's first-ever "CRM Excellence Award" as the best overall B2B implementation that year. According to Gartner, one of the key criteria for Boise's selection was the breadth and depth of the company's change management program, and its effort to facilitate adoption of its new customer-oriented strategy.

In 2003, Boise announced that it was acquiring office supply superstar OfficeMax, a chain of retail office supply stores catering primarily to small businesses and consumers. (Since then, Boise has rebranded itself as OfficeMax.) While Boise had not had a retail presence before, its One Boise initiative formed a strong basis for integrating OfficeMax into its overall customer strategy, and for understanding what key change management and adoption activities were required.

By 2004, Boise had already accumulated more than $23 million in total contribution from its One Boise initiative. Even more important than cost savings, customer retention is up dramatically, and sales are up for Boise's most valuable customers, as well. The firm now has good customer-profitability data, which is yielding steady benefits on a customer-by-customer basis. For instance, relying on this data Boise chose to discontinue working with one of its largest customers, a group of hospitals that apparently cost it money with every sale. And a senior executive visited another customer's headquarters with data to show how the company was one of Boise's least profitable accounts, winning a price increase over two years.

Using its customer data all the way down to the end-user level, Boise also provides its own suppliers with much more incentive for doing business. According to one supplier:

> "When we present internally to [our company's] marketing now, the Boise team has much more powerful data than the Staples or Depot team...which allows us to get more resources...In fact, Boise has better data than we ever had internally."

Successful ROC adoption is a leadership issue

Inculcating a customer-oriented culture, and giving priority to the overall return generated by customers in the long term as well as the current period – require the direct attention and intervention of a firm's CEO. This was certainly one of the reasons Boise succeeded with its One Boise initiative while Company Z's effort failed.

A 2004 IBM-study based on in-depth interviews with hundreds of business executives around the world concluded that the biggest factors differentiating successful customer-oriented technology initiatives from unsuccessful ones involved managing the change well, in order to create the right culture and to facilitate adoption:

> "Differentiating steps are not the big-ticket items, such as technology implementation or customer data integration; rather, they are the human-oriented steps such as change management and process change...It all comes down to culture, including top-down, ongoing support of senior executives and clear links to overall corporate goals."

According to this study, nearly three out of four companies implementing such initiatives place ownership for it with sales, marketing, IT, or some other department, as Company Z did. Only a quarter of firms assign it to a corporate-level team, as Boise did. Yet, the study showed, when such a program is owned at the corporate level it has a 25% to 50% greater chance of success as long as there is a strong management team that works together well. Surprisingly, IBM found that senior management actually *impeded* success in more than a third of the firms surveyed, because the customer-oriented initiative at their own firm was viewed as "useful," but not "critical."

Ned Barnholt, recently retired CEO and Chairman of Agilent Technologies, once asked us what type of behaviors he should expect of his leadership team, if they were to adopt fully a customer-oriented point of view. He wanted to know what he should expect his leadership team to *do* differently, if he were successful in motivating them to want to make this type of a corporate transformation at Agilent. Together, we brainstormed this issue and concluded that, at the very least, an enthusiastically on-board leader would:

- *Accumulate expertise* in the area of customer-focused strategies and relationship management, and become an informal "cheer-leader" for the ideas involved. Customer-specific competition is a relatively new discipline, requiring not just computer technology but also new marketing, sales and customer service tactics. Few companies are competent in it yet, so the discipline required to maximize ROC is not very well known. A leader will make an effort to find out more about it, attending workshops or seminars, reading books and articles, and calling in experts – becoming fluent in this type of thinking, and facilitating that fluency so everyone has a common language and philosophy.

- *Sponsor pilot projects* and shelter the people involved in them. This transformation must be engineered and implemented in pieces, if it is to be successful at all. Pilot projects designed to prove the concept and measure benefits in terms of ROC will be required, but in budget-tight times a loss-producing pilot can easily get jettisoned. A leader who supports this transformation will provide sponsorship for proof-of-concept pilot projects even when they lose money.

- *Measure success differently*, establishing not only new metrics, but also new reward structures. A leader will root out inconsistencies and conflicts in the company's rewards and incentives programs, and try to create a better alignment with the goal of maximizing Return on Customer.

- *Cross boundaries* to generate enterprise-wide results. Customer-specific actions are rarely product-specific or business-unit-specific. When the enterprise seeks to treat different customers differently, in an integrated way across all touchpoints, there will be conflicts among departments and functions. Leaders recognize this and will actively cross boundaries in order to make the new processes work.

- *Directly interact with customers.* Customers are, in the final analysis, at the center of this transformation. Leaders recognize this, and want to meet them, talk with them, watch the focus groups, visit the customer sites, and so forth. There is no substitute for direct experience.

- *Communicate and live by customer-oriented values.* The CEO and senior management team have an overriding and indispensable role in both communicating the values of the company to employees and others, and in reinforcing them with their everyday behavior.

Formal communication is the easy part – you do that with policies, tools, training, and performance measurements. But values are also communicated in the actions and behaviors of senior managers themselves. (We met a CEO who told his executives he wanted them to build customer value, but every morning his first question to his team was "How much product did you move yesterday?") Employees must know, both formally and informally, that the firm values taking the customer's perspective, as well as earning and keeping the customer's trust.

Genuine leadership is required for this kind of corporate transformation, because it involves an extreme form of adoption and change management. What it amounts to is practically a reinvention of the firm. The difficulty of "changing over" to this relatively new type of technology-facilitated customer-specific competition is great enough that, even today, the most distinctively successful customer-oriented initiatives are in the hands of new entrants – companies created from scratch, beginning their corporate lives with access to the computer-based and interactive technologies necessary to build and maintain individual customer relationships.

Attitude is as important as altitude

JetBlue is one of the new-entrant American airlines, renowned on Wall Street for its low costs and high profit margins, and renowned among passengers for both low prices and technology-rich customer service. At JetBlue, information systems are critical to the company's operational efficiency, but these systems also allow the firm to cultivate the right orientation within the firm's employee base. At one Gartner conference on CRM, analyst Ellen Kitzis commented that JetBlue Airways had doubled its IT investment that year in order to gain a competitive advantage once the market bounced back. But more than simple technology and data are involved in this airline's investment. According to Kitzis, JetBlue "believes the average wait time online should be one minute. They believe the pilots should have access to [the name] of every passenger on the plane."

JetBlue also uses technology to ensure that its own people and resources are deployed not just efficiently, but effectively. The airline's reservations center actually operates "virtually," with more than half the reservations agents interacting with customers while working in their own homes. According to Blue Pumpkin, the solution provider, this innovative organization increased service levels by 38%, boosted agent productivity by 30%, and generated a 50% improvement in management workload per agent, among other gains. Perhaps the true sentiment at the airline, however, came from Julie Strickland, a JetBlue contact center manager: "To be a customer-centric business, you first need to be employee-centric."

Is that right? Do you have to be employee-centric in order to be customer-centric? We can't prove it but we don't know of any exceptions. While maximizing Return on Customer sounds like a purely financial goal, the fact is that it requires a customer-oriented perspective to be adopted wholeheartedly by the employees. You can't really legislate this in your firm. People have to *want* to do it – mentally and emotionally.

Not all transformations are the same

Transforming your organization, culture, information systems, and value chain in these ways will require immense change – not just to processes and technologies, but to mindsets, culture and, in some cases, personnel. You'll have to rethink how your employees interact with customers, how products and services are positioned both externally and internally, and how your employees are trained and compensated.

One important difference between making this kind of change, as opposed to other types of change, is that it really does affect everyone within your organization's entire ecosystem. As tempting as it may be to assign a customer initiative to sales and marketing, or to customer service, we've already seen that this is a recipe for failure. Trying to increase your Return on Customer will involve people playing different roles in different departments, across the entire enterprise. Everyone has to understand the initiative and want to undertake it.

But a second, very important characteristic of this type of change is that it is actually quite easy to explain to your employees and partners. The goal of your new operating model will be to provide a more realistic mechanism for increasing the value of the company, but the real world "take away" can be stated simply: to treat customers fairly and openly – the way you would like to be treated if you were a customer. The unifying goal for everyone at your company is to *become* the customer – to get inside each customer's head and to see things, honestly, from the customer's own perspective.

Everyone is going to understand this proposition because, after all, we are all customers somewhere. In contrast to other types of change you might have introduced from time to time – computer system upgrades, reorganizations, and the like – it won't be hard for even your most junior employees to grasp the underlying idea behind moving to a Return on Customer perspective. So an important tactic for making a more successful transformation is, essentially, to sell the "whole vision" first, even though you may choose to implement the transformation itself on an incremental basis, from pilot project to pilot project, letting each small success beget others, and so forth.

Whatever you do, the truth is it's not going to be easy. But look carefully at the differences between the firms that have succeeded (like Tesco and Boise Office Systems and JetBlue), and compare them to those whose efforts have failed (like Company Z). The successful firms invested time and energy to develop new "soft" skills – skills that really consisted of a whole family of activities, including collaboration, team building, active listening, and negotiation. This is not necessarily something you can script in detail, but rather, these foundation skills are developed in order to achieve the benefits of integration throughout the enterprise.

Successful firms engaged their leadership and reinforced these collaborative activities with pay for performance and customer-oriented incentive compensation. Successful firms typically set up standards and motivate people, but then allow them the time and space to work through and develop local initiatives and solutions.

By contrast, the call center reps at Company Z were handed a technology solution that wasn't even ready yet to be implemented. True, they were motivated to increase sales, because that's where the incentive compensation lay. The only problem was that an exclusive focus on immediate sales conflicted with the more balanced objective of

Company Z's customer initiative, undermining the success of the program. Compensation should have been the primary motivator for this organization, but, because it was never aligned with the program's goals, it ended up being a major obstacle.

In addition, Company Z's call-center initiative required *all* the reps to participate, from Day One – there were no dedicated reps to nurture the profiles of their own bank of customers, no "firelighters" to kick-start the culture change. If Company Z's informal leaders – the most savvy and successful reps – had been brought in to help develop the effort, they probably would have coached and encouraged the other reps, because *they* would have needed everyone participating so that they could have the information to handle their calls and increase their own chances for success.

In the end, it boils down to this: To maximize your Return on Customer, you have to put customer interests at the forefront of every employee's mission. When your employees' primary objective is to see things through the customer's eyes, then no matter how complex or unprecedented the situation is, they are still likely to do the right thing, adding value rather than destroying it.

One more thing to keep in mind, however, is that from your customers' perspective, your company's "behavior" might involve a variety of actors other than just your own employees. Your dealers, brokers, agents, and outside sales reps must all adopt the same basic philosophy of cultivating the trust of *your* customers – treating customers fairly and openly, the way they would want to be treated if they were customers themselves. Your ability to deliver on the value proposition to your customers will depend on your ability to manage the customer's overall experience, considering all the various partici-pants in your own value chain, from raw materials all the way down to the store clerk or salesman putting your product in the customer's hands.

9. Delivering Value *to* Customers to Build ROC

Vision without action is a daydream.
Action without vision is a nightmare.

Japanese proverb

It is easy enough to create a vision for influencing your customers' behavior. At some point, however, you must go from planning and strategy and culture change – to *execution*. Action, not just vision. Initiatives must be implemented; things have to happen. To change your customers' behavior, in other words, you must first change your firm's behavior. *ROC is not just a metric, it's a way of life.*

But what do we mean when we talk about the "behavior" of a firm? The way to answer that is to look at it from the customer's perspective. For a customer, your company's behavior consists of everything done or said on your behalf or for your benefit. This includes every action by any of your employees, of course, but also the actions of your agents or representatives, your dealers or brokers or suppliers, even the store clerk at the retail counter who collects the money for your product.

In essence, the customer perceives his own experience with your brand, your product, or your company in terms of all these different actions by different participants in your firm's value chain. If you want to maximize your Return on Customer, you have to manage that experience as rationally and competently as you can. You have to align the actions of all these different parties, with their own different interests, to make your customer's overall experience a positive one – one that will create value for your business. Your customer sees your firm, with all its many products and functions and people, as one company. But do all your firm's various pieces see each customer as one customer, to be treated accordingly?

Power to the employees!

An important characteristic of almost all truly successful customer-oriented initiatives is employee empowerment. The right culture will lead employees to *want* to solve customer problems and ensure customer satisfaction, but they must be *empowered* to do so. If the mission of the firm is to create lasting enterprise value by maximizing Return on Customer, then the individual employees themselves should have the capacity to take the actions necessary to do so, one customer at a time.

The Ritz-Carlton Hotel Company operates more than 50 hotels around the world and is renowned for its personalized customer service. The company has won the Malcolm Baldridge National Quality Award twice (1992 and 1999) – the only hotel firm ever to win this award, and the only service firm to win it twice. Through the operation of a "Leadership Center" the company permits other firms to benchmark its own highly successful culture of service excellence, customer retention, and employee retention. Ritz-Carlton service employees are taught that they should think of themselves as "Ladies and Gentlemen serving Ladies and Gentlemen."

Ritz-Carlton literally coined the now-popular term "empowerment," as it applies to employees. After a highly selective screening and hiring process, even new employees are given the authority to commit up to $2,000 of the hotel company's money to resolve a guest's problem. According to an article in *Expert Magazine*:

> *Clearly, an employee cannot evade difficult situations by uttering, "That's not my job." Job descriptions become irrelevant when guest satisfaction is at risk. Ladies and Gentlemen step outside job boundaries, and no one questions their right to act—because they have an overriding obligation to settle issues.*

Indeed, Ritz-Carlton employees have an overriding obligation to keep their customers' trust. What the firm wants is to ensure that every guest, without exception, has a delightful overall customer experience, every time that customer touches the company.

FedEx, the global package delivery service, is a business that has long prided itself on quality and customer service. FedEx, like Ritz-Carlton, has won the Baldridge Award for quality, and they also share their best practices with other firms in regular benchmarking seminars. According to Scot Struminger, VP of IT for Corporate Headquarters Systems at FedEx, "We know that customer loyalty comes from treating customers like you want to be treated."

Every day some 600,000 people call in to FedEx's 56 call centers around the world, and another 2.4 million access the company online. In 2002 FedEx implemented a comprehensive IT upgrade that provided unified, all-inclusive customer profiles to the reps handling calls, and instituted "closed loop" problem-resolution processes. A key part of FedEx's program is empowerment of the customer service representatives, each of whom is trained to handle the vast majority of problems on their own initiative and authority. The result: Not only has daily call volume dropped by some 89,000 calls, saving the company money, but also customer satisfaction has improved significantly. And FedEx reps have become more loyal, too. Employee attrition has fallen by 20%.

Stena AB is a Swedish company operating several different lines of business, mostly involved in maritime activities, including passenger ferries. In the late 1990s, Stena Line's Irish Sea ferry route, which runs between Scotland and Northern Ireland, carried some 1.5 million passengers annually, and was plagued with a terrible customer service reputation. Complaint letters outnumbered compliments by four to one. That's when Stena's management decided to assign a new managing director, Alan Gordon, to improve the ferry's service. Gordon said the first thing he and his management team did was to ask the staff what was wrong, and the answer came back in four parts:

- *Internal communication.* Employees either didn't know what was going on or didn't believe what management told them was going on.
- *Training.* Employees felt strongly that the company should invest in training, in order to "get it right" with customers.

- *Change management.* Employees did not feel involved, because management's style was to communicate decisions rather than to gain participation and share responsibility.
- *Attitude of staff toward one another.* The simple fact was that when someone on staff did something very good for a customer they were sometimes actually ridiculed!

Over a five-year period, Gordon launched a comprehensive training program and implemented twelve different major initiatives in the service area, putting employees themselves in charge of fixing the problems. The company calculated that a typical good customer had a lifetime value to Stena of some £15,000, based on 20 years of traveling back and forth, so Gordon's charge to employees was to figure out how to keep such a customer well served, satisfied, and loyal. The team benchmarked with other companies with well-known reputations for efficient and courteous customer service, such as Southwest Airlines and Stew Leonard's in America.

Besides involving employees in the culture change at Stena, Gordon's team also empowered individual employees to identify and solve customer problems on the spot, by approaching passengers directly, within a few minutes of disembarkation on each voyage. Every employee at Stena, from stewards to cooks and deck-hands, is empowered to commit up to £1,000 to satisfy a complaint or resolve any problem. Again, this is a company where no employee can plausibly say, "It's not my problem."

Gordon maintains that his customer team at Stena is composed of nothing but "enthusiastic amateurs" when it comes to service, but they must be doing something right. In 2002, compliments outnumbered complaints from customers by three to one. The random survey of customer satisfaction (100 passengers per week), has shown a steady uptick in the proportion of "very good" overall ratings – growing from just 22% in 1999 to nearly 60% in 2003.

When companies like Ritz-Carlton and Stena empower their workers to spend money to satisfy customers, few employees ever find it necessary to spend very much. However, just the fact that an employee knows he or she is capable of doing so has a tremendous transformative effect on the organization. Now *everyone is in charge of increasing the firm's Return on Customer,* and they are acting at the molecular, individual customer level. Only by creating an employee culture like this can you ensure that all your employees and managers, dealing with the myriad of customer situations and unanticipated problems they encounter every day, do the right thing, adding value rather than destroying it.

It's hard to overstate the importance of having the right corporate culture when it comes to empowering employees and implementing a customer initiative effectively. Customer-oriented programs can be conceived and architected in a highly sophisticated way, supported by brilliant strategy and state-of-the-art technology, but successful implementation depends not just on whether your employees know what to do, but also whether they *want* to do it and are *empowered* to do it. Employees have to understand, embrace, and advocate for the basic mission. If they don't, then even the most forward-thinking plan will fail.

Even worse than simple failure, a poorly-implemented program will actually backfire. Two New Zealand professors, after surveying nearly 1,000 consumers, found that when customer-relationship programs are implemented poorly, they actually do harm to a firm. That is, a well-intentioned but poorly implemented customer-relationship initiative is worse than useless – it is damaging to a firm's business, eroding customer satisfaction and reducing customer loyalty. Moreover, this study found that the harm done by a poorly-implemented program exceeds the benefit to be gained from a well-executed one. But you shouldn't find this surprising, because you already know that maximizing Return on Customer is an optimization problem.

In addition to employees, however, you have to worry about your channel partners – all the various retail stores, dealers, brokers, warehouse operators and sales people who interact with your customers but aren't part of your firm.[1] Depending on your industry, you may or may not "own" your distribution channel. It's a great deal more difficult to manage the customer's experience if you don't have the authority to "manage."

---

[1] Some describe this task as "Partner Relationship Management," or "PRM." We don't care what you call it, as long as you can make sure each customer's value to your firm is not destroyed anywhere along the way, even at the hands of your channel partners.

How BMW improves the customer experience – at the dealers

BMW sells 275,000 cars annually in America through a network of over 340 dealers. Nearly all of the company's American dealerships are owned independently, and about two-thirds of BMW dealerships also sell at least one other, unrelated brand of car. BMW has a strong interest in how car-owners and prospective owners are treated at each dealership, but the dealer and his employees do not formally answer to BMW. The dealership is a completely separate business, with its own operating costs, its own business processes, and its own ideas about how BMW owners should be treated. Dealers have contractual obligations to BMW, but these obligations do not necessarily extend to every aspect of how an individual consumer is actually treated. In this regard, BMW's situation is similar to that of most other car manufacturers, and to the situation faced by companies in other categories when they make a product that is delivered or serviced through a network of independent distributors.

Shifting gears

BMW has spent many years and millions of dollars carefully crafting its "ultimate driving machine" brand promise. Today, with new technologies making it possible to track consumer relationships individually and to treat different consumers differently, BMW wants to improve on the customer experience in a way that amounts to nothing short of a cultural shift for the company and its dealer network. But while the dealers all have significant obligations under their franchise agreements, the simple fact is that no legal agreement could possibly anticipate all the nuances involved in personalized customer service.

So BMW has devised a plan to encourage its independent dealers to treat retail customers consistently, reliably, and in a high-quality way – a manner designed to delight them with their BMW experience. The car company's goal is to make the dealer into a BMW "hero" for the customer. Before this can happen, however, the dealer must not only know what is expected, but must also be enthusiastically onboard with respect to the overall idea. Moreover, the dealers must clearly agree on what the BMW customer experience should actually consist of at every different touchpoint.

As an initial step, BMW Corporate has designed and begun implementing "dealer modules" to help shape the way dealers interact with owners and prospective owners in various situations. These modules cover a variety of topics, including specific processes that mark the brand's relationship with an individual owner across different stages of the customer lifecycle – new vehicle delivery and initial ownership, the end of a lease, managing sales leads, and showroom traffic.

Each module is independently administered, and involves fact finding and analysis by BMW's field sales staff as well as training and review on the part of the dealer's employees. Field sales managers are encouraged to use their own knowledge and insight to select the most appropriate first module for each dealership, and then to begin the module with a "diagnostic" to see how the dealership is currently handling the key elements for the specific process. Then, the field sales staff provides the dealership with an assessment – highlighting areas of strength as well as areas that need improvement to enhance the specific process examined. The Marketing and Sales Operating Manager and the dealer management team agree on opportunities with the greatest potential for impact and agree on an action plan. This typically includes both "quick hits" as well as long-term initiatives. Then, once a dealer implements the first module, they'll move on to the next one, and the next, and so forth.

Consider how the lease-end module would work, for instance. First, the diagnostic is designed to identify whatever special programs a dealer now has in place to win over the continuing allegiance of an owner at the end of a lease. Then, through a series of one-hour interviews with Client Advisers who have a mix of tenures at the dealership, BMW's field sales folks determine how customers are currently handled at the end of their lease, and assess the dealership's readiness to change. Questions raised range from an exploration of systems and tools already in use, to an examination of the attitudes and beliefs of the dealer's personnel. Does the service department have the capability to recognize customers who are near the end of their lease when their car is brought in for service? Do the sales and service people coordinate their treatment of individual lease-end customers?

Based on the findings in the lease-end diagnostic, the company first maps out a set of opportunities for improvement, and then lays out a series of steps designed to improve the dealership's handling of lease end, along with an Action Plan to ensure that they are implemented capably and in the manner intended, along with regular Action Plan Updates. The overall objectives for the lease-end module address not just the dealer's perspective, but also the *customer's* perspective – that is, how the customer actually experiences the end of a lease. BMW wants its dealers to use lease-end interactions to get customers excited about their "next" BMW. They want dealers to assume the onus of communications, and to coordinate the management of lease-end treatment across the sales and service functions at the dealership. Basically, the company wants a lease-end customer to experience a seamless and simple process involving special treatment or offers designed to encourage a new vehicle purchase.

Success of the modules is gauged by a set of results-oriented metrics as well as dealer-behavioral metrics. Measured results include straight-forward data such as changes in the dealer's overall repurchase and re-lease rate, broken down by client adviser (salesperson) and service manager. The dealer behaviors being measured clearly put the onus on the dealer for managing the customer's experience. But if things go right, once a dealer implements the lease-end module, each customer whose lease expires will encounter communications and offers from the dealer that work in harmony with BMW's overall brand objectives, and with the company's customer treatment strategy for that customer.

Mike Sachs, BMW's Customer Experience Development Manager, says the company has two primary objectives for its Performance Management Approach, or "PMA," as it is called around the halls of BMW. The first objective is to ensure the customer's delight with their BMW experience. After all, the dealership is the location for most customer-interactions with the company's brand. "So," according to Sachs, "our first PMA objective is to ensure customer delight. We want to have customers out there selling for us. We want them to be advocates for the dealers, as well as for our brand."

But the second objective, Sachs says, goes right to the heart of car culture. "We can create good products and we can do good marketing. But dealers need to be able to attract and retain the kind of people who want to make car-retailing their career and believe in delighting customers. Our goal as the manufacturer is to support them with the right processes and tools such as the PMA modules. But, fundamentally the customer experience is driven by interactions with people. If our dealers can't attract and retain the kind of people who *strive* to turn customers into lifelong advocates – then there's no way to win."

"No way to win." That's the fix you're in if you don't think carefully about what it really means to maximize the overall return you get on your customers, not just in terms of current sales, but also any increases in the customer's lifetime value. Enrolling everyone in the organization – indeed, everyone in the firm's ecosystem, including independent channel partners who deal with your brand and your customers – is vital.

Zurich Insurance emphasizes "tripartite" relationships

Clearly, dealing with customers through intermediaries can be challenging. It's a bit easier to manage your customer's experience with your channel partner when your partner is at least operating under your own brand name, as BMW's dealers do. However, when your channel is completely independent it gets tougher. An independent distributor's proposition, after all, is based on offering a variety of providers' products – your competitors' products as well as your own – in order to find the best solution for the customer. So you have to look carefully at the value proposition with your channel partner if you want to have any influence at all.

For many years, the commercial insurance business had been characterized by a great deal of price-cutting and bargain shopping. This was particularly the case in the mid-to-late 1990s. Brokers controlled the customer and shopped all the major players to drive prices down. The result was a buyers' market, with customers asking for better pricing and cover, brokers managing the route to market, and insurers competing aggressively on price.

In the past few years, the insurance market has changed dramatically, however, as it became apparent that risks had been underwritten at uneconomic rates and a few high-profile insurers collapsed. New regulations, external market factors, and reduced investment returns forced the industry to reevaluate what's important. The year 2001, which saw the collapse of Independent Insurance, followed by the September 11 attack, exemplified what is now key – stability and protection from catastrophic loss. The issues of financial stability, credibility, and insurers' ability to cover previously unimaginable types of loss, overtook the focus on premium levels. Corporate customers wanted to know that the capital they invested in insuring their assets was well-placed, and they wanted to play a more active part in managing their risks and stabilizing their premiums. Risk managers were clamoring for a chance to satisfy themselves with respect to the stability and competence of their underwriters.

In this environment Zurich Insurance focused itself on strong underwriting integrity, and their British commercial business unit began trying to move closer to its larger, mid-corporate customers. In doing so, they formed strong tripartite relationships with brokers and customers to bring value to the table that the broker was unable to bring alone. By working with many brokers, including three key global players in the British market – AON, Marsh, and Willis – the company designed an unprecedented, direct contact strategy. It proposed to give these brokers' corporate clients direct access to key underwriting decision makers at Zurich, one of the world's largest and most respected underwriters. Zurich would listen to their needs, gain a deeper understanding of their business, and boost these customers' confidence in the soundness and safety of their coverage. The program added real value to the tripartite relationship, addressing many concerns the brokers themselves were dealing with – clarity over underwriting and pricing decisions, claims evaluation, increased communication, and risk management.

New roles were developed, including a Claims Account Manager – a first in the commercial arena – to work directly with each corporate customer and their dedicated claims teams, in order to process claims more quickly and efficiently. Also, recording key information on a custom-built 'Insight' system enabled simple structured contact from dedicated teams of experts to provide the contact and servicing that target business customers needed. According to Steve Green, Major Customer Manager at Zurich's British commercial unit:

"I wanted to build something simple that everyone could access and was easily understood. It enabled the Major Customer Servicing Teams to record information about customers, link to customer websites and an external business information provider and news aggregator. Managing the relationship with a few hundred major customers does not require sophisticated technology – the ability to use the information recorded is far more important than storing accumulated data that is of no use."

The results of the initiative have not only increased profitability for the company, but also created an area of specialization that now accounts for close to a quarter of total income at Zurich's British commercial business, even though it accounts for less than 1% of the policy count. Both customer acquisition and retention rates are up, enabling the company to plan over the longer term, while providing customers with more pricing consistency and stability. Not only have Zurich and its corporate customers benefited from this new initiative; the brokers have, too. Sometimes, as Zurich's case shows, doing simple things well, in an open and transparent way, can go a long way to breaking down traditional taboos and establishing long-term successful relationships.

Recipe for success

Professor George S. Day of the Wharton School at the University of Pennsylvania cites a survey Wharton conducted of executives in some 352 different businesses, which confirms the importance of both culture and empowerment. According to Day, the survey points out three important success criteria for any company hoping to improve its "customer-relating capabilities." All three of these success criteria are important, but the first one, "orientation," has to do with attitude, really, and may be more important than anything else. The Wharton study's three success criteria are:

- *Orientation.* Your whole enterprise should be focused on goals related to customer retention and value creation. In successful transitions these goals are shared by everyone in the firm, and not limited to sales or marketing. It is more difficult if your current practice grants one function or department or business unit "ownership" of the customer, because in that kind of environment essential customer information is often hoarded by those closest to the relationship. Day also says that if your tradition is one of celebrating customer acquisitions through individual efforts, then this will hinder progress, too. Customer orientation, in essence, must be embedded in your company culture – it must reside within your corporate DNA. "Orientation" is the real secret behind the kind of success enjoyed at Stena and Ritz-Carlton.

- *Configuration.* Day calls this "the alignment of the organization," to be achieved with "incentives, metrics, organizational structure and accountabilities." He says that a genuine customer-oriented configuration will involve, among other things, incentives based not just on sales, but rather on lifetime value improvement, customer satisfaction, and retention (or what we've called "leading indicators" of lifetime value change). Modifying your organization structure is also critical, because ROC metrics will create new individual responsibilities within your firm, and a traditional, product-oriented organization structure cannot always accommodate these new responsibilities. We'll discuss the organizational implications in more detail in Chapter 13, when we introduce a structure based on managing portfolios of customers. But configuration is also important when it comes to managing a customer's overall experience with your firm, and it underlies the initiatives by BMW and Zurich.

- *Information.* Finally, the Wharton study shows that, while information is vital to success, it "contributes little to a superior capability." In other words, information and technology are necessary but not sufficient for competitive superiority. It is essential to have the right technologies in place so you can make customer information available at various touchpoints, engage customers in cost-efficient interactions, and deliver your products or services in a more customer-specific way. But the Wharton survey also showed that information technology, by itself, could not provide a competitive advantage. Despite this limitation, Day reports, "when we asked our interview respondents how their time and money were being allocated for building the capability, almost everything was being spent on databases, software, and data mining." This is indeed what we saw at Boise, where the information systems provided important advantages, but the company's orientation and configuration were more critical to the overall success of the One Boise initiative.

These three issues – orientation, configuration, and information – go to the heart of what is different for a company that focuses on overall Return on Customer, rather than focusing solely on current income. Managing the overall experience of a customer with your brand, your product, or your business requires a comprehensive approach to culture, organization, and information.

But taking a Return on Customer approach also requires careful attention to your supply chain. Think of it this way: If you want to treat different customers differently, then the "back end" of your company must be capable of doing what the "front end" learns that your customer needs. For that simple reason, customer insight must be integrated not just into the behaviors of your dealers, brokers, and other channel members in the demand chain, but also into the actual operation of your supply chain.

Knowing and doing: Supply chains matter

If you try to implement a customer-centric initiative on top of a weak or poorly integrated supply chain, you'll merely provide your customers with a clearer view of your inadequate logistical capabilities. Customer treatments have to be backed up by a capable, flexible, responsive, and fully integrated supply chain. If you can't do that, then you can expect three types of problems:

- *Under-delivery.* Your front-office processes will increase interactions with your customers, and customer expectations, as well. If your back office can't soon deliver what your front office promises, customer dissatisfaction will skyrocket.

- *Over-delivery.* Customer processes that don't provide "cost trans-parency" into supply-chain information may result in delivering products or services to customers that are simply unprofitable for your firm. Treating different customers differently must occur within your company's own, real-world constraints of costs and capabilities.
- *Lost share-of-customer opportunities.* Without integration, the supply chain can't capitalize on the customer insights that a Return on Customer perspective uncovers. This means new supplier partner-ships, that intelligently and profitably increase the scope you offer, are less likely to materialize, and will be more difficult to manage when they do.

In the mid-1990s, Volvo found it had an excessive inventory of cars at midyear that were painted green. Looking to reduce the inventory, the sales and marketing group began offering a host of discounts, deals and rebates on green-colored cars to distributors. Sales of green cars soon picked up. However, the company's supply chain planning group was not aware of the campaign and erroneously concluded that customer demand for green cars was the impetus behind the spike. As sales increased, the supply-chain group decided to produce even more green cars to meet perceived demand. The end result: At year's end, Volvo had an even greater inventory of green cars.

Many firms have paid penalties like these because they failed to realize the connection that must exist between supply chain and demand chain. The results often include poorly supported new product launches, or simply uncoordinated customer service actions, but the root cause is a left-hand-right-hand problem: Supply chain and demand chain must work together.

Provided that demand chain and supply chain are well coordinated, a firm can launch customer-specific initiatives that speak to individual customer needs in ways that ensure lasting, productive, and more prof-itable relationships. If the supply chain and demand chain are inte-grated into a single "value chain," then customers won't know and won't care where one part of the value chain stops and another part picks up. For customers, it simply isn't relevant whether the various connected parts of a manufacturing and service "ecosystem" are owned by a single entity or bound together by agreement. Customers just see a great product or service, tailored to meet their own needs.

"SPAR" is the brand name of a chain of more than 19,000 grocery stores and outlets operating in 33 countries and generating some €20 billion in worldwide sales annually. SPAR refers to itself as a kind of "soft" franchise operation, because most of the stores carrying its brand name are owned by independent operators, while the company itself is the wholesaler for the stores in the chain, providing most – but not all – of the products sold by member stores. SPAR's customers are the store operators themselves, and the company performs many services for them, in addition to wholesaling. For instance, for some storeowners, SPAR does the books and minds the payroll.

One of SPAR's innovations worth a closer examination is in Austria, a relatively strong market for the firm, where it has a 30% share. In 2003, SPAR Austria implemented a system that preloads its wholesale deliveries to a store in the same order in which the items are displayed on that store's shelves. So, as the stock clerk rolls the pallet of groceries down the aisle at his store he can effortlessly find the next items for each shelf, a greatly simplified process that saves considerable time and cost for the storeowner. The ease with which SPAR Austria's products can be placed on a store's shelves provides an incentive for the storeowner to rely as much as possible on SPAR, rather than going to the trouble of dealing with an additional supplier, even if for a few items the other supplier might offer a more advantageous price.

Of course, each store's configuration is different, so SPAR's preconfiguration requires the firm to maintain an up-to-date record of each store's individual configuration. But it must also *act* on that information cost-efficiently, by changing the actual product delivery configuration for each store. SPAR is able to do this by relying on a mass-customized warehouse supply operation. Until this program was launched, the configuration of grocery products as they left SPAR's warehouses was not something that would have been considered a "customer-facing" activity. Mass-customizing those configurations, however, and thereby treating different customers differently, is definitely a customer-facing action; it perfectly illustrates that trying to draw a line between "supply chain" and "demand chain" activities is not only difficult, but pointless.

If you can integrate customer insight into your supply-chain activities, the payoff can be substantial. A 2002 Deloitte Research survey of nearly 250 major consumer businesses and their executive teams in 28 countries found that "Consumer businesses that effectively integrate their customer management and supply chain operations are twice as profitable as competitors that do not." According to the survey, such businesses were "two to five times more likely to achieve superior performance in sales, market share, customer service, and other key measures, *and much more likely to generate higher shareholder returns.*"

Shareholder return – that's the key: generating a higher shareholder return, whether your shareholders number in the dozens or the millions. When your people make their decisions based on maximizing Return on Customer, what they are really doing is ensuring that their own actions, within their own divisions or operating units, are aligned with the corporate goal of maximizing shareholder return. At the corporate level, however, ROC has additional implications. Among other issues, for instance, it should play an important role in deciding where to allocate capital, or what types of business combinations make the most sense. We'll take an "enterprise perspective" on ROC decision-making in the next chapter.

10. ROC and the Economics of Your Enterprise

Suppose a customer calls your firm to complain and the complaint doesn't get resolved. When this happens, the customer's lifetime value goes down *immediately*. They may not actually defect to a competitor for some time, but the likelihood of their defecting has suddenly increased, and the probability of buying more things from you has just as suddenly declined. When this customer hangs up the phone after such an unsatisfactory experience, your company loses value *at that very moment*. You might as well have gone to the bank yourself, drawn the money out, and burned it in a little bonfire in your office.

A customer can create value for your business in two different ways – first by spending money today (increasing the company's current-period cash flow), and second by spending money tomorrow (increasing future cash flows, because the customer's lifetime value increases). It's important to recognize that the value your company creates or destroys with an increase or decrease in the customer's LTV is just as important as the value you get from current cash flow.

Customers have free will and memories, so the treatment they receive from you today has an effect on the value they yield not only today but also in the future. How you treat parts and supplies on the assembly line today has nothing at all to do with their future cost to you. But how you treat customers today has everything to do with their future profit for you. Today's treatment of a customer or prospective customer needs to be justified not just by the lateral cash flow generated from quarter to quarter, but also by the longitudinal value created or destroyed over the long term – that is, by the degree to which it alters the customer's LTV. It works like this: If you have to use up customer equity to make today's numbers, then today's numbers don't look so good after all.

In this chapter we're going to discuss some of the implications of using ROC as a corporate metric of success. We're going to make comparisons with other success metrics and accounting quantities, and frankly it isn't going to be very pretty. If you have an economic bent, we hope you find it interesting, but in case you aren't so inclined, we've broken the chapter into specific sections. We'll summarize the basic argument for each section in the very first paragraph. It won't hurt our feelings if you're not interested in the logic behind these conclusions – just read the first paragraph of each section and you'll get the gist of the argument.

Customer equity: A capital idea

Your firm's customer equity is an important intangible asset, somewhat like capital. You want to track your company's use of capital to avoid destroying value unintentionally (or using it up too fast). In the same way, you also want to track your firm's use of customer equity. Unlike capital, however, with the right actions on your part your customer equity can actually be replenished and increased even as you employ it to generate current cash flow from customers.

Tracking ROC at the enterprise level allows you to avoid eroding your value as a business. When ROC declines, or even turns negative, watch out, because your company may be destroying value, rather than creating it. A negative ROC often means you are using up customer equity faster than you're generating current-period cash flow. It could also be negative if your customer equity doesn't grow enough to offset a current-period loss or expenditure. (That can happen, for instance, when a company spends a lot of money on customer-oriented technology without fully understanding how to create long-term customer value with it.) Any firm that doesn't track ROC might easily adopt programs that lead to unintended value destruction – programs that may generate better current-period profits at the expense of "using up" even more value from the customer base.

If customers, as a scarce resource, can be thought of as a productive asset for a business, then customer equity is something like capital, and Return on Customer is a metric that could be compared to Economic

Value Added.[1] "EVA®," as it is known, is a measure which accounts for the cost of the capital required by a business, giving companies a more accurate picture of the value they actually create with their operations. Two businesses with identical cash flows are not identically valuable, if one firm requires more capital than the other to produce those cash flows.

Even if a firm measures its success in terms of return on assets, its financial results can still be deceiving unless it factors in its cost of capital. According to one EVA proponent, IBM's corporate return on assets was over 11% when it was at its most profitable, but at the same time it faced a realistic cost of capital of nearly 13%. So even though it seemed "profitable," you could argue that IBM was not actually creating value for its shareholders.

You may be unaware you are diluting your capital unless you measure EVA, and *unless you measure Return on Customer you will most likely be unaware you are diluting your customer equity*. To compare the likely economic impact of alternative actions you should always know how much *capital* each action will require, but you should also know how much customer equity will be consumed.

Customer equity, however, is not a tangible piece of capital equipment or material, like a building or a machine. It is instead one of the most intangible of assets, and this fact distinguishes how you use it, consume it, alter it, and replenish it during the routine course of business. Lifetime values are partly a function of attitudes and predispositions, so they can change as quickly and easily as those attitudes can, perhaps with something as simple as a price change, a new service policy, an ad campaign, or a news story. Customer equity can easily evaporate into thin air. One well-publicized violation of customer trust, for instance, will vaporize a great deal of customer equity, the way the Enron scandal eradicated the value of Andersen's customer base.

Or, with a brilliant new product or marketing offer, such as Apple's iPod and its music downloading service, a firm's customer equity can grow enormously, nearly overnight. It's not just your current customers who create value for your company, but your future customers, as well – your prospective customers. If yours is like most firms, you acquire a fairly steady stream of new customers in the routine course of business. If you are expanding rapidly, perhaps in a new or growing category, a great deal of your customer equity will

[1] Economic Value Added® and EVA® are registered trademarks of Stern Stewart & Co.

actually be in the form of the LTVs of customers you don't yet have, but reasonably expect to acquire in the future.[2]

Physical capital is consumed in the ordinary course of business, no matter how carefully a firm is managed. That is the nature of capital. Machinery and factories and truck fleets and other assets are gradually used up, as they are employed to generate current cash flow.

Something similar, but again not exactly the same, could be said of customer equity, which represents a store of value that must be consumed, sooner or later (otherwise, how could a customer's lifetime value ever be realized as profit?). Suppose you had a fixed set of customers, each of whom had a completely predefined pattern of future patronage, known to you in advance. When you receive cash from any of these customers, you are actually drawing down the customer's lifetime value by the same amount. In other words, as time goes on, each customer's previously expected future cash flow is simply converted to current cash flow. No value is created or destroyed with this kind of transaction, simply converted. The Return on Customer is zero.

But of course there's no such thing as a fixed set of customers with a completely predefined patronage pattern, is there? Customers can change their minds at any time. A customer may simply decide to buy more from you, or to buy less, or to stop dealing with you altogether, or to recommend a friend to you, or to cash a competitor's coupon, or to pay online rather than by check, or to move out of the country, or to declare bankruptcy, or to sell a subsidiary. Customers make these decisions by themselves, of their own free will, and while you can predict their decisions, you cannot "completely predefine" them.

Moreover, your customer base is a fluid, constantly changing set of customer relationships, with existing customers leaving and new customers coming in all the time. Your own current actions influence the future behavior of your existing and prospective customers in many ways, both positively and negatively. The way you treat customers today will to a large extent determine how predisposed those customers are to buy from you in the future.

In other words, while it may be mathematically correct to say that a customer's lifetime value declines with a purchase by the amount of

---

[2] Predicting the growth rate and value of an expanding customer base is no easy task, but there are accepted statistical methods to do so. See our discussion of this in Chapter 4 and in Appendix 4.

the purchase, it's unrealistic. When a customer buys a new car, for instance, the car dealer might think that his LTV has just declined by the amount of profit in that car – because there is now one less future purchase in the customer's lifetime value. Or, the dealer could see the sale transaction itself as an opportunity to influence the customer positively, to change his future behavior and *increase* his currently projected LTV. Providing great service, or simply remembering the customer's preferences – such actions by the dealer could create a greater willingness on the customer's part to continue purchasing, or to purchase additional services. The dealer could maintain the car, finance it, insure it, maybe even wash it regularly. The car owner might have two spaces (or three) in their garage. They might have a 15-year-old-daughter who will need a used car soon. They might recommend the dealer to their friends or colleagues. It's conceivable that a good dealer could, through their own proactive initiative, double or even triple the otherwise-projected LTV of the customer. Every interaction is an opportunity to increase a customer's lifetime value, and a sales transaction is a perfect opportunity to try.

Return on Customer versus Total Shareholder Return: ROC = TSR

Return on Customer and total shareholder return[3] are each based on cash flows. But ROC can be broken down and measured in terms of the lifetime values of small subsets of customers, making it a more useful metric for guiding everyday business decisions. Not only that, but because ROC is composed of hundreds, or even millions, of data points, it will provide an inherently more stable measurement of the rate at which a firm is actually creating value.

As we saw in Chapter 1, Return on Customer is nearly the same thing as Total Shareholder Return. ROC and TSR simply represent different ways to quantify the rate at which a company is creating value. To calculate the current value of either metric requires you to predict your firm's future cash flow, either by predicting the perform-

---

[3] See the discussion in Chapter 1, on page 23, for the definition of "total shareholder return."

ance of your various business units, or by summing customer lifetime values. But your company's future cash flow is the underlying basis for both your market value as a firm, and your customer equity.

There are some important differences between TSR and ROC, however. First, because a public company's past share price is a matter of record, TSR can be precisely measured on an historical basis, while ROC cannot. Return on Customer can never be *actually* measured, even on an historical basis, because there are no market prices for customer lifetime values. Nevertheless, knowing your actual shareholder return over the last twelve months does not tell you the rate at which your firm is creating shareholder value *today*. You can't know for sure what your share price will be next month, any more than you can know what your cash flow will be.[4] So to calculate TSR as of this minute, you still need to project your cash flows and do an analysis.

But this brings us to a second difference. Unlike shareholder return, Return on Customer is built from the bottom up, by analyzing many different groups of customers. As a result, it is inherently a more stable and reliable metric for predicting enterprise-wide cash flow. With discounted cash flow analysis, your company's value is calculated based on the projected performance of its individual operating units, each of which must be evaluated relative to trends and growth patterns in its own market. While each unit's cash flow projection might result from an analysis using a few dozen data points, ROC is likely to be based on several thousand individually calculated data points – possibly millions.

Another advantage of ROC, compared to TSR, is that Return on Customer is prescriptive, partly because it's a bottom-up metric with many more data points, but also because of where those data points come from. By using ROC, you are analyzing your company's shareholder return in terms of the individual groups and subsets of customers that are actually creating value. This means you'll have much more insight into the economic consequences of your day-to-day tactical decisions. You'll have a clearer picture of where the leverage is for creating more value, where your vulnerabilities are, and what types of activities should receive priority. You would always use discounted cash flow analysis to evaluate things like capital investment allocations,

---

[4] Theoretically, an economist would assume that a company's current share price reflects the marginal investor's superior knowledge of the firm's most likely future cash flows, and therefore of its true value.

new ventures, business combinations, and the like. But a discounted cash flow analysis built from the bottom up, using individual customer lifetime values, should provide a great deal more confidence that your analysis is accurate.

ROC is a scalpel, not a hatchet.

Spend money to make money: Using ROC to allocate capital investment

Many different considerations should go into decisions regarding which business units and activities to fund with your company's capital. Return on Customer is an important criterion, also. If you don't analyze the ROC implications of the activities you're funding, then you may end up exacerbating a problem rather than accelerating a solution.

One of the most important business decisions you can make is how to invest for growth. Which activities, which business units, or which new ventures should your business fund, and how much should it invest in each? There are many different factors to consider, of course, and you have to evaluate every proposed capital investment on its merits. But the Return on Customer metric should definitely be included in your evaluation.

Because customers create whatever value you have, so you should base your company's investment decisions on the groups of customers affected, and the degree to which each group can create value for your firm. These groups might represent the customer bases of different business units, or they might be subgroups that benefit from particular programs or initiatives, or different customers engaged with the firm through different sales channels.

In general, high-ROC business activities should be funded first, while low-ROC businesses should only receive capital allocations once opportunities for high-ROC investment have been exhausted – unless, of course, there is a possibility for using a capital infusion to convert a low-ROC activity to a higher ROC. ROC is not only a better metric for allocating capital investment than sales, profit, or cash flow, it is often a better metric than customer equity itself.

To see how this could be so, let's consider a set of hypothetical business units of a company, each of which has a different configuration of revenue, sales, customer equity and ROC, as shown in Table 10.1 below. At this company, Unit J is clearly the biggest and most profitable operation, with £150 million in annual revenue and a profit of £20 million. Dig below the surface, however, and we see that while Unit J has £200 million in customer equity, it is consuming this equity rapidly in order to turn its profit. Its calculated ROC is a negative 5%, meaning that it used up customer equity in excess of its reported current-period profit. Unit J is eating itself, and spitting a profit out every year, but this obviously cannot continue. Units K and L each have positive ROC as well as healthy profits, although they are each smaller than Unit J.

	Unit J (mm)	Unit K (mm)	Unit L (mm)
Revenue	£ 150	£125	£100
Profit (Loss)	£20	£10	£5
Customer Equity	£200	£150	£70
Return on Customer	–5%	15%	30%
Implied change in customer equity	£(30)	£12.5	£16
Total value created (destroyed)	£(10)	£23	£ 21
Year 2 Customer equity	£170	£162.5	£86
Year 2 Profit	£17	£11	£6
Year 2 ROC	–5%	14.5%	30%
Year 2 change in customer equity	£(25.5)	£14	£ 20
Year 2 total value created (destroyed)	£ (8.5)	£24	£ 26

Table 10.1

Now, if a company's management were to encounter this kind of situation, the right thing to do first would be to try to redress Unit J's situation, perhaps by retooling its offering to customers. This might or might not involve a capital investment. However, for the purposes of our discussion, let's make the assumption that each of these units has appealed to management for an injection of capital, and no one is planning to make any major process or business model changes. What will probably happen is that a capital injection for any of these units will have the effect of facilitating, magnifying, or accelerating that particular unit's current activities. So the question we need to answer is: Which unit's activities are most worthy of such leverage?

If the investment decision were based on revenue, profit, or the level of customer equity calculated at each business unit, then Unit J would receive the capital infusion, because it has higher values in all three categories. But because of Unit J's negative ROC, this unit is actually destroying value, while both Units K and L are creating value. If we simply supported and encouraged J with a further capital injection, because it's the bigger operation, and assuming we get no change in business process or practice, then all we would be doing is destroying our firm's value at a faster pace![5]

Now compare Units K and L. The ROC at Unit L is twice as good as Unit K's (30% compared to 15%), but L has less than half as much customer equity to start with, so Unit K actually creates more total value, at least in Year 1. However, if ROC remains the same for each unit, then sooner or later Unit L will overtake K and actually create more total value, as it does in our example during Year 3.

The point of this exercise is not to show that capital investment decisions should be based solely on Return on Customer, but that the Return on Customer metric should be carefully considered, along with other criteria, in making those types of decisions. You shouldn't make critical decisions like this without knowing how well each of your units is actually creating enterprise value.

Business combinations that maximize Return on Customer

Business combinations often promise more than they deliver. By using Return on Customer to evaluate the outcome of a merger or acquisition, you can ensure that real value is created, rather than just accounting optics.

Business acquisitions, mergers, and joint ventures should be evaluated with similar attention to Return on Customer and customer equity, rather than simply profit or revenues.

---

[5] It's important also to realize that even if Unit J's ROC were positive, this argument would apply just as solidly, as long as the ROC at Units K and L were higher. Maximizing overall ROC requires a firm to favor, support, or expand those elements of the customer base having the highest ROC first. While every capital investment must be evaluated on its own merits, a dollar spent to leverage an ROC of 20% will create more value for the firm than a dollar spent to leverage an ROC of 19%.

Companies increasingly desperate to satisfy their shareholders' demands for top-line growth often resort to mergers and acquisitions. But while business combinations can produce ever-bigger conglomerates with more and more buying power and market dominance, sooner or later industry consolidation always reaches a limit. Moreover, two businesses that don't make much profit independently can hardly be expected to make more just because they are strapped together. Often, all that really happens is that a few accountants and HR folks lose their jobs as duplicate overhead functions are eliminated. But do small synergies like this really qualify as "growth"? When business combinations fail to produce lasting success, the most brilliant financial stars are the very ones that fade the most quickly – think Vivendi, Tyco, WorldCom, Enron.

Recently enacted financial regulations and accounting conventions seem to support the idea that growth by business combination has been over-used by companies trying to please their shareholders. American accounting rules now make the "pooling" of assets in a merger unattractive in most situations, eliminating what was previously a sure-fire method for making a business combination appear more valuable. Companies must now also write down the cost of acquired assets when the objective value of those assets declines significantly, and acquiring firms are no longer allowed to amortize the good will value of their acquisitions. No matter what side of the economic debate you're on with respect to the wisdom or effectiveness of each of these specific rules, there can be no doubt that they evidence a general dissatisfaction with the former accounting regime, under which mergers and acquisitions were much more useful financial instruments for growing a firm's apparent value.

But from a purely financial standpoint, think about what it would mean to apply the Return on Customer metric when evaluating a business combination. Two firms will have two different customer bases and two levels of customer equity and profit. But both firms together will have a combined level of customer equity and profit, and if either firm has something to offer the customers of the other, then the customer equity of the combined entity is likely to be greater than the sum of the two separate firms.

Customer "synergy" is often an explicitly stated rationale for a merger, but in truth most firms are quite poor at exploiting such synergy. If, on the other hand, the managers of the combined firm have experience in creating a culture of customer trust, and are committed to creating long-term value as well as short-term profits, then such synergies are much more likely to be realized. The result will be that the ROC of the combined entity will be greater than the ROC of the two independent entities, calculated based on their own independent levels of profit and customer equity.[6]

It is a perilous activity for any business to combine itself with another, or even to launch a joint venture with another. But Return on Customer can help us determine whether real value is or is not being created with such a combination.

We can itemize all the benefits of using Return on Customer to aid in such decision-making, but the overriding rationale is quite simple: ROC respects the fact that customers are a constrained resource. For the vast majority of companies, customers are probably the single most constrained resource there is. *Additional capital is always available for good investments, but additional customers aren't always available, even for good products!*

Capital allocation to customers is not the hardest part of your task. Capital can be allocated to products, if necessary, and products can be allocated to customers – so any company with the right information systems in place can make the connections. The hardest part remains ROC's predictive requirement: You need to know how customers will change their future behavior based on the treatment they receive from you today.

It will require lots of experimentation and refinement to get this right, and then to be sure the management team and employees understand and buy in to the whole argument of creating a culture based on customer trust. Once this is in place, however, your insights will provide a tremendous competitive advantage, which is what strategy is all about. There may be economic barriers to driving this strategy in some businesses or business units, but the ROC metric will tell you that, and point you to places where it is more feasible.

---

[6] If two independent entities, A and B, merge to create entity AB, then the merger creates real value if $ROC_{AB} > ROC_{A+B}$, where:

$$ROC_{AB} = \frac{\pi_{iAB} + \Delta CE_{AB}}{CE_{AB}}$$

$$\text{and } ROC_{A+B} = \frac{\pi_{iA} + \Delta CE_A + \pi_{iB} + \Delta CE_B}{CE_{Ai} + CE_{Bi}}$$

Return on Customer is clearly a very useful economic tool for evaluating the actual financial effects of your company's actions. But what if you don't work for a company? What if you don't have customers, because you work for the government? What relevance would ROC have for government agencies? We'll talk about that in the next chapter.

11. ROC the Government

In 2004 Edward Prescott, an economics professor at Arizona State University and a senior monetary advisor to the Federal Reserve Bank in Minneapolis, won the Nobel Prize in Economics, sharing it with Finn Kydland, a Norwegian. According to the Royal Swedish Academy of Sciences, Prescott's work on "the time consistency of economic policy" was one of the reasons they awarded him the prize.

The "time-inconsistency problem" concerns, among other things, how to evaluate the long-term impact of short-term macroeconomic policies. Consider a central bank's responsibility to control inflation, for instance. No one wants inflation. Sooner or later, inflation's bad for just about everybody. But if unemployment is high, a government can drive it down in the short term by increasing the money supply, although this is almost guaranteed to boost inflation, leaving everyone worse off in the long term than they were before.

Governments face the same dilemma businesses face, when it comes to balancing long-term value and short-term results. It's a serious dilemma, as evidenced by the fact that Prescott and Kydland earned a Nobel for trying to resolve it. A business can resolve this short-term/long-term dilemma by measuring Return on Customer. But what can governments do?

The ROC argument raises an obvious question with respect to governmental entities and other nonprofit organizations. For most (although perhaps not all) government organizations the very concept of trying to value the enterprise in terms of future cash flows received from "customers" is meaningless. Needless to say, it isn't appropriate for a government entity to rank customers (or citizens, or taxpayers) by their "value" to the enterprise, and this obviously has an impact with respect to how Return on Customer principles should be applied to government agencies – or even *if* they should be applied at all.

Let's start with a definition of the organization's mission. It's easy to state the primary mission for a business – it is to create economic value, both in terms of current profit and the long-term value of the enterprise itself. You can accomplish this mission more effectively if you measure success in terms of the return generated on individual customers. Return on Customer provides a direct "translation" of a company's primary mission, allowing the firm to transfer this mission without distortion, from the enterprise level all the way down to the customer-specific level.

For government organizations, however, the mission statement is not so simple. Every agency has, of course, a primary mission or function. The police are charged with making society safer, the tax authority wants to ensure that citizens pay their taxes, the education folks want to make kids smarter, and the health people want to keep people in good shape. The value of accomplishing any of these missions is not easily translated into direct economic terms, although applying utilitarian economics can help.

For most government organizations dealing with issues other than foreign policy or national security, the primary mission is composed of some mixture of providing services to citizens or corporations, and getting citizens or corporations to do or not do certain things. To accomplish its mission, an agency must constantly balance the service experience it provides to a constituent against the cost of providing that experience. But crafting the right experience, while balancing the short-term and long-term costs required to deliver it, is exactly the kind of optimization problem we've been talking about throughout this book. The management principles that apply to Return on Customer involve using a customer orientation to streamline your overall operation, balancing short-term and long-term benefits. These principles make sense even when an organization does not rely on the formal economics of ROC.

Start with the self-evident proposition that any organization set up to serve the needs of constituents, taxpayers, donors, beneficiaries, or others will be more effective at delivering a satisfactory experience if it takes a "customer" perspective, and tries to see things through the eyes of the people whose interests it is supposed to be serving. Taking this perspective is important even if the organization doesn't actually try to estimate customer lifetime values. Imagine a gymnast doing a series of backward handsprings, one after another, and ending in a back flip.

The back flip at the end of the gymnast's run looks just like a hand-spring, except that this time no hands actually touch the mat. In some ways, this is analogous to a government entity applying the principles in this book. The motions and rhythms are developed based on what companies do when they have paying customers and a financially measurable mission, but the government's own execution of the move-ment takes place with "no hands" touching the profit mat.

In a nutshell, you could say that we think all organizations – profit making and nonprofit alike – should *want* to do back flips for the constituents they serve, with or without hands!

The point is, the principles of management will be nearly the same for governments and non-profits as they will be for profit-making companies actually measuring customer equity and Return on Customer. Taking actions today that positively affect future constituent attitudes and behavior will be accomplished at lower cost with some constituents than with others. And earning the trust of constituents will be central to running a smooth, cost-efficient operation. That's right – it will likely cost *less* for a government agency to run a more constituent-friendly organization.

Almost all governments around the world are trying to figure out how to streamline their operations by taking full advantage of computer tech-nology and the Internet. But the most forward-thinking governments realize that success is predicated not on the technology, but on taking a truly customer-centric view of the government's role. As private-sector service and interactive accessibility have improved throughout the last decade, consumers have begun to demand the same kind of treatment from the government agencies they must deal with.

Accenture ranks Canada as the world's most advanced government when it comes to e-thinking. On the Canadian government's own website, the mission is stated quite clearly:

"The overall objective of the GOL [Government Online] initia-tive is to increase the availability of online federal services. The approach is both citizen-/client-centered and 'whole-of-govern-ment.' In practical terms this means improving citizen/client satisfaction by designing services in response to their needs, rather than those of government organizations, while increasing the efficiency of service delivery."

Still, there is also the question of cost-efficiency. No matter what an agency's basic mission is, a natural tension will exist between cost minimization and experience maximization. Return on Customer economic principles can help manage this tension in a way that optimizes the overall benefit.

A taxing experience

Consider how Inland Revenue manages this tension when it comes to generating better compliance among employer taxpayers. With the largest active "customer" base of any government organization in Britain, and also one of the most diverse, ranging from single parents to multinational corporations, Inland Revenue needed to develop a plan for delivering better service to these taxpayers.

In 2001, Ian Schoolar became Inland Revenue's first ever director of marketing and communications. He was charged with developing a plan for delivering a higher level of service to all customers. Among other things, this required Schoolar to ensure that customers would be treated in a consistent manner across all channels, including the organization's website, its contact centers, and more than 300 "enquiry centers," which are essentially retail touchpoints, usually situated in mid-grade retail or office sites, and mainly used by people who want face-to-face contact because of their circumstances (such as the elderly, or those with poor English), or who have complex tax affairs but don't use an accountant, for example the self-employed.

Schoolar tackled his mission by setting up a seven-step process to:

1 Help customers understand Inland Revenue's mission
2 Segment the customer base
3 Understand the needs of those segments
4 Design and offer products and services to meet those needs
5 Engage all employees to help them understand the new customer strategy
6 Make the new processes understandable to constituents
7 Ensure the best use of communications.

He knew that in order to change the way Inland Revenue approached customers he would have to create an entirely new culture within the agency, focused on customer needs. Every employee would have to adopt a customer-oriented attitude. "It's about...trying to put ourselves in our customers' shoes," he said, adding, "...each and every person has the ability to build the brand we want to have."

To make it happen, he engaged a Swedish consulting group to develop interactive "learning modules" that brought just four employees together at a time, to discuss how to help customers. All 80,000 Inland Revenue employees participated in the process in these small discussion groups, designed to teach everyone how to adopt the citizen's perspective and then apply it to improve Inland Revenue's dealings with its constituents. Not only did the process help employees to understand and embrace the organization's new mission, but Inland Revenue also collected best business practices.

One of the services Inland Revenue provides to employer taxpayers, for instance, involves Business Support Teams of about 600 people, who help employers with their payroll obligations. Although this team visits employers' workplaces, Inland Revenue learned that most employers prefer to pick up the phone and talk to someone. Armed with this insight, Schoolar has begun to make improvements in the organization's call centers and to upgrade its database-sharing. The organization now attaches behavioral and demographic segments to the customer base, and has begun to determine which programs are most "profitable" (cost efficient) for which groups.

Every government agency in Britain has been assigned a number of "PSAs," which are "Public Service Agreements" – essentially, what a business would call "management objectives." At Inland Revenue, there are three PSAs:

- Improving taxpayer compliance
- Creating a more customer-friendly experience
- Holding costs down

It's easy to see that the department's primary mission is the first PSA, which ensures that the government can collect taxes. This is the fundamental reason for Inland Revenue's existence. The other two PSAs involve the means used to accomplish the first PSA. Better customer experiences will lead to more satisfied citizens, more willing to pay the fair taxes they owe. Holding costs down ensures that customer experiences are only improved in a cost-efficient, judicious way.

But these latter two PSAs are at odds with each other. If cost were no object, the customer experience could be made even better, and if customer experience were not important, then costs could be made much lower. This is an optimization problem much like the one faced by businesses when they try to balance the amount of short-term profit harvested against the long-term value created. In this case, however, the "optimum" path for a governmental department will depend on how that agency has set its primary mission. In Inland Revenue's case, compliance is indeed the primary mission, but it must be defined in a very broad sense. The fact is that the department must also render a number of services to taxpayers that go beyond pure tax collection – providing information, answering questions, and simply providing access for citizens who have complaints, grievances, or special needs, for instance.

One of Inland Revenue's many initiatives in this area focuses on its relationships with employers, who withhold and pay the income taxes due from their employees. The department is implementing a "channel management" strategy designed to encourage more cost-efficient employer behavior (primarily involving a greater use of electronic services) while also providing a better and more satisfactory experience to the employers themselves. In the government's "preferred scenario," shown in Figure 11.1, employers will receive more customized, satisfactory service, but they will also use more cost-efficient channels for interacting with Inland Revenue, largely as directed by the agency.

With this effort Inland Revenue hopes to improve compliance, eliminate information and processing errors, and make more timely collections of tax payments, when they are due. At the same time, the agency wants to reduce the burden many employers feel, in terms of paperwork and time-consuming procedures. The goal is to improve compliance by raising employers' general level of satisfaction with the overall process, while encouraging a greater use of more efficient online services.

The financial results of these customer-oriented initiatives are quite significant, although the agency is reluctant to release specifics. Some of the customer-oriented process improvements include 80% first contact resolution on inbound inquiries, and a significantly accelerated take-up by businesses of the e-filing and e-services channels. The net present value of anticipated cost reductions is nearly £25 million.

These cost reductions are directly attributable to changed behaviors and streamlined operations on the part of the organization's employer taxpayer customer segment – in essence, it represents for Inland Revenue a £25 million increase in the customer equity of that segment.

Obviously, governments work with highly sensitive personal information on citizens – and not just tax authorities, but judicial agencies, licensing bureaus, welfare offices, and other departments. In fact, nearly any government department that works with individual citizens may from time to time have to handle information that a citizen might justifiably regard as "private and personal." But so do companies. In fact, any time an organization of any type – public or commercial – deals with an individual citizen or consumer, it's possible that personal information will figure in the transaction in some way. But any time personal information is involved, it's also possible that the person involved might feel, in some way, vulnerable.

If you want to earn the trust of your customers, you have to be prepared to deal carefully with that vulnerability.

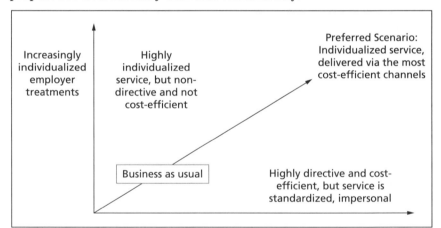

Figure 11.1: **Increasing Channel Direction by the Government**

12. Violate Your Customer's Trust and Kiss Your Asset Goodbye

In a recent *Washington Post* article, Margaret Webb Pressler asked readers to consider why women are so loyal to their hairdressers, and what other retailers could learn from salons about building loyalty. It's easy, really. You sit in the chair and pour your heart out. And the stylist takes notes – about the evolving formula for your hair color as well as the outcome of the party you're giving for your husband's high school buddies. Just before your next appointment, she reviews her notes about you from six weeks ago, and so the first question you're asked is not "What color did we do for you?" (she knows that already) but "How did the party go?" She picks up where you left off. She doesn't ask the same thing twice. She's *relevant* to what's going on in your life. She uses *insight* to advise you about what happens next. And if she doesn't want a scandal on her hands, she keeps quiet about what you tell her. Anything else, and you wouldn't depend on her as much. You wouldn't *trust* her as much.

If you have to fill out the same forms over and over, or explain your problem *again* after you thought it was already resolved, or (our favorite) repeat out loud the same account number you just punched into the telephone handset, then your trust in the competence and perhaps even the intent of the company you're dealing with is compromised. This could be just another company trying to separate you from your money. In order to save a customer the indignity of telling us the same thing over and over, without even putting them on the payroll, we need to get information, reassure them that the information is safe with us, and then use it to provide some type of individualized treatment, which is their payoff for having taken the time to let us know them better.

Protecting your customer's privacy pays *you* interest

Protecting privacy will help you build a customer relationship based on trust. The reason for protecting customer privacy is not just to avoid litigation, or federal fines, or a disastrous public relations debacle. Privacy is one of the most tangible manifestations of trust. What is more, if you know that customers are your scarcest resource then you'll understand naturally that information about your customers is your primary mechanism for creating value. Embracing and internalizing this philosophy is much more important to the success of your privacy protection effort than memorizing the bullet points in a written privacy policy. Fact is, for a company committed to Return on Customer, the data interests of the customer and the company will come into perfect alignment. The customer wants you to protect their information. You want to protect your financial asset.

Customer-specific strategies require customer-specific information. Yet many consumers are naturally reluctant to reveal "personal" information and entrust it to a corporation, creating an inherent conflict that can only partly be resolved by adopting a watertight personal privacy and data protection policy. Customer data is the fuel that powers all your company's different value creating activities. But like most fuels, it must be handled with extreme care. One thoughtless slip could significantly damage your reputation with your customers and destroy a great deal of shareholder value.

Some of the warning signs that your company may be close to a privacy implosion include:

- You have no formal privacy policy.
- Your formal privacy policy is vague or weak.
- Your formal privacy policy is documented in 15 small-print pages of contractual clauses and legal language.
- You have no central privacy group, empowered to take action.
- Your line personnel are not sufficiently committed to the idea of acting in the customer's own interest.
- Privacy issues at your company are governed entirely by lawyers, rather than those with responsibility for growing customer value.

- You're constantly engaged in efforts to extract more data from existing customers.
- You offer limited choice and consent options for permission-based marketing.
- New or existing privacy legislation impacts your industry, but the precedents aren't clear yet.

The likelihood that your company will encounter a serious privacy protection problem has a lot more to do with your attitude toward customers than it does with the bench depth of your legal department. The wrong customer orientation, to use Professor Day's term (Chapter 9), will almost certainly defeat even the best policy.

Does your company do business in that parallel universe where customers have no memories and every purchase event is a standalone, isolated transaction? Are you focused, with laser-like intensity, on maximizing current-period cash flows, without being sidetracked by changes in customer lifetime values? If the answer to either of these questions is "yes," then you'll see no *business* reason not to strip mine your database and sell whatever information will bring a price. In the parallel universe, privacy protection is not a business issue at all, but simply a matter of regulatory compliance. If it's not illegal, why not sell it?

Outside of the parallel universe, however, your interests as a business align pretty neatly with your customers' interests. If you see your customers in terms of their continuing role as your sole source of value creation, then maintaining their trust is imperative for maintaining your firm's health, and privacy protection will no longer be just a regulatory issue, but a business tool. Your customers want you to maintain their privacy and security, and you *must* protect their data in order to remain competitive. If you are maximizing your Return on Customer, then not only are you getting the most overall value from the value proposition, but your customer is, too.

To many customers, the way customer data is used and customer privacy protected is a strong indicator of trustworthiness in a company. The Ponemon Institute, an Arizona-based privacy think tank, regularly examines consumer trust with respect to dozens of American companies. Relying on a survey of American consumers, the institute ranked companies from top to bottom in terms of perceived trustworthiness, in the eyes of customers. It's interesting to note the differences in how privacy is handled by the most trusted firms, relative to the least trusted.

**DIFFERENCES BETWEEN THE MOST TRUSTED (TOP 20)
AND LEAST TRUSTED (BOTTOM 18) COMPANIES**

Characteristics	Top 20	%	Bottom 18	%	Diff
Full time privacy leader (CPO)	15	75%	3	17%	58%
Privacy reports through corporate law (General Counsel)	10	50%	10	56%	-6%
Privacy function with budget	14	70%	5	28%	42%
Privacy governance integrated with marketing & CRM	13	65%	5	28%	37%
Clear and concise policy posted to the website	14	70%	2	11%	59%
Well-defined redress program	13	65%	3	17%	48%
Uses permission management process to manage privacy preferences	9	45%	1	6%	39%
Uses third-party auditor or seal program	14	70%	1	6%	64%
Has reporting authority to board	12	60%	3	17%	43%
Privacy governance integrated with IT security	15	75%	8	44%	31%

Source: Survey by Ponemon Institute & TRUSTe, released June 11, 2004.

Table 12.1

It ought to be obvious that privacy violations will undermine your customers' trust in your company, making it difficult to achieve your basic mission, which is to maximize Return on Customer. The only task is to decide what actions will do the best job of protecting individual privacy (and thus enable a trusting relationship) while still providing enough fuel to power your various customer-specific activities.

Privacy protection in the parallel universe

Unfortunately, for most companies the question is not how customer insight can be used to add value for customers, or to improve a customer's life, or to make things simpler, less expensive, or more convenient for the customer. Instead, for most businesses the primary question is how customer insight can be employed to extract more money from the customer. How can we sell this customer more stuff, or reduce the costs of serving the customer, or identify the most lucrative prospective customers, by using the detailed information we now have? With respect to personal customer information, most companies act as if they were residents of the parallel universe.

But this is an extremely shortsighted view on the part of any company. Not only does it completely disregard the issue of customer trust, but it also leads a firm to focus on short-term revenue gains at the expense of eroding long-term customer value. As a customer, you expect the company you do business with to make a profit from your transaction. Just because they make a profit doesn't mean you wouldn't trust them. But if they make an unseemly profit on you, by taking advantage of you in ways that you have no power to influence, or by recommending products or services not in your best interest, or perhaps even by working behind your back without your knowledge, then your trust will be broken.

The problem is that many companies view customers in a way that is, if not overtly hostile, at least obliviously self-oriented. Customers exist primarily to be separated from their money, and a successful business extracts the most money from these customer "targets," while incurring the least cost. While it's true that lots of firms make a concerted effort to combat this attitude by declaring that the customer is king, or the customer is at the center of the business, or the customer is always right, this effort represents an uphill battle if, as is usually the case, a company is unable to document any economic benefit from it. A firm that is not focused on Return on Customer is not *financially* committed to earning the trust of its customers, which is why it always seems like such an unnatural act.

As a result, at most firms the company's publicly proclaimed customer-friendly policy is actually not very credible, and can easily be overturned to meet short-term financial objectives, which are paramount. In early 2002, Yahoo! reset the self-selected privacy preferences of its millions of subscribers (see Chapter 2), sending Yahoo! users a lengthy email notification that included this statement, buried in the middle of the fourth paragraph:

We have reset your marketing preferences and, unless you decide to change these preferences, you may begin receiving marketing messages from Yahoo! about ways to enhance your Yahoo! experience, including special offers and new features.

If you were getting email at Yahoo!, or if you had ever registered there for chat sessions or games or other activities, Yahoo! changed all your preferences to "yes – contact me." This included not only 13 different "enroll me" categories for email information and offers (translation: spam), but also a ticked box instructing Yahoo! that it was OK to contact you "via phone at [your number]," or "via U.S. mail at [your address]." They had a subscriber's home phone and address already, if they had ever given it to any Yahoo! merchant or partner. Yahoo's email to its users began with the statement "Your privacy is very important to us here at Yahoo!," but after reading the message only a yahoo would have believed them.

In fairness, of course, many of Yahoo!'s excellent services and benefits are offered completely free of charge, and it's not at all unreasonable for a company to want to "monetize" its customer base. The problem was that because the company's only metric of success was its currently reported financial numbers, this money-raising initiative probably destroyed a great deal of long-term customer value during the process of raising current-period profits. It is an issue that could easily have been handled differently – and probably *would* have been handled differently – had Yahoo!'s corporate culture been oriented around earning the trust of its customers. Interestingly enough, this kind of culture would have provided Yahoo! with a much clearer focus on building permanent shareholder value, regardless of the daily fluctuations of its share price.

This is not an isolated example. The plain fact is that what Yahoo! proposed doing was no different than what is already done by a wide variety of companies that collect individual customer information, including banks and credit card companies, phone companies, magazine publishers, and others. In 2002, American consumers began receiving letters from phone companies, insurance firms and financial services companies, advising them about their newly legislated rights to prevent these firms from disseminating (that is, selling) their personal information. The letters themselves, and the public rationales put forward by spokespeople for these firms, defied all reasonable standards for the truth. What they told consumers they wanted was to "provide a high level of service to people," or to "help consumers learn about new products and services." But what they really wanted was to be permitted to continue to earn a profit by selling personal data.

So: Violate your customer's privacy and you violate their trust. It's that simple, right? No, actually it's not at all simple.

The many faces of privacy

In the first place, different people have different levels of sensitivity with respect to protecting their own privacy. In fact, just agreeing on a definition of privacy protection can be problematic. Three people discussing privacy protection might think they mean the same thing. But one means: "I don't want you to know anything about me." Another means: "It's OK for you to know something about me, but I don't want you to tell anyone else." And the third means: "Leave me alone."

What influences customers to share their personal information? A survey on the state of customer trust showed that customer responses such as "gives me control of how my information is used," "keeps customer information safe," and "open and honest about their business" far outweighed "has best value." A study by Accenture confirmed this finding. *Customers are willing to pay more if they trust a company.* In addition, fear of inadequate privacy protection has compelled half of consumers to reject or cancel doing business with a company. And two-thirds of respondents reported "aggressive marketing" as the factor that undermines their trust in business. Business respondents cite positive customer service, company reputation, or length of relationship as the most positive influences on trust.

Respecting your customers' privacy while using personal data to benefit the customer involves a difficult balancing act. Without data you can't personalize a customer's treatment, providing convenience and better service. But if you use too much data you risk creating "too much" personalization value for the customer, offending them with a level of intimacy that you may not have earned. Because every customer makes his own judgment with respect to how much is too much, you have to undertake this balancing act for every customer, individually.

Moreover, different cultures have different takes on the importance of privacy protection. In some societies consumers are more prone to take a "them against us" perspective. "Those big corporations are just trying to use what they know about me to sell me more things I don't really need." In other cultures, personal privacy barely hits most consumers' hierarchy of needs at all. So the issue of customer insight and privacy protection can become a great deal more complicated for any multinational enterprise attempting to use Return on Customer as a unifying measure of corporate success.

Then there is the problem of execution. It's one thing to have a policy, but something else entirely to enforce it effectively. In July 2004, for example, the Federal Trade Commission settled a year-long battle with Gateway Learning Corp. after bringing charges for "alleged unfair and deceptive practices in connection with its rental of customer information to third parties." Gateway Learning agreed to hand over to the FTC the $4600 it earned in renting out its customer lists. Even though doing this was in direct contradiction of its own privacy policy, the most likely explanation for Gateway's action is simply poor internal coordination. Folks in one department at the firm weren't talking to folks in another department. In other words, while Gateway probably had good intentions, these intentions were subverted during the routine, day-to-day operation of the business. The company's lawyers simply can't watch every outbox.

Good intentions are clearly not enough to avoid a privacy problem. Competence and execution also count. To ensure that your own privacy policy is properly implemented, you must pay attention to how your day-to-day business activities might affect it. Do you partner with other companies to render services to your customer? Are you accountable for your partner's privacy policies? If you give a customer's personal information to an outside company, is that a violation of the customer's privacy? What if you give it to another division within your own firm? What if you give it to an outside company that you are partnering with to render services to your customers? How do you track, and act on, a customer's level of sensitivity about their own data? So long as you secure customer data, is that enough, or do you still need to provide a way for worried customers to be reassured 24/7?

Are these questions too difficult? Then take a simpler, more straightforward test: Call your own call center several different times, masquerading as a customer, and ask about how the company will protect or use your personal information. Ask what options you have to manage the process. Tell someone you have a complaint about how your own privacy was violated, and ask to speak with someone about it – then see whom they connect you to. Ask if your name or personal details have ever been given to any other firm, and whether that firm will be bound by the same privacy protection principles.

The answers to these questions will come more easily if your company has a culture based squarely on earning your customers' trust – treating your customers the way you'd like to be treated yourself, if you were the customer. This seems to us not only to be the surest way to avoid privacy problems, but it also has the advantage of maximizing the rate at which you can create shareholder value. (Nevertheless, one Chief Privacy Officer insisted to us that the "privacy problem" mostly involves data security and legal compliance. We predict she'll be watching a lot of outboxes.)

Regulatory authorities around the world are taking an increasing interest in questions such as these. The questions are different for different agencies, different countries, and different types of information, but the issue goes way beyond the law, the regulations, or the courts. Jennifer Barrett, Chief Privacy Officer at Acxiom Corporation, puts it this way: "Law cannot generate trust. It creates the floor we walk on."

If the law is the floor you walk on, then customer trust is the air your company needs to breathe.

One last question: At your company, who's actually in charge of privacy protection? Who sets the policy, and who enforces it? Yes, you certainly need legal beagles to make sure you don't cross any regulatory lines, but shouldn't you put someone in charge who understands the interrelationship of customer value, enterprise value, and trust?

Responsible Information Stewardship®

There is a straightforward method for simplifying many of the complex issues that surround the problem of privacy protection. It involves adopting the customer's perspective and putting policies in place that are considerate, fair, and *responsible*. We have a term for this holistic approach to the problem: "Responsible Information Stewardship®." The "RIS"[1] approach involves several key elements:

- *Process management.* Performance-based measurement systems, including scorecards that take account of privacy protection and data security issues. Verification procedures should be based on external authorities. Enabling technologies that ensure security and privacy protection need to be implemented.
- *Education and awareness.* Classroom training for employees, partners, and anyone with access to sensitive or personally identifying information. Use facilitated training, e-learning, and other mechanisms for disseminating the right practices.
- *Monitoring.* A formal process for identifying privacy and data-protection risks. Identify vulnerability areas not just within the core business units, but also within and among all the associated databases, software applications, and outside parties that might have any access to sensitive data for any reason.
- *Communications.* Policies, corporate communications, employee handbooks, compliance procedures and crisis-management interventions.
- *Enforcement.* The formal mechanism and due process for responding to consumer or employee issues and concerns.

If you don't adopt this kind of a holistic approach to protecting privacy and securing data you can easily run into problems. For one thing, when you collect too much data you're likely to have cumbersome or inefficient information processing, storage and document-retention processes. You'll also probably end up wasting a great deal of time and energy simply trying to manage information you don't really need. In addition, the more information is collected the more likely your employees and managers are to make mistakes with their indi-

---

[1] Responsible Information Stewardship® and RIS® are registered service marks of Peppers & Rogers Group, a division of Carlson Marketing Group.

vidual roles and responsibilities. A lack of understanding coupled with too much personal information can easily lead to a privacy breach.

If maximizing Return on Customer is your goal, however, then you'll find that protecting privacy is not a constraint on your business at all, but rather a tool for creating more value, faster. If your customers can trust you with their personal information, then you'll be free to tune your whole organization and management structure to the customer frequency. You can manage your relationship with each individual customer for your mutual benefit. The only thing you now need to succeed is a management structure that's capable of treating different customers differently, and this is what we'll take up next.

13. Managing Portfolios of Customers to Build Enterprise Value

Your company has a lot of moving parts, and you have, over the years, put managers in charge of those various pieces. That's why you have product managers, assembly line managers, brand managers, contact center managers, finance officers, human resources directors, customer experience managers, branch or franchise or store managers, a website designer, sales directors, IT managers, territory managers, regional managers, and the list goes on and on.

But often a company finds that its organization has difficulty taking the customer-specific actions required to boost Return on Customer. For instance, a single customer might buy more than one product or service from a company, and might engage with it through two or more channels, but which product manager or channel manager should be "in charge" of the firm's actions with respect to that customer? Consider the issues at your own company:

- Who's managing your firm's customer relationships, setting objectives for each customer and determining the right actions, across all product and service lines?
- How should you measure the success of such a customer manager?
- What authority should a customer manager have over the other moving pieces in your firm, in order to maximize ROC?

These are some of the questions we'll address in this chapter, as we examine the role of the "customer portfolio manager."

The buck stops...where?

Managing the overall process of customer-specific competition is one of the thorniest issues facing companies today. How can you hold your organization accountable for creating value with customer-specific treatments that might vary considerably across your customer base? Who will be "in charge" of your treatment of a particular customer, when that treatment spans different products, different sales channels, or different business units? To focus on improving the value of a specific customer or group of customers, over time, you have to resolve the conflicts among all your various product-oriented and brand-oriented business units, which means someone, somewhere in your company, has to be *in charge* of the customer's relationship. This gets at the heart of *relationship governance*.

Fail to resolve these conflicts, and your customers will see your actions as uncoordinated or even irrational. This is exactly how the majority of American consumers see their banks today. During the 1980s and 1990s, practically the entire American retail banking industry began "productizing" their operations, hiring brand managers and product managers from other industries, and trying to streamline their marketing efforts. They put different managers in charge of specific products, such as retail lending, credit cards, mortgages, investments, and checking, and each operating unit frequently had its own bottom line, not to mention its own set of customer and account data.

On the surface, this had the benefit of streamlining a bank's operating costs, making a large, multiproduct bank easier to manage. But when banks then began trying to cross-sell their products, problems became obvious to customers immediately. Every product was pitched to every customer, with marketing messages that were more or less independent of whatever banking services the customer already used. Naturally, this irritated customers, because it was apparent that even though they might already be purchasing several products or services from the bank, the bank was virtually oblivious.

Nor was the problem quickly resolved, because few people at a bank would take it on board as a problem, and even when someone did they had little authority to do anything about it. Product managers and brand managers were in charge, and they were rewarded not for the growth of customer equity but for product sales. Yes, customer responsiveness was gradually eroding, across all products, but what could you do about that?

Whenever the problem of customer coordination was identified at a bank, it was inevitably described as an information-technology problem, rather than a management problem. Everyone thought the bank simply needed its computer systems to render a "single view" of its customers, and if all its product-line databases could share customer-specific information, then rationality could be restored. The real problem, of course, was not IT, but organizational structure. When a bank is organized by product line no one has responsibility for developing a single view of any particular customer, and even when that view becomes available, no one has responsibility for acting on it.

Customer-specific management

The problem faced by retail banks is similar to the one all companies face, when they have no mechanism for measuring the value they create through their customer-specific actions. If, on the other hand, you measure success in terms of Return on Customer, then you have to organize your business by customer, rather than by product.

Return on Customer operates well at the enterprise level, but one of its biggest advantages is that it can quantify the shareholder return your firm earns from various day-to-day actions.

Return on Customer can be measured for any non-overlapping group of customers, because every unique group of customers has its own customer equity and generates its own current-period cash flows. ROC can therefore be applied to various operating units and departments within a larger organization, while still retaining its integrity as a metric of shareholder return, enabling you to measure the actual rate at which you are creating shareholder value with your day-to-day tactical activities, affecting even small groups of customers. With ROC you can distribute the task of creating shareholder value to individual managers and business units, each of whom can be placed in charge of a nonoverlapping group of customers – what we call a customer *portfolio*. Moreover, because different types of customers present different opportunities for creating value, to maximize your overall

Return on Customer you *must* break your customer base down into smaller and smaller bits. The logic for this might seem clear, but implementation is not quite so straightforward.

The "molecular" granularity of ROC gives it an extraordinary usefulness for ensuring that tactical, in-the-trenches decision-making conforms to the broader corporate objective. To change a particular customer's behavior (and increase your ROC for that customer), your company will have to interact with or behave toward them in a way that is influenced, not just by your knowledge of their value to you, but also by your insight into their individual needs and motivations. This insight will probably be based on some categorization of customers, but no matter how well you categorize your customers, when you interact you'll be dealing with *individual* customers – not with categories, or segments, or even with portfolios. In other words, maximizing Return on Customer requires you to treat different customers differently, and to do so in a customer-specific way. Fortunately, ROC can also measure your success with customer-specific activities.

Inherent in the idea of maximizing ROC is the notion that you will assign different objectives, strategies, and actions to different customers, in the same way that a product-line company applies different objectives, strategies and actions to different product or service offerings. So, for every customer you must ensure that someone – some single authority – is "in charge" of setting the strategy and carrying out your company's actions, with respect to that customer. Ideally, every customer will be the direct line responsibility of a single customer portfolio manager, whose job will be to:

1 Set the strategy for each customer in the portfolio.
2 Ensure that these customer-specific strategies are carried out.

We have deliberately used the term "portfolio" in describing the customer management function, rather than "segment," because we are talking about a non-overlapping customer group.[1] The customer

---

[1] Market segments can easily overlap, and often do. This is one of the primary reasons why many customers, and particularly the most valuable ones, are over-solicited, and it's why their interactions with a firm are often not coordinated. A "portfolio" of customers is a group of customers for whom the firm is in fact managing its overall interactions and offerings in a coordinated way. So, while a customer portfolio is technically a type of market segment, most segments are not customer portfolios. In the Endnotes for this chapter, you'll find a more complete discussion of "segments" and "portfolios."

portfolio manager can be thought of as a kind of "traffic cop" who coordinates a firm's interactions and transactions with respect to the particular customer's portfolio, across all product and service lines, and through all channels, deciding when and how to offer which products or services to that customer. For this reason, every customer should be placed into one and only one portfolio, and portfolios will never overlap. (Of course, while we say customers are being "managed," what we really mean is that the firm's own actions are being managed, in a customer-specific way. Perhaps a more precise but cumbersome term would be "customer-specific manager.")

In a B2B environment, customer management often takes place at the hands of the company's relationship manager or account manager for each client. The relationship manager "owns" the relationship, and is free to set the policies and communications for their own individual clients, within the boundaries set by the enterprise. At most firms that employ key account management, the relationship manager is held responsible for keeping the client satisfied and loyal, as well as profitable. Discounts and price changes are only offered with the key account manager's approval. And while most such companies do not formally estimate an individual client's actual lifetime value, in strict financial terms, many do have a process for ranking clients by their long-term value or importance to the firm. A relationship manager who improves the value of the client's relationship to the company will be rewarded.

Hannover Life Re measures relationship managers based on customer value

Hannover Rückversicherung AG is a large, German-based reinsurance firm. Hannover Life Re is one of four strategic business units at the Hannover Re Group, representing all life and health activities of the group and ranking third among the top global life reinsurers. Since 1999 it has measured its success in terms of how much value it can create with its several hundred customers, mostly large life insurance companies and other financial services firms laying off the risk of life insurance and other policies they've written for their own customers. By sharing these risks with the reinsurer and pooling them with others, an insurance company can minimize the probability of financial loss. Reinsurance firms like Hannover Life Re facilitate this by taking long-term contracts (called "treaties") from their customers to cover them for various risks. The very nature of the business therefore demands long-term, trusting relationships between insurer and reinsurer.

Hannover differentiates its clients based on both their loyalty and their value. Loyalty differentiation is a function, not only of the size of a firm's book of business with the company, but also of its treaty renewal behavior. In Hannover Life Re's lexicon, clients fall into four value tiers: loyal customers, habitual customers, variety seekers, and switchers. Within each of these groups, there are finer gradations of loyalty. To assign different clients to different value tiers, the firm uses a set of questions administered by the regional relationship managers, including such things as whether the client has a strategic partnership (ie. intensive product development) with Hannover Life Re, the share of business, level of sophistication and innovation of insurance products, the client's proactivity in the market, and the type and intensity of services rendered by Hannover Life Re. According to Axel Heinemann, Senior Vice President, Customer Relationship Management at Hannover Life Re, "We mathematically value these questions, and with this tool we have an excellent and proven method of deriving a 'loyalty factor' for each client."

The firm also differentiates clients according to actual and potential value. According to Heinemann, the company begins by "assessing the actual value of existing treaties. We figure out the present value of future profits from last year's new business assignments: however, we also have new treaties, from either new customers or current customers, which is our potential value. Using a mathematical formula, we then derive the customer lifetime value."

Once a year all regional relationship managers submit their customer plans, containing customer loyalty status and lifetime values to the head office. "We combine these numbers," according to Heinemann, "and come up with a number in euros. Everyone is obliged, on each and every treaty, to come up with that euro amount. First we do this by treaty, then we add up the treaties to derive a value for each and every customer." Calculations of customer lifetime value and growth potential define the criteria by which relationship managers are judged and rewarded for their next year's business-building activities.

This number is, in a sense, the company's value-creation "objective" for each customer. But Heinemann is quick to add that the financial objective assigned to each relationship manager is only 80% of the actual value and 60% of the potential. By hedging the numbers somewhat, he says, he can get his managers to produce their numbers more willingly and objectively.

Grouping customers into portfolios

When your company engages in customer-specific activities, you are operating at the molecular level of the individual customer. If you just have a few, very large customers, then each molecule is visible to management. You can pay individual attention to customers by assigning key account managers or relationship managers to oversee each of them, one at a time. It's when the customers are smaller that grouping them into portfolios becomes a useful management idea.

Because you can apply ROC to large or small groups of customers with confidence that it will still maintain its integrity as a metric of shareholder return, you can use ROC to evaluate tactical situations even when the molecules are tiny, relative to your company. When you deal with consumers as customers, or even with small and medium businesses, your individual customers will be all but invisible to other management lenses and tools. But with ROC you can refine and sharpen your treatment for each type of customer, and evaluate the actual value created with each different treatment. The most persuasive offering to make to a utilitarian shopper, for instance, will almost certainly be different from the one that appeals the most to a status-seeker. Your objective for a high-value customer will be different from your objective for a low-value customer, and so forth.

As we've already seen, customers are different not only in their value to your firm, but also in terms of what they need from it. By ranking customers into tiers based on the amount and type of value they represent, you can gain insight into where the most attractive sources of value creation lie within your customer base. And by differentiating customers according to their own needs, you can gain insight into the actual motivational triggers to use, in order to stimulate more value creation.

For portfolio management to work, it is absolutely critical that you have accurate and reliable insight into the value and needs of your individual customers. If you don't know what a particular customer needs, then you have no way to motivate the customer to change behavior in a way that creates more value. If you don't know a customer's value, then you have no way to prioritize your activities between that customer and other customers, and no way to measure your success.

But which type of customer differentiation should we rely on in assigning customers to individual portfolios? Is a portfolio of customers similar in terms of value or needs? Answer: Either or both, depending on the granularity of your effort. Most firms find that some combination of customer differentiation by both value and needs is appropriate. And don't forget that in most cases a customer's value is correlated with needs – that is, customers with a certain type of need, or a certain type of identifiable behavior, tend to be more or less valuable than customers with other needs. The real problem is how to decide which portfolio fits which particular customer the best.

Hypothetically, for instance, suppose one of your bank's customer portfolios is made up of married couples with school-age children. The portfolio manager shapes the bank's communications to these customers based largely on their need to plan for college and eventual retirement, as well as their current need for borrowing – mortgages, car loans, and so forth. Now suppose one of the mothers in this portfolio is suddenly widowed, and inherits a sizable insurance payout. You have a portfolio manager who handles newly wealthy clients (mostly heirs), and another one who handles single mothers. But which portfolio manager should be given responsibility for this customer? Or should she continue to receive the hard-working family-oriented messages she was getting when her husband was alive? Obviously, such situations require judgment and individual decisions. No matter how sophisticated your analysis, in reality you will never be able to define all of the different situations your customers will find themselves in. But the point of managing portfolios of customers is not to write down in advance the rules for creating value from every customer, but simply to do a better job of anticipating and meeting the needs of the customers who create value for your business.

Portfolio managers: Authority and accountability

The tools a portfolio manager ought to have available include literally every type of action or communication that the company is capable of rendering on a customer-specific basis. This means the portfolio manager should control all addressable forms of communication and interaction – direct mail, interactions at the call center and on the website, and even (as far as possible) scripts and talking points for face-to-face encounters in the store, at the cash register, or during meetings with sales reps. Ideally, the portfolio manager would also set or approve the pricing for customers, extending any discounts, charging premiums, and imposing or waiving service charges and fees. (In some industries, and in some countries, regulations will inhibit or bar customer-specific pricing, or they may restrict the use of direct mail, or other communications vehicles. But when this is the case, these tools should simply be treated as noncustomer-specific, and thus not available for the portfolio manager's toolbox.)

In sum, the portfolio manager should "own" not just the communication of the offer but also the offer itself, with respect to the customers in the portfolio. The company will still be creating and marketing various programs and products, but the portfolio manager will play the role of "traffic cop" with respect to determining whether, how, and when these programs and products are offered to his customers. He will likely allow some offers to go through as conceived, he will adapt other offers to meet the needs of his own customers, and he may block some offers altogether, choosing not to expose the customers to them. The actual treatments of individual customers – including communications and offers – will have to be "mass customized" through the application of business rules, and one of the portfolio managers' primary responsibilities will be to oversee the business rules that govern your firm's relationships with the individual customers in the portfolio.

The fact that ROC is measured as a rate, rather than as a fixed quantity, simplifies the task of evaluating portfolio managers and holding them accountable. Portfolios will consist of different amounts of customer equity to begin with, depending on the types of customers within them. A portfolio composed primarily of Most Valuable Customers, for instance, is likely to throw off a great deal of current profit, while a portfolio of Most Growable Customers represents more of an opportunity for increasing lifetime value. Other portfolios are likely to have more promising new-customer acquisition possibilities, and so forth. But for each portfolio manager, ROC will gauge the efficiency with which value is created from the value started with.

Managing customers in portfolios allows you to parse your entire customer base into nonoverlapping units of value creation – and remember that *each customer is a value creation unit.* Since the measurement of success is identical for each unit, you can subdivide your business into nearly autonomous, but ultimately synchronized, business units, each striving to increase shareholder return in its own way and with its own customers.

It is never completely simple, however. While you may want to evaluate a portfolio manager on the basis of Return on Customer, many things will have an effect on ROC other than the offers and customer-specific communications that are under the actual control of the portfolio manager. A bad bit of press, or a stunning piece of advertising, for instance, are each likely to have significant effects on any portfolio's customer equity. Poor product quality or shoddy service delivery, or letting a competitor sneak in a terrific new product will damage Return on Customer. In other words, you can hold portfolio managers accountable for ROC, but you can only grant them authority over a few of the tools and levers for increasing it.

Thus, a portfolio manager's accountability will almost certainly exceed his authority, although he will have a strong interest in making up the difference through persuasion and influence. Just like the product or brand manager whose success rests partly on clearing away obstacles that might inhibit the successful distribution of the product, the portfolio manager must also clear away obstacles. An expensive but pointless advertising campaign, for example, will impose a burden on every portfolio manager's ROC, and in a business measuring success in this way, the portfolio managers themselves will likely complain the loudest. So even though they may not have formal authority to control nonaddressable communications, or customer service standards, or product development, they will certainly have a big influence on such policies. (Note, however, that the interest a portfolio manager shows in controlling noncustomer-specific costs, such as advertising, will depend to a certain extent on how you choose to allocate those costs in calculating lifetime value. See Appendix 2 for a more complete discussion.)

The central goal of managing portfolios of customers is to provide a rational, cost-efficient way for a company to treat different customers differently. Rationality implies that the company is collecting and processing information on its customers' current behaviors and making conscious decisions regarding desired future behaviors.

Unlike data mining, however, which has an uncertain outcome, the kind of customer analytics required by portfolio managers will work the other way around. That is, rather than starting with the raw data and trying to synthesize it in ways that reveal hidden opportunities, customer portfolio managers will begin with the business objective for their customers and work backwards to figure out what they need to do next, based on the data available. The method will rely on a great deal of testing and experimentation to uncover value drivers that help the firm achieve its objectives.

CAPABILITIES MANAGERS (PRODUCT MANAGERS REINCARNATED)

Even when a company institutes a system for measuring its success in terms of the value it creates through its customers, the actual processes for making products and delivering services must still be competently executed. Moreover, it is important to ensure that production and service delivery serve the actual needs of the company's new line managers – its portfolio managers, who are measured by the Return on Customer they generate and as a result now have "bottom line" responsibility for value creation.

Portfolio managers are the executives who will be the most closely attuned to customer needs, and they will uncover unmet needs, in the routine course of their job. A portfolio manager might learn, for instance, that some customers would become more valuable to the firm if they could purchase extra warranty and repair services. But the portfolio manager cannot actually produce and deliver that service or product. There must be some place in the company for this request. The company needs to have an ability to respond to customer inputs by deploying its capabilities differently, or by developing and deploying entirely new capabilities.

So, in addition to the managers who are charged with overseeing your relationships with individual customers, you will need "capabilities managers" as well. The role of a capabilities manager is to deliver the capabilities of your enterprise to the portfolio managers – in essence, to figure out whether you should build, buy, or partner with other firms to render any new products or services that might be required by customers. Capabilities managers are something like "product managers at large." The products and capabilities they bring to bear, however, will actually be marketed not directly to customers but rather to the portfolio managers in charge of the firm's relationships with customers.

In many cases, to deploy new capabilities you'll need to engage in strategic alliances with other firms. There are a variety of reasons why you might choose not to develop new capabilities for yourself – including, most obviously, the problem that new capabilities can sometimes require a different organizational structure, or a completely different set of skills and talents, and these might not advance your firm's core competitive strategy (see Chapter 7).

Because the portfolio manager's tools consist of individually addressable offers and communications, one of their principal activities will likely be testing one offer or message against another. Testing and customer analytics, however, represent complex and specialized disciplines, and in many companies they will be provided by a central source to all portfolio managers.

In the same way that a product manager can tap the marketing department for preapproved sales collateral, with the right look and feel for the brand, a portfolio manager needs to be able to tap the marketing department for the right analysis of the portfolio's transactions and leading indicators, and the right "preapproved" testing and validation methods for learning more. The marketing and marketing research people, in turn, will be relying on the firm's customer database or data warehouse. At most firms, this kind of standardization will create a kind of "market" in testing and analytics, so that important learning from one portfolio rapidly disseminates to others.

The problem faced by retail banks, for example, has always been that an organizational structure built to facilitate brand management and product management holds no one accountable for creating more overall value from particular customers. The sophisticated marketing organizations at most large retail banks have access to whatever testing and analytics are necessary to monitor the profitability of their offers, on a campaign-by-campaign basis, but few banks have yet set up the same type of sophisticated marketing organization for the purpose of measuring – and improving – their Return on Customer for different types of customers.

A decade-long initiative at CIBC

Canadian Imperial Bank of Commerce (CIBC) is one of North America's largest financial institutions, serving more than nine million customers and offering a constellation of services, including retail banking, wealth management, consumer and corporate lending, credit cards, and commercial and institutional banking. In the early 1990's, CIBC's retail banking organization began its long transition toward becoming a more customer-centric operation, when it implemented technology allowing it to compile a centralized database of customer information. It soon found that success would require aligning its organization and management around customers, rather than around products.

However, rather than collecting and organizing as much information as possible about each customer, CIBC chose, as Tesco did, to collect and maintain a bare minimum of customer data, so as to maximize the accuracy and completeness of its customer information on a regular basis. Even this effort required 18 months to complete, because the bank's culture was oriented not around customers, but around "accounts" – which were the products that CIBC's various business units sold. A single customer with multiple accounts was treated as if that customer were multiple customers.

So first the bank linked customers to the accounts, and then grouped the customers into economic buying units (families, households, businesses), called "connections." Portfolios of between 200 and 10,000 connections were formed and assigned to the business units, to be managed based on calculations of individual customer values and growth potential. Altogether, 17 different product systems tie in to the database so that even if a customer has multiple account numbers, there will still be only one customer number.

By focusing its analytics efforts on customer values, rather than account sales, CIBC soon began discovering some quite interesting things about its business. For instance, it found that there was no good correlation between a customer's value and the number of accounts maintained by the customer. Nor could profitability be predicted simply from the number of funds managed for a customer.

CIBC's overall premise was that optimizing by customer would create at least as much value as optimizing by product, because the net present value of the firm was equal to the net present value of its customer relationships. But optimizing by customer rather than by product meant a number of changes in how the bank approached all its marketing tasks, as shown in Table 13.1.

John Moore, CIBC's Senior VP, Personal Banking and Customer Insight Relationship Marketing, maintains that the database and its associated analytics have "enabled us to get the *right* share of customer." What he means is that, not only can the bank sell more effectively to its customers, but it can also monitor the customers to ensure that each has the right products to meet his individual needs – second mortgages for homeowners, for instance, or retirement savings plans for working couples. Optimizing by customer, from CIBC's point of view, first involves optimizing the customer's experience – that is, maximizing the value the customer is realizing from the bank.

Task	From	To
Target	Single-product focus	Customer-driven, multi-product focus
Timing	Seasonal	Ongoing, or event-triggered
Channel	Stand-alone channels	Integrated multichannels
Offer	Product-feature driven	Tailored to segments
Measures	Market share, volume	Customer profitability

Table 13.1: **Marketing Task Migration at CIBC Based on Product Versus Customer**

One of the key responsibilities for portfolio managers at CIBC is developing and approving the business rules that govern how customers in the portfolio are treated. At first, this process involved standardizing the way messaging occurred at the bank – the number, type, and order of communications to customers. But over time, event-driven messaging came to be driven by a series of "if...then" rules, documented by the business managers, and standardized by the relationship marketing people at the bank.

The analysis that underlies the bank's efforts to tailor its offers and communications to different customers typically involves more than 500 variables, each of which is weighed for relevance and predictive power. The bank is constantly trying to understand what factors drive value creation for specific types of customers. And, in order to ensure it is capturing not just short-term profit but long-term value, depending on the marketing campaign or event, it will sample outcomes over longer periods of time.

According to Moore, "Contact opportunities for any given customer are limited, so we have to carefully select our messages and offers. We evaluate results based on a balance of both the campaign's immediate profitability and a three-year ROI, which takes into account overall three-year expected value from the contact. This includes attrition impact and cross-sell opportunities driven from this conversation." However, he says, when they do the final evaluation of each campaign, "the three-year ROI figure is how we measure a campaign's actual success."

The results of CIBC's program are not evaluated based solely on mathematical analysis and computer data, however. Certainly, for a complex business with millions of customers and dozens of product offerings, technology is an indispensable tool. True success, however, will occur only when employees actually use the technology to act in the interests of their customers – as if they were customers themselves. This is the not-so-secret ingredient in this bank's recipe for success. Moore put it this way:

> "Shared customer history is one of many important initiatives underway to improve customer satisfaction. It helps our front line have the right conversations with customers – by giving them fingertip access not just to contact history but also to the products the customer currently has with us, products and services they are likely to need, and whether there are any outstanding issues that need resolving. Combine this with outstanding needs-based selling skills and an integrated set of products that meet a customer's lifetime needs, and you're demonstrating to customers that you know them, value them, and are working to delight them at every point of contact."

As Moore implies with these comments, CIBC does not see this as an issue of technology and analytics alone. Customer management requires you to create a culture that values the customer's interests – a culture in which employees are constantly trying to see things from the customer's perspective. This not only generates a higher Return on Customer, but it also delivers the most value to customers. Moore's own incentive pay is based on a "Balanced Scorecard" approach, which weights the three-year ROI on the bank's campaigns as well as current profitability at the customer-segment level.

"DAY IN THE LIFE" OF A CUSTOMER PORTFOLIO MANAGER

It's not too difficult to visualize a customer manager's job in a larger, B2B company – one that might even have a key account management structure already in place for certain clients. Even retail banking is not hard to conjure, because at least every retail-banking customer is in regular, direct contact with the bank itself. But what would a customer portfolio manager's job look like in a more consumer-oriented firm?

Hypothetically, let's suppose you were one of five or six customer portfolio managers in, say, a branded electronics firm selling through retailers as well as online. Your firm doesn't have direct contact with every single customer it sells to, because about 20% of your customers have bought one or more of your products at a retail store, but never contacted you in any way – no product registrations, no calls to the help line, no complaints or service requests. But you do have identities and reasonably accurate (although not perfect) contact details for the other 80% of your customers.

Your particular customer portfolio, Portfolio 3, is one of the more valuable groups your company sells to, made up of younger (under 40), techno-savvy single males with incomes over $40,000. Testing has shown that the type of channel your customers prefer says a lot about how they respond to offers. For this reason, you're considering whether to divide your portfolio into three sub-portfolios, one for retail-only shoppers, one for customers who shop principally via catalogue and on line, and one for multichannel customers.

Last week your staff instructed the web team to begin intercepting every tenth Portfolio 3 online customer with a single five-point scale "satisfaction" question at the end of each successful shopping visit. The goal is to correlate answers to this question with these customers' future purchases, in order to develop a better database of leading indicators of lifetime value change. You already track "abandoned shopping carts" (online shoppers who picked out merchandise, but terminated their shopping transactions before carrying through with their purchases) and this data has proven somewhat useful in predicting future behavior. What you're trying to do now is refine your understanding of the successful shopping visits, on the theory that perhaps not all sales are equally "successful" in terms of intent to repurchase. However, you also want to track any positive or negative changes that arise from the interception itself, which is why this test only goes to 10% of shoppers. This week you're having yet another meeting with the sales department, trying to figure out if there isn't some way to gather a similar data point for retail customers (with an eye toward identifying a greater proportion of them earlier, as well).

The main project on your agenda today, however, is the quarterly marketing staff review meeting. You can't prove it yet, but you're pretty sure that the current advertising campaign, featuring a prominent professional quarterback, is doing nothing for Portfolio 3 customers. It may even be having a negative effect on your heavy multichannel users, many of whom don't consider themselves sports people at all. You talked yesterday with both Tom and Natalia, who manage Portfolios 4 and 1, respectively, and they have similar concerns. In today's meeting the three of you plan to object to the size of this year's ad budget and to put votes in early for a change in direction next year. It's ironic that you'd have to make this case, because the whole campaign was put in place to appeal primarily to your particular type of customer. You want a chance to take just a slice of the $20 million advertising budget and spend it on increasing the lifetime values of Portfolio 3 customers with more relevant offers and higher level service.

Then there is the brainstorming meeting with the Chief Privacy Officer and two subordinates this coming Friday. The new privacy policy is great, as far as it goes, but while most of your online and multichannel customers aren't overly concerned about your firm's privacy protection practices, you know for a fact that a significant proportion of the retail-only shoppers in Portfolio 3 are worried about the issue generally – not just with respect to your company, but with respect to all online vendors. So Friday's meeting is to see if there isn't some way to put the details of the new privacy policy in front of them, even though they don't visit your website.

Finally, within a month you hope to have a realistically vetted financial plan for how much current income and lifetime value could be created from your own customers if you could offer music and videos as a regular part of their electronic equipment purchases. Buy a new DVD player and get X number of DVDs delivered over the next Y months. Buy a new laptop with personal listening device and get Z free downloads. These offers won't appeal to very many customers outside Portfolio 3, so it's not really something that "corporate" is interested in, but if you can build a case for how this kind of service would increase your customers' intent to purchase, or their purchase of warranty services, then you might have a shot at it.

The ROC "hurdle rate" is 8%. Projects that don't return at least an 8% ROC don't get approved anywhere in the corporation. The "stretch goal" for Portfolio 3 is 20%. If you can achieve a 20% ROC for the year for Portfolio 3, the bonus plan for you and your staff will pay out at 150% of allocation. Last year, your first year in the job, you achieved 16%. This year, you plan to do better.

Transitioning to customer management

It should go without saying that few companies can simply paste a customer-management structure onto their existing organizations. This change, in terms of success metrics, management roles and responsibilities, and the required capabilities of the enterprise, is profound. In truth, the "transition" never actually ends, because there will always be additional steps you can take to improve your relationships with customers. Nevertheless, if you start as a well-oiled product-marketing organization, it requires a good deal of planning to take the first steps toward customer management.

In making this transition, you should always remember the first rule of wing walking: Never let go of what you're holding on to until you're holding on to something else. In other words, your transition must be conducted without giving up the "old way" of competing too hastily, because you will have a continuing need to generate earnings. You can't simply put your business on hold while you try to start up something completely new.

The organizational and cultural transition to customer management represents a genuine revolution for your company, but it is more likely to be successful when it can be treated as an evolution. There are at least two ways to speed this evolution process: the "picket fence" strategy, and segment management.

The Picket-Fence Strategy. What if you were to place just a few of your customers into portfolios, then add a few more, and a few more? You would be operating under two different modes, likely with two different compensation models, and with different rules applied to the customers you've placed into portfolios. In essence, you need to fence off the portfolio customers and treat them differently from the remainder of your customer base. As the transition progresses, the number of customers behind this "picket fence" will increase.

If you've ranked your customers by value, you can prioritize your transition so as to place the most valuable customers behind the picket fence first. This transition strategy is especially compelling for companies that already identify their customers individually, during the natural course of their business. Companies such as banks and financial services firms, telecommunications companies, personal services businesses, some retailers, and many B2B companies with internal sales organizations are probably already singling out their high-value customers for individual attention. If a retailer, for instance, has identified any customers at all who merit special treatment, it is likely they are the store's very high-volume, repeat spenders, and the "special treatment" might easily include assigning personal shoppers or relationship managers to watch over the individual interests of such customers. Your goal, with a picket-fence transition strategy, should be to extend the idea and automate it, codifying the business rules that are being applied.

Remember that your customer portfolio manager will own the business rules for determining all of the communications that customers receive. This means that direct mail pieces should not go to a customer behind the picket fence without the initiation or approval of the portfolio manager responsible for that customer. Over time, as technology makes it better and more cost efficient to process customer information, and as your company gains more knowledge and confidence in the process, you can expand the picket fence and put more customers behind it.

Segment management. Another way to transition your organization to customer management is by deploying segment managers. The picket-fence transition is a customer-specific process that places an increasing number of customers under management – adding individually identified customers to the "customer management" process gradually. By contrast, segment management involves identifying groups of customers (rather than individuals, per se), and giving segment managers an increasing number of roles and responsibilities with respect to their segments. For example, a consumer goods company might have different segment managers in charge of different types of customers, based on demographics. One segment manager might be in charge of retirees, while another might be in charge of young, childless couples or young adult singles. Each would set objectives for their own segment, and help develop specific offers or marketing communications targeted to the segment. But many, if not most, of the customers within the segment being "managed" in this way will not be identified, individually.

Therefore, the most critical missing ingredient in segment management (relative to customer management) is direct, interactive contact with individually identified customers. Nevertheless, segment management is an appropriate transition plan if you have a business in which it is difficult to identify and track customers individually. The picket-fence transition works better for companies like banks, telcos, and retailers, while segment management works better for consumer packaged goods, for instance. (Such firms might have highly developed customer management organizations for dealing with retailer customers, but they are unlikely to have the identities of more than a microscopic fraction of their consumer customers.)

A segment manager can't control your company's interactions with the individual customers in his segment, but can advocate in favor of product and service configurations more likely to appeal to them, or for advertising and promotional messages more likely to persuade them. A segment manager can make these arguments across the variety of different products and brands your company might offer.

Company J's transition to portfolio management

Here's an actual example of one company's transition. Significant revenue losses in 2001 cast a pall on Company J's future marketing plans. This global transportation and shipping company found itself in serious danger of losing money for the second straight year. Accelerating internal and external pressures were driving costs up, holding revenues back, and threatening the company's franchise with both consumers and businesses. Despite a number of new products and services on offer, the firm's resources were still not strategically aligned to drive genuine value creation, and although the company's publicly stated strategy was to be "customer-focused," many of its actual operating practices did not reflect this focus at all.

To break through this miasma of unprofitable processes and self-defeating product strategies, Company J implemented a comprehensive system for managing its millions of customers separately, breaking them up into portfolios. The firm had 3 million actively measured and managed business accounts in America, along with some 16 million passively measured accounts. It also had occasional, routine interactions with tens of millions of retail consumers.

For its business customers the firm created a financial model for calculating a three-year NPV, or net present value, of customer contribution.[2] It then identified some of the leading indicators of value creation, and made some "best guess" estimates as to each customer's potential value, as well. The company mapped out all the interactions it had with these various customers, throughout its overall organization, identifying the key value drivers in each type of interaction wherever possible. Its goal was to trace specific value creation opportunities for particular customer types, and track these opportunities back through the actual touchpoints that would affect those customers.

One of the problems Company J soon faced, however, was a surfeit of data. The Chief Marketing Officer and the marketing executives received volumes of data weekly, but no real analysis. Forced to compile, analyze, and synthesize the raw data before marketing decisions could be made, the firm's marketing staff found that it was always behind schedule and trying to catch up. As a result, a great deal of expensive management time was wasted on low-value activities. Chronic delays in processing and analyzing the immense volumes of raw data led to missed opportunities and often inappropriate or inadequate actions, based on obsolete insight.

By grouping its tens of thousands of business customers into distinct portfolios, Company J's marketing department was able to apply different analytics-based strategies to different types of customers, and hold specific managers accountable for the results, in terms of ROC value creation.

In order to prioritize its efforts and assess its progress, it was important to assign potential values to these customers. Many did not have individual account managers assigned to them, however, and it didn't seem practical to do individual questionnaires to the field sales force on each customer. So the company decided to assign potential values based on a proxy formula. The firm first categorized each of its business customers by the four-digit SIC code (Standard Industrial Classification) most appropriate to it. Then it looked at the average volume of business done in its category by all the companies in that SIC code, on a per-revenue-dollar basis. Any company below that average was assigned an amount of growth potential equal to the difference between the average and their current level. This was a conservative, but still very useful, formula for estimating growth potential.

---

[2] See Appendix 1 for a definition of "net present value."

Company J also set up a central customer analytics function – a professional staff concerned primarily with processing the raw data into useful insights, on which action could be taken. But the analytics staff served the function of customer management, so rather than simply sifting through the numbers to find interesting opportunities, they always started with the business-building objectives for different customer portfolios, and worked back into the data to find possible solutions. This group's goal is to apply the most advanced analytical and modeling capabilities to the data, in order to first understand current customer performance, and second predict the likely future behavior of these customers. From this feedback, the company was hopeful that its portfolio managers could figure out the best ways to foster customer retention and growth, and to ensure that new-customer acquisition efforts were more efficient and productive.

To understand the power of this approach, it might be useful to trace one particular group of business customers, in terms of how the firm's actions were designed to improve this particular group's Return on Customer. The company had categorized nearly 20,000 medium-sized businesses as "Most Growable Customers" based on their likely potential values. Again, based on a three-year net present value, these businesses were found to have an actual value of $140 million, but a potential value of some $465 million. Needs-based analysis of these business customers identified three distinct profiles, which the company labeled "urgent shippers," "basic shippers," and "emerging marketing companies." The company set out specific, and different, strategies for each of these three portfolios.

Over 4,000 of these customers were categorized as urgent shippers, with a total potential value of more than $200 million. The agreed treatment strategy for urgent shippers was education. If the company could provide education on its shipping processes and other options to these customers, then it could realize more of this group's potential value, driving up the portfolio's Return on Customer. The interactive and communications channels available to the firm to carry out this mission included an inside sales team (telephone based), direct mail, and a website. These medium-sized business customers were not large enough, by themselves, to warrant a dedicated field sales staff, which focused on large enterprise customers.

For this group of some 4,000 customers, the leading indicators of value creation were identified as revenue, revenue per company, close

rate, and sales per day. In general, these drivers each had a positive correlation with a customer's NPV, and so small increases in each of these
leading indicators could be linked to implied increases in overall value for
the portfolio. An all-in marketing investment of approximately $100,000
in the first year generated a $1.2 million increase in profit and estimated
customer lifetime value, equating to a Return on Customer of some
1,200%.

Company J's experience provides a nice picture of the role that portfolio managers play in creating value for a firm. The company's
marketing staff, relying on analytics performed centrally, is carrying out
the portfolio management function at present. But as the program
develops strength, individual groups of customers will be directly
assigned to portfolio managers for oversight. By assigning responsibility
for individual customers to individual portfolio managers, we immediately solve the customer-governance problem, freeing up the manager to
pursue the proper course of action with each customer. Ultimately, the
portfolio manager's overall performance will be measured and evaluated
based on the Return on Customer they can achieve with their portfolio.

In other words, it's clearly possible to manage your firm's customer-
specific activities, but you have to have a customer-specific management structure to do it, and a customer-specific metric of success. You
also have to have support at the very highest level in your company.
We're not just talking about the CEO's support. We're also talking about
the CEO's bosses – the shareholders and owners of the firm. That's what
we'll cover in the next chapter.

14. Who Moved My ROI? Shareholder Value, Investing, and Customer Trust

One should always play fairly when one has the winning cards.

Oscar Wilde

Return on Customer is a metric that tracks the genuine value created by your customers. What is remarkable is that it can not only give you a winning hand, economically, but it will also turn your company into a better place to work – a fairer, more ethical organization. Adopt ROC as your metric of success and you will become a *better company*. But this will only happen if you actually embrace the idea wholeheartedly.

We can't really say it emphatically enough – once you buy into Return on Customer, you're going to be turning your business on its head. Rather than just worrying about how many new customers you acquire, you'll have to worry about what *kinds* of new customers you acquire. Rather than just counting how many products you sold this quarter, you're going to tabulate how much shareholder value your customers created for you this quarter.

This is a different dimension of competition we're talking about here. It's not the kind of competition they taught you in business school.

The principles of ROC

We can summarize the argument for Return on Customer in seven basic statements:

1 *Customers are a company's scarcest resource.* Capital is global and mobile. Products and services abound, and have even become commodity-like. Globalization has kept costs down, while stirring up intense political debate about the role of free trade. Today, nothing is as scarce as customers.

2 *When companies don't treat customers as a scarce resource, they focus excessively on the short term.* Shareholders want long-term value, but current-period numbers tend to drive the financial community. Companies willingly sacrifice long-term value for short-term results, creating a culture of bad management, and a crisis of inadequate – maybe even unethical – corporate governance.

3 *Return on Customer is a balanced metric, focused on the scarce resource.* By measuring the total value created by customers, ROC helps a firm optimize the tradeoff between higher current-period cash flow and increases in lifetime value. The ROC metric is equal to Total Shareholder Return, and can be allocated to subsets of a firm's customer base.

4 *Taking the customer's perspective is the first step to drive ROC up.* This means earning the trust of customers, treating the customer the way you'd like to be treated, and protecting privacy. It requires creating an employee culture of trust, empowering employees to solve customer problems. It is a major transformation that, in the end, creates not just a better-run firm, but a better, more ethical firm as well.

5 *Maximizing ROC requires treating different customers differently.* You must understand customer differences, analyze and track the leading indicators of LTV change, make tactical decisions based on ROC, and manage customer relationships in nonoverlapping portfolios.

6 *ROC creates better leverage for your competitive strategy.* You can use ROC to enhance your structural advantages, and guide the direction of your business growth and expansion.

7 *Success requires not only your CEO's active support and advocacy, but it requires your shareholders to buy in as well.* The improvements in your

company's productivity and culture will pay off right away, but if you don't teach investors to hold you accountable for ROC, they'll continue to hold you accountable only for current-period results. Investors should be interested in ROC because it's a short cut to Total Shareholder Return. But you'll face a challenge in helping all of them understand this.

Educating investors

Yes, with this seventh principle we have circled right back to where we started – with investors and financial analysts. In the final analysis, no matter how persuasive the arguments for *Return on Customer* have been, your efforts to maximize ROC will be stymied if the financial community doesn't allow you to optimize long-term value creation as well as current-period earnings. So you're going to have to teach the analysts to watch the metrics that are important to you, and to watch them consistently.

Let's say that, having now read our book, you buy into "Return on Customer." Let's say you now understand how vitally important it is to create a culture of customer trust, in order to earn the maximum possible return from customers – not just in terms of current-period profits, but over the long haul as well. You plan to begin setting up the metrics and analytics functions necessary to track leading indicators of lifetime value changes, and you plan to start asking ROC questions before evaluating your firm's business plans and making important business decisions.

You might find yourself wondering why you should tell any of this to investors, or to the financial analysts who follow your firm's progress, given that your competitors would quickly learn of your plans. Why not simply keep your ROC initiative secret, in order to preserve whatever competitive advantage it might provide?

There is an easy answer to this question: If you don't get the financial community on your side, sooner or later your effort to measure success and manage your business in terms of Return on Customer will falter. It is inevitable – repeat, *inevitable* – that if your own metrics do not align with those being used by your shareholders to evaluate your firm's performance, eventually your shareholders will win the argument. Their metrics will trump yours, because it's their company, not yours. You're just part of the hired help.

In early 2004, Costco, the American-based chain of warehouse stores, saw its stock hammered by Wall Street analysts who maintained, essentially, that the company was simply not focused enough on short-term profits. According to *Business Week*, Costco:

> "...handily beat Wall Street expectations on Mar. 3, posting a 25% profit gain in its most recent quarter on top of a 14% sales hike. The warehouse club even nudged up its profit forecast for the rest of 2004. So how did the market respond? By driving the Issaquah (Wash.) company's stock down by 4%. One problem for Wall Street is that Costco pays its workers much better than archrival Wal-Mart Stores Inc. does and analysts worry that Costco's operating expenses could get out of hand. 'At Costco, it's better to be an employee or a customer than a shareholder,' said Deutsche Bank analyst Bill Dreher."

To Deutsche Bank and other firms following this company's stock, the Costco model leaves too much money on the table. Rather than hiring more staff to shorten checkout lines, the analysts say, the firm should save that expenditure in order to generate more earnings. These analysts are comparing Costco's model with Wal-Mart's, and they find it lacking.

But what if Costco's practices have the effect of increasing customer loyalty and preference, boosting lifetime values and creating additional value in the form of customer equity? What if Costco's business policies are actually improving the company's shareholder return? The problem is that because Costco has not tried to measure changes in lifetime value, they have nothing to show their investors.

We could go on with this story, but the point is that at least in Costco's case Wall Street obviously doesn't "get it" when it comes to talking about maximizing not just the profit taken from the customer but the actual *value* of the customer, as a productive asset. Even for companies in subscription businesses – like cable television firms and telecom companies – financial analysts often just *count* the customers owned as a way of valuing these firms, and pay little if any attention to the lifetime values of those customers.

Customer counts, as a short-term measure of corporate value, can also be "gamed" by aggressive managers, just like current-period profits or revenues. This is, in fact, what seems to have happened at least among some firms. In July 2004 the Securities and Exchange Commission (SEC) initiated a probe into how a number of telecom and cable firms report their customer counts to Wall Street, sending letters requesting information to about 20 companies. When it doesn't matter to Wall Street what *value* a customer has, then any customer will do, and these numbers have now been distorted enough that the SEC feels it necessary to step in.

Clearly, it's critical to educate investors and analysts if you want to succeed with a Return-on-Customer perspective for your business. But don't despair; it might not be as hard as it looks. For one thing, it's definitely in your shareholders' interest to measure success in terms of Return on Customer. After all, they already measure success in terms of Total Shareholder Return. What you need to do is educate them with respect to how TSR can now be broken down into smaller, tactically useful units of customer-specific ROC.

But second, many firms have successfully convinced their investors that future value (as opposed to current earnings) should be factored into their current stock price. Financial analysts certainly understand the concept of a company having to invest operating funds today, as a current-period cost of generating long-term benefits. Pharmaceutical companies, for instance, spend heavily on research and development. But Eli Lilly spends 19% of its annual sales on R&D. That's about four percentage points more than other pharma companies. Although such heavy R&D spending has depressed the company's profits in the short term, the P/E of the stock is higher than its peers. Why? Because of the depth of the company's pipeline of new drugs pending release, analysts expect earnings gains of 15% annually over the next several years.

In other words, at least when they're dealing with the "comfort zone" of product development, the financial community clearly does understand the benefit of deferring some profitability in order to boost a company's future earnings. Translating this thinking into the realm of the customer is all you'll really be asking of them. Stated differently, financial analysts cannot simply dismiss your argument on the basis of logic. Your job is to educate them on the wisdom (and financial reliability) of customer-oriented investment.

In any case, you probably do have some time to work with – perhaps several years. You can begin building a business case for the ROC metric gradually, without eliminating any other financial metrics. Adopting ROC as a metric of success *now* will begin to make your company a better place for employees to work and a more attractive company for customers to buy from, as well as a more valuable investment for shareholders (even though they may not realize it as fast as you do). You'll have to continue to meet your analysts' current objectives, but you're certainly no worse off for starting on the ROC journey now, and educating investors along the way.

There is strong circumstantial evidence that Costco is actually creating more overall value than Wall Street is giving it credit for, but it's only circumstantial. Although Costco pays its employees more per hour, its work force is a great deal more productive than Wal-Mart's, with lower turnover and less training expense, not to mention a happier, more satisfied and cheerful set of employees coming face-to-face each day with customers. *BusinessWeek* compared Costco with Sam's Club, the Wal-Mart operation with which it competes most closely, and found that "the 102,000 Sam's employees in America generated some $35 billion in sales last year, while Costco did $34 billion with one-third fewer employees." Moreover, in the last five years, "Costco's operating income grew at an average of 10.1% annually, slightly besting Sam's 9.8%."

So, while Wall Street laments the earnings Costco forgoes by paying employees more than its competitors pay theirs, the truth is that a number of other financial measurements seem to stack up in the company's favor. The problem may simply be that Costco has no unifying, all-encompassing metric to reassure its investors with respect to the appropriateness of its expenditures designed to ensure competent, happy employees and satisfied, loyal customers. Fine and good to have loyal employees and customers, an analyst might say, but *how much* is that benefit really worth?

The lesson should be clear: If you don't want your own stock downgraded because you've invested wisely in raising your customers' LTVs, then you're going to have to do some prework. You're going to have to educate the moneyed interests.

This is important, because one of the linchpins of any effort to maximize ROC – building customer trust – could easily be mistaken by analysts as taking too soft a line on customers, leaving money on the table, not collecting all the profit you could. If you cultivate an employee culture based on treating customers the way they themselves would like to be treated as customers, this could easily sound soft and fuzzy to a cold-blooded numbers person in the financial community. Your defense has to be ready. You don't want to have this kind of culture misunderstood as a one-sided act of charity on your part. You want to convince the investors in your firm that creating this culture is actually in *their* interest, as investors. You have to be able to demonstrate the link to shareholder return.

So get your program going, make a start at changing your company's culture, think through the role of technology and metrics at your firm, and then work this whole idea into your regular conversations with "the analysts." These folks are nobody's fools. They have to be pretty smart or they wouldn't earn mega bucks. But if you don't educate them on what it means to measure a leading indicator of LTV change, then who will? If you don't show them how it's *in their interest* to monetize the customers you serve not just during this current period, but over each customer's lifetime, who will?

Remember: The only value your company will ever create is the value created by your customers – the customers you have now, and those you will have in the future. Your task is to ensure that you get the most possible value out of each and every one of your customers, both now and in the future.

Take the customer's perspective to maximize your Return on Customer. By maximizing ROC, you'll be maximizing shareholder return as well.

Appendix 1
Discounting Made Simple

If you had a choice between receiving money today and receiving the same amount of money next year at this time, which would you choose? Right: Getting the money today is always better. But how much better is it, exactly? When we talk about discount rates, all we are really doing is trying to quantify the amount of preference a business has for receiving immediate cash, when compared to receiving cash at some point in the future. We are quantifying the time value of money.

Businesses must use discount rates to evaluate the costs and benefits of their various actions, because the cash expenses and benefits of these actions will be realized not just now, but at varying times in the future. Does it make sense to invest £1 million today in order to generate a profit of £1.5 million three years from now? The answer depends on how much it's worth to you to have money today, versus having money sometime in the future. When predicting future events, there is always some risk that positive cash flows won't be as positive as anticipated, or that negative cash flows will be even more negative than expected. How a business evaluates that risk is what discounting is all about.

A discount rate is expressed as an annual percentage, like an interest rate, or a rate of return. Let's say you apply a discount rate of 20% when you are evaluating the financial consequences of your own company's actions. This means the future cash required to equal what you have on hand today will be greater by 20% per year. Your firm would therefore consider £1.2 million one year from now to be worth the same as £1million today. At a 20% discount rate, £1 million is the "present value" of £1.2 million, received in one year.

However, there is no single, correct discount rate to use when trying to analyze a business problem. The discount rate you use will depend on your company's assessment of the desirability of future cash versus current cash, and this is a subjective judgment. It will vary with your business situation, the risk you see in your business, the inflation rate, and so forth.

You can evaluate your own personal discount rate with a simple experiment. Suppose a bank were to offer to pay you either £11,000 one year from now, or £10,000 today. Which would you choose? If you choose the £10,000, then what you're saying is that your discount rate must be greater than 10%, because having £11,000 one year from now is actually worth less to you than having just £10,000 today. But what if the offer were either £10,000 today or £13,000 next year? If you now choose the £13,000, then we know that while your discount rate is greater than 10%, it is less than 30%, because for you £13,000 in one year is more valuable than £10,000 today.

But now let's introduce some additional complications. First, suppose it's not a bank offering you £13,000 next year, but an individual person – a person you don't really trust very much. If this were the situation, would you take the £10,000 today, or wait for him to come across with the £13,000 next year? The more risk you foresee, the more discounting you should apply.

Or suppose you've been made redundant and you're already three months behind on the mortgage. Even if it were a bank making the offer, would you wait a year for £13,000, or would you take the cash today, instead? You'd probably take the cash, if you thought you could hang on to your house and keep your life together until you got another job, right?

Obviously, when evaluating a business situation, a manager must factor in the company's cost of capital, general economic trends, the expected rate of inflation and other factors. But in addition, managers must take into account the subjective situation. If a company has a high current need for cash, it will probably apply a higher discount rate when evaluating the value of future cash flows (meaning that cash in hand now is worth relatively more, compared to cash later).

And of course, if a manager understands a customer better, and manages a portfolio of customers better, he should be able to reduce the risk of future cash flows, which in turn reduces the company's cost of capital, thereby increasing customer equity.

Appendix 2
Lifetime Value Accounting Issues

The actual value of a customer to a business can be defined and calculated in different ways. Is LTV the net present value of the future stream of *fully allocated profit* from a customer? Or would it be more appropriate to talk about the *marginal financial contribution* of the customer? Or should we instead stick to *free cash flow*? Each of these economic values has its advantages and disadvantages.

Fully allocated profit

One big disadvantage of using fully allocated profit when defining LTV is that many of the costs incurred by a business cannot be reasonably attributed to individual customers; instead, they must be allocated according to some criterion or formula. Under what criterion, for instance, should the cost of an ad campaign be allocated to the customers who are the targets of the campaign? Should each customer be allocated an equal portion of this cost? How do we account for the cost of reaching people who are exposed to our messages but aren't even in the target market? Should the cost be allocated in proportion to product sales, so that customers who buy the most products bear a greater proportion of advertising costs? The same questions could be asked with regard to allocating the depreciation costs resulting from building a new manufacturing facility, or the operating costs of running the facility, or the funding of new product research and development.

On the other hand, while cost allocations can be arbitrary, ensuring that *all* costs are in fact allocated to specific customers does have some management advantages. Eventually, the firm will have to assign individual managers the responsibility for maximizing the ROC of particular groups of customers (see Chapter 13 on Managing Portfolios of Customers). Allocating all costs to individual customers under some criterion or another will ensure that these managers have an incentive to influence how the firm commits its resources, even at headquarters level.

Marginal financial contribution by customer

Another way to assess the value of a particular customer is to calculate the cost to the company if the customer simply disappears from the customer base, while everything else remains constant. The most accurate way to address this is to think about the customer's marginal financial contribution, rather than fully allocated profit – but the exact figure would depend on the particular customer or group of customers being analyzed. The contribution-based customer equity of a group of customers must be calculated not by adding the individual LTVs arithmetically, but by "rolling them up," while factoring in previously unallocated costs as the roll-up accumulates bigger and bigger groups of customers. A cost that cannot be fairly ascribed to a single customer (and so does not figure in the customer's own contribution-based LTV) might be easy to attribute to a group. When considering the customer equity of a customer group, previously "unallocated" costs should be bundled into the calculation according to a simple rule: Unallocated expenses are those that would still be incurred even if that customer or group of customers were dropped from the customer base, while everything else remained constant.

For instance, suppose a business services firm selling to retailers, wholesalers, and other distribution companies were to target independent grocery retailers for a trade magazine advertising campaign, along with a direct mail program with follow-up phone calls. In such a case, the expenses associated with the direct mail and phone effort would be allocated to each individual customer, and would be figured into the customer's contribution, as would any other "addressable" expenses, including email, sales calls, and the like.

The cost of the trade magazine campaign, however, would not be allocated to any particular customer's contribution LTV, because even if the customer were to disappear from the customer base the advertising expense would still have to be borne by the company. On the other hand, the cost of the trade campaign *should* be included when the individual customer LTVs are rolled up to calculate the customer equity of the target market – that is, independent grocery retailers as a group – because if that entire group of customers were removed from the customer base, there would be no trade campaign expense.

Thus, as contribution LTVs are rolled up to calculate the customer equity of larger groups of customers, a greater proportion of costs will be figured into the total. At the top level, when calculating customer equity for the whole firm, all enterprise costs would be incorporated. In this way, the management decisions that have to do with both individual customers and groups of customers will be more directly related to the actual customer-equity consequences of those particular decisions.

However, a contribution model might hamper management's effort to minimize costs and allocate resources efficiently. We know of one American-based global business services firm, for instance, that has assigned its customers to individual portfolio managers and evaluates those managers according to a contribution-based LTV model. This firm has an expensive brand advertising campaign involving famous sports personalities, and very few of the portfolio managers feel that the campaign is doing much good with their own customers. If it were up to them, they'd cancel the advertising altogether as a waste of money. But because the campaign's cost is not allocated to them in calculating customer equity for their own particular customers, none of the managers has any real incentive to object to it, nor even to complain to HQ about its ineffectiveness.

Cash flow

Perhaps the most direct and economically "pure" LTV calculation is based on free cash flow, rather than profit. Free cash flow is the ingredient that goes into the most widely used and accepted economic valuations of a company or a business operation. In calculating LTVs, using a cash-flow model helps to eliminate some of the complex issues that would otherwise be introduced by a firm's capital investments, and its depreciation and amortization of those investments.

For instance, consider just the capital costs that can be directly attributed to a firm's effort to strengthen its customer relationships. It will cost money to launch any overt program designed to improve customer relationships, strengthen loyalty, increase cross selling, or streamline the way customers are served, and in addition to the ongoing expenses of operating the program, some capital investment and "set up" costs are also likely to be involved. All these costs should be directly reflected in the LTV calculations in more or less the same way as other costs are. In the fully allocated profit model, the capital expenses required for, say, building a call center to improve customer service, or installing new customer database software, will generate depreciation to be allocated to individual LTVs in the same way all other depreciation is allocated. One might ask, however, whether this paints a fair picture of the actual ROC on such a program. Instead, if we use the fully allocated profit model of LTV, we might want to back out customer-specific capital expenses and treat them differently – perhaps as cash-flow entries, rather than as depreciable capital expenses. The contribution model of LTV has a similar problem.

Such a calculation can be based on either fully allocated cash flows or marginal cash flows, and as with the contribution model, LTVs based on marginal cash flow cannot simply be summed to derive customer equity, but must be rolled up as more and more cash flow costs can be allocated to larger and larger customer groups. The most important advantage of the cash-flow model, however, whether marginal or fully allocated, is that it is no longer necessary to reconcile capital and depreciation accounts, either for the enterprise itself or for any group of customers within it. Among other things, this means that the direct effects of any investments made to strengthen customer relationships will be more accurately captured in a cash-flow model of LTV.

Appendix 3
Lifetime Value Equations and Examples

It would be useful at least to understand the process by which you could construct a workable set of LTV equations for your own company. Our recommendation is that you proceed in two steps. First, set up an "as if" LTV equation – that is, an equation that could calculate a customer's LTV reasonably accurately, written out just "as if" you could actually obtain the data required in the equation. For instance, LTV might be the expected number of purchase transactions from a customer each year, times the number of years the customer is expected to remain loyal, times the discounted net present value of the margins on those purchases each year. Industries vary immensely in structure, however, including their distribution channels, their technologies, and the frequency and nature of customer purchases, and each of these factors will affect the actual form of the LTV equation. There is no shortage of mathematical models, financial tools, and computer software for plotting customer LTVs in a variety of industries.

Your "as if" LTV equation will never be completely accurate, because there will always be additional factors that could be included. A customer indicates they are willing to refer your company to their friends, but what's the likelihood or value of that referral? What extra cost is incurred in handling a less informed service inquiry? How likely is a customer to default on an invoice? How influential is the customer among their friends or colleagues? Despite the fact that no equation can capture all the factors going into a customer's future behavior, your goal should be to compile a reasonably good set of the first-order variables likely to determine most customers' lifetime values, and these are the variables you put into your "as if" LTV equation.

After you write the "as if" LTV equation, your second step should be to figure out how to estimate the values of the variables you have written into it, using the data you actually have available. A comprehensive customer-transaction database makes a big difference. With such a database you can break your customer base up into smaller groups of like customers, and examine each different group's history of transactions, using your "as if" equation to calculate the value of different types of customers over a several-year period. Then you can correlate these approximate LTVs with other variables in your database in order to determine, so far as possible, the real drivers of customer value – in effect, modeling the behavior of your customers in the past in order to predict their behavior in the future. What you're looking for, ideally, are variables that were not in your original model, but have an influence on the model – and variables that you can influence with your company's actions.

The "as if" LTV equation for your own company should reflect both the structure of your industry and the practicality of acquiring or inferring the data you require. With respect to the car industry, for example, the ideal car-buyer LTV equation developed for use by a manufacturer might include such factors as the most likely frequency of purchase, the likelihood that a customer will remain brand loyal for the next purchase, the margin on such purchase, the likelihood additional services will be purchased and the margin on those services, and so forth:

LTV = (Expected purchase frequency) × (loyalty probability)

×

[(expected model of repurchase) × (margin on expected model) +
(expected options purchased) × (margin on options) + (probability of
using manufacturer financing) × (likely face value of a financing contract)
× (finance contract profit margin) + (after-sales probability) × (expected
after-sales revenue) × (after-sales profit margin)]

×

(adjustment for net-present-value discounting).

In the car business, remember that the manufacturer is actually capturing only some of the customer's total lifetime spending, while some is captured by the dealer. The truth is, the same car customer will have one LTV to the manufacturer, and a different one to the dealer.

If we were to attempt an LTV model for, say, the pharmaceutical business, the first step would be to decide which particular set of customers we were trying to value. In America, a pharmaceutical manufacturer serves four principal constituencies, each of which creates value for the company: consumers (patients), prescribers (doctors), payers (insurance firms, and others who pay for the products), and dispensers (that is, the pharmacies who fill the prescriptions). Each of these customer types has a role to play in the complex task of creating enterprise value for a pharmaceutical company. The LTV equation for prescribers, who are probably the most influential customer type served by a pharmaceutical company, might go like this:

LTV = (total number of scripts for client's products written by prescriber)
×
[(average price per script) – (total number of scripts for client's products written by prescriber) × (COGS/total number of scripts)] – (costs of prescriber detail calls) – (direct marketing costs) – (samples costs) – (costs of call center interactions)
×
(adjustment for net-present-value discounting)

Of course, it won't be easy to get this data, and in many cases much of it will be virtually impossible to get. If you have, say, five years' worth of spending and profit margin data for your customers, for instance, then you'll want to calculate the lifetime values of these customers based on this history, mirroring as closely as possible the actual "as if" equation you wrote. This will give you the retrospectively calculated LTV's of different customers with different spending patterns.

Your second step is to use whatever data you have available currently to find any correlations with the outcomes of your "as if" LTV formula, calculated retrospectively. So, for instance, suppose your database includes a notation for whether a customer has initiated a customer service inquiry in the past year, and whether that inquiry resulted in a satisfactory outcome or not. Statistical analysis then shows that satisfactory service inquiries are correlated with 5% higher spending, on average, in subsequent years.

Other data that can often be correlated with future spending levels include a customer's most recent overall spending level, and spending levels in other departments or divisions, the customer's source (that is, did they come in based on the referral of another customer, or based on customer acquisition campaign A or campaign B, and so forth), the customer's age and gender, and perhaps even the customer's income level and socio-economic status. The data you have on specific customers can come from a variety of sources, including not just your own customer database, but third-party databases, syndicated customer surveys, and the like.

The result will be a lifetime value algorithm very much like the department store example shown in Chapter 4, in the section "ROC and tactical decision-making."

Getting to the root cause

When using an algorithm based on correlations with past data, you must be prepared to address the issue of "causality." In the department store example, it's great that multidepartment spending is *correlated* with higher customer lifetime values, but does that necessarily mean that such spending actually *causes* a customer's lifetime value to increase?

This is not a trivial issue, because within the piles and piles of data available in a customer database, there will likely be a number of correlations that are not actually related by cause at all. Some factors that look like they make a difference will actually be caused by other factors. For example, there is an obvious correlation between the amount of children's breakfast cereal a consumer buys and the number of children in the family. But it's important to get the causal relationship right. Discounting the price of cereal might increase the purchase rate, but it's unlikely to increase the number of children. On the other hand, if you can increase the number of children, you might then sell more cereal, as well. In the department store example, suppose what actually happens is that customers who buy sets of complimentary products in multiple departments are actually the ones who are more valuable in LTV terms. That is, it's possible that the effect driving higher lifetime values for multiple-department shoppers has to do with women who buy jewelry to go with the blouse they purchased, or men who buy CDs with the electronics they purchase. It's possible that this type of shopper is naturally of more value than other types of shoppers, and there may be enough of them to show a strong correlation between multiple-department shopping and higher LTV.

Obviously, if this is what's going on, then simply offering a coupon or sweepstakes entry to a single-department shopper won't have the effect on LTV that you think it will. It will probably increase the rate of multiple-department shopping, but for completely different reasons, and among customers who have different motivations than the ones that are actually accounting for most of the higher lifetime values you've tracked. It won't matter much that a shopper who came in for a book ended up also buying a CD to get the coupon, because that is unlikely to drive a significantly higher LTV.

Statistical methods that deal with the problem of causality go beyond mere regression and correlation analysis, which are essentially descriptive in nature, and often not very explanatory. One modeling technique, known as Structural Equation Modeling (this method underlies the RSx tool mentioned in Chapter 6), involves linking variables that can be observed (indicators) to variables that can't be observed, in a formal, statistically valid procedure. Another technique is based on Bayesian analysis (named after an 18th-century Presbyterian minister who moonlighted as a mathematician). Bayesian methods are based on "a mathematical rule explaining how you should change your existing beliefs in the light of new evidence." Essentially, Bayesian analysis maintains that the more times you see the sun rise in the morning, the more *confident* you should be that it will actually rise the next morning. This kind of analysis might prove especially useful for evaluating real-time, ongoing events (tracking the click streams at a website, for instance), rather than analyzing batches of data (such as a direct-mail campaign).

Causality can also be inferred more confidently by using control groups to test your actions. If you want to test the benefit of a particular customer treatment, you can compare the behaviors of customers given the treatment to the behaviors of statistically identical customers not given the treatment. These and other sophisticated statistical techniques are yet another benefit of computer technology, without which they would not be practical at all.

For further research

A number of alternative definitions of lifetime value and customer equity abound in the academic and trade literature. As is the case with any subject that has evolved over years through the contributions of many academics and practitioners, the customer valuation literature is rich – and it can be confusing.

Think about customer valuation from a hierarchal (and roughly historical) viewpoint. At its most basic level, the term "LTV," or lifetime value, while not used consistently, in general refers to an estimate of a customer's future economic worth. That worth – especially within the older traditions of direct and database marketing – is in practice often restricted to a prediction of revenue only. The reason is simple: The objective, in such situations, is not to generate a point estimate of the dollars-and-cents value of a customer, but only to rank customers from most valuable to least. The argument for the exclusion of fixed costs in the computation was that those costs don't reflect customer behavior so much as marketing management behavior, and the net impact may basically be subtracting a constant from each estimate. The rationale for the exclusion of variable costs was practicality: These costs have traditionally been, for many organizations, simply too difficult to capture and maintain reliably. To add even more confusion, it should also be noted that despite the name, "lifetime" has in practice typically been computed not for a customer's "lifetime," but usually for the next twelve-month period (direct marketing firms), or perhaps for the next two or three years (consulting firms). The LTV or lifetime value term is also sometimes used to refer to a customer's overall lifetime of spending in a category, even though that spending may be spread among several competing suppliers. This is not what we mean, however. When we use the term, we are referring specifically to the value a customer represents to a specific company. The customer's total value to all companies in that category might be more appropriately talked about in terms of "potential value," a concept we have introduced in Chapter 5.

(For additional background, see Appendix 2 for a discussion of the accounting issues associated with lifetime value or LTV, and for sample equations.)

When an estimate of a customer's duration is incorporated into a LTV prediction (ideally, with fixed and variable costs considered), the term CLV – or customer lifetime value – has sometimes been used. For example, Bolton, Lemon, and Verhoef (2004) define CLV as the "net present value of all earnings (i.e., revenues less costs) from an individual customer," where "all earnings" is inclusive of multiple customer behaviors. These behaviors encompass "length" (retention), "depth" (purchase frequency), and "breadth" (cross-buying).

The term CE – customer equity – often appears in the literature as a super-ordinate concept encompassing CLVs for a portfolio of customers. More precisely, CE is used to denote the sum of CLVs for all present and future customers (Rust, Lemon, and Zeithaml (2004)). As Blattberg, Getz, and Thomas (2001) explain, "a firm's total customer equity equals returns on acquisition plus returns on retention plus returns on add-on selling across a firm's entire customer portfolio over time" (page 24).

ROC – Return on Customer – is defined as the rate at which a business is able to create value from any given amount of customer equity. It is the sum of a firm's current-period cash flow from its customers, plus any changes in customer equity, divided by the total customer equity at the beginning of the period. Instead of thinking about customer equity, ROC looks at the *change* in customer equity. ROC extends the CE concept by introducing it into the mainstream of business management decision-making, on the one hand, and on the other hand by allowing a level a granularity that enables the planning of actionable marketing initiatives for specific groups of customers, on the other hand.

Because the nomenclature "CLV" is not widely used outside of the academic arena, you'll find the more commonplace "LTV" designation employed within this book. However, remember that we use the term LTV with the understanding that the emphasis is on profit.

Although this list is by no means exhaustive, here are a number of articles and books that present various ways to understand the LTV (lifetime value) concept as well as its use and limitations.

- Andrews, Katherine Zoe, "Optimizing Customer Value and Resource Allocation," *Insights from MSI*, pp. 1, 2, Winter 2003–4. Offers a straightforward value analysis with attendant prioritization and treatment strategies.
- Berger, Paul D., Ruth N. Bolton, Douglas Bowman, Elten Briggs, V. Kumar, A. Parasuraman, Creed Terry, "Marketing Actions and

the Value of Customer Assets: A Framework for Customer Asset Management," *Journal of Service Research*, Vol. 5, No. 1, August 2002, pp.39–54. Develops a framework for assessing how marketing actions affect customer LTV. Based on four critical actions: Database creation, market segmentation, forecasting customer purchasing behavior, and resource allocation.

- Berger, Paul D. and Nada I. Nasr, "Customer Lifetime Value: Marketing Models and Applications," *Journal of Interactive Marketing*, Vol. 12, No. 1, Winter 1998, pp.17–30. Presents a series of models for calculating LTV to take it beyond the traditional direct marketing concept.

- Blattberg, Robert, Gary Getz, and Jacquelyn S. Thomas (2001), *Customer Equity: Building and Managing Relationships as Valuable Assets*. Boston, HBS Press. Focuses on measuring so that marketers can allocate resources wisely between acquisition and retention efforts.

- Bolton, Ruth N., P.K. Kannan, and Matthew D. Bramlett, 2000, "Implication of Loyalty Programs and Service Experiences for Customer Retention and Value," *Journal of the Academy of Marketing Science*, 28 (1), 95–108.

- Bolton, Ruth N., Katherine N. Lemon, and Peter C. Verhoef, "The Theoretical Underpinnings of Customer Asset Management: A Framework and Propositions for Future Research," *Journal of the Academy of Marketing Science*, vol. 32, 2004, no. 3, pp.271–292. Proposes CUSAMS – customer asset management of services, claims that CUSAMS enables service organizations to make a comprehensive assessment of the value of their customers, and to understand the influence of marketing instruments on them. Examines leading indicators of key customer behaviors reflecting the length, depth and breadth of customer/service-organization relationship: duration, usage and cross-buying.

- Gross, Neil, "Commentary: Valuing 'Intangibles' Is a Tough Job, But It Has to be Done," Aug 6, 2001, *BusinessWeek Online*. If companies can account for intangibles on a balance sheet when there's a merger or acquisition, why not all the time? Worries that FASB will never buy it because any whiff of subjectivity leads to a label of "voodoo accounting."

- Gupta, Sunil, Donald R. Lehmann, and Jennifer Ames Stuart, "Valuing Customers," *Journal of Marketing Research*, February

2004, pp.7–18. Makes the case that much of the financial value of the firm depends on assets not listed on the balance sheet, e.g. brands, customers, employees, knowledge. Demonstrates how valuing customers makes it feasible to value firms, inc. high growth firms with negative earnings. Study examines Capital One, Ameritrade, E★TRADE, Amazon.com, and eBay.

- Gupta, Sunil, and Donald R. Lehmann, *Managing Customers as Investments: The Strategic Value of Customers in the Long Run*, Wharton School Publishing, 2005. Gupta and Lehmann are professors at the Columbia Business School, and Sunil Gupta has been a Visiting Scholar at the Teradata CRM Center at Duke University. This book appeared just as we entered the copyediting stage of our own book, and we are glad to list it for the reader. While its focus is still primarily on investment choices surrounding marketing decisions, it is the best discussion we've seen yet of ROMI or "return on marketing investment."

- Kordupleski, Ray, *Mastering Customer Value Management: The Art and Science of Creating Competitive Advantage*, Pinn-Flex, 2003.

- Lenskold, James D. *Marketing ROI: The Path to Campaign, Customer, and Corporate Profitability*, McGraw-Hill, 2003.

- Malthouse, Edward C., and Robert C. Blattberg, "Can We Predict Customer Lifetime Value?" in *Journal of Interactive Marketing*, Vol. 19, No. 1, Winter 2005, pp.2–16. Argues that the feasibility of predicting the future profitability of customers depends on the probabilities and costs of misclassifying customers. Proposed that of the most valuable 20% of customers, 55% will be misclassified (and not receive special treatment), and of the bottom 80%, 15% will be misclassified (and receive special treatment), if treatment decisions are based on historical transaction data (such as RFM used by database marketers).

- Mathias, Peter F., and Noel Capon, "Managing Strategic Customer Relationships as Assets: Developing Customer Relationship Capital," White paper, Columbia University, 2003. Refers to customer equity as CRC (customer relationship capital), discusses six steps for creating and acquiring the future customer wallet (using only B2B applications. Noel Capon is a professor at Columbia: http://www.gsb.columbia.edu/whoswho/full.cfm?id =55764; Peter Mathias is CEO of Mathias and Company: http://www.mathiasco.com/about.html.

- Mulhern, Francis J., "Customer Profitability Analysis: Measurement, Analysis, and Research Directions," *Journal of Interactive Marketing*, 1999, Vol 13, no. 1, Winter, pp.25–40.
- Niraj, Rakesh, Mahendra Gupta, and Chakravarthi Narasimhan, "Customer Profitability in a Supply Chain," *Journal of Marketing*, July 2001, 65 (3), 1–16. Emphasizes the need for individual customer profitability calculations if customer lifetime values are to be determined.
- Parasuraman, A. 1997 "Reflections in Gaining Competitive Advantage Through Customer Value," *Journal of the Academy of Marketing Science*, 25, 2, 154–61.
- Rust, Roland T. Rust, Katherine N. Lemon, and Valerie A. Zeithaml, "Return on Marketing: Using Customer Equity to Focus Marketing Strategy," *Journal of Marketing*, Winter 2004. Presents a strategic framework that enables competing marketing strategy options to be weighed on the basis of projected financial return. LTV = frequency of category purchase, average qty of purchase, brand-switching patterns, firm's contribution margin. Based on "what-if" evaluation, and focuses on return on advertising, return on loyalty programs, return on corporate citizenship. Defines "customer equity" as the total discounted lifetime values summed over all of the firm's current and potential customers.
- Rust, Roland T., Valerie A. Zeithaml and Katherine N. Lemon (2000) *Driving Customer Equity: How Customer Lifetime Value is Reshaping Corporate Strategy*, New York: Free Press.
- Stahl, Heinz K., Kurt Matzler, Hans H. Hinterhuber "Linking Customer Lifetime Value with Shareholder Value," *Industrial Marketing Management* 32 (2003) 267–79. Emphasizes increasing importance of ability to evaluate market strategies against ability to deliver shareholder value, therefore acquisition and maintenance of customers must result in improved cash flows and shareholder value. Argues that customers are assets, and increase shareholder value by accelerating and enhancing cash flows, reducing cash flow volatility and vulnerability, and increasing residual value of the firm.
- Srivastava, Rajendra K., Tasadduq A. Shervani and Liam Fahey, "Market-Based Assets and Shareholder Value: A Framework for Análisis," *Journal of Marketing*, January 1998, Vol. 62, pp.2–18. Develops a conceptual framework for the marketing-finance

interface and its implications for the theory and practice of marketing. Asserts that assets are based on customer relationships, channel relationships, and partner relationships, which increase shareholder value by accelerating and enhancing cash flow, reducing cash flow volatility, and increasing residual value of cash flow.

- Thomas, Jacquelyn S., Werner Reinartz, and V. Kumar, "Getting the Most out of All Your Customers," *Harvard Business Review*, July-August 2004, pp.116–23. Builds on the Return on Marketing Investment literature by asserting that profitability of customers matters more than their raw numbers, or their loyalty.

- Woodall, Tony, "Conceptualising 'Value for the Customer': An Attributional, Structural, and Dispositional Analysis." *Academy of Marketing Science Review* [online] 2003 (12), available: http://www.amsreview.org/articles/woodall 12-2003.pdf. Notes that "customer value" is used in literature to portray both value from supplier to customer and vice versa. This author calls the first of these two "value for the customer," or VC.

- Woodruff, Robert P., 1997, "Customer Value: The Next Source of Competitive Advantage," *Journal of the Academy of Marketing Science*, 25 (2), 139–53.

- Zeithaml, Valerie A. (2000) "Service Quality, Profitability, and the Economic Worth of Customers: What We Know and What We Need to Learn," *Journal of the Academy of Marketing Science*, 28 (1) 67–85.

Appendix 4
The Economics of Customer Equity

An intuitively compelling case can be made that the value of a firm's customer equity is virtually the same as the value of the firm itself, as an operating company. However, a firm's value reflects not just the value of its current customers, but its growth potential, as well. A firm that is rapidly acquiring new customers will generally have a higher market value than a similar firm that is not acquiring new customers. So our own definition of "customer equity" explicitly includes the LTVs of not just current customers, but *future* customers, as well.

Valuing future customers

In most businesses it's possible to estimate the rate at which new customers are being added to the customer base. Figuring the customer equity attributable to new customers is then simply a matter of calculating whether the average LTVs coming in are increasing or decreasing (obviously, one purpose of "look-alike prospecting" is to increase the average LTV of newly acquired customers).

In addition, as shown in Chapter 4 (in the section "What is the value today of a customer you don't yet have?"), it should be possible to make reasonable assumptions about the probability that any single prospect will become a customer, along with the lifetime value they would have if they were to become a customer. If you can do that exercise across the whole universe of prospects, then you have a way to calculate the total customer equity of not just your current customers but your future ones, as well.

However, in some situations your firm could be in a more fluid market situation. Perhaps you have a completely new product or service, or you are competing in an explosive new category. One of the most useful mathematical tools for analyzing a rapidly growing customer base is known as "Bass Diffusion Theory," a mathematical technique first suggested in 1969 for calculating the rate at which product or service innovations can be expected to diffuse throughout a market. Essentially, the Bass model works by fitting a kind of S-shaped curve to the market, based on estimates of the total market potential for a new product or service, along with a coefficient of innovation and a coefficient of imitation. The model can be adapted to account for step changes in pricing or product improvements, as well. (This is the model that was applied in the Columbia Business School study, which attempted to estimate customer equity for rapidly growing companies like Amazon and E*TRADE cited in Chapter 6, on page 104.)

Customer insight drives the discount rate down

In analyzing business ventures, a higher discount rate is often applied to account for the fact that the outcome of the venture cannot really be known in advance. (We apply a discount rate to calculations of the net present value of future cash flows, in order to take account of the risk that these cash flows might not materialize in the magnitudes that we are predicting, or that they might not materialize at all.) In general, riskier ventures should be evaluated using higher discount rates, and vice versa. In assessing a fairly straightforward financial transaction in a low-inflation economic environment, it might be appropriate to apply a discount rate of, say, 6 to 8%. When assessing the launch of a completely new business, on the other hand, it would be more appropriate to apply a discount rate of 10% to 15%, or even more.

The same exact principle applies when calculating a customer's lifetime value. Lifetime value is based on the net present value of future cash flows attributable to the customer. The accuracy of our predictions about a customer's future behavior – and the cash flows that this behavior will generate – depends directly on the level of insight we have today into the motivations and needs of our customers. When we know little about our customers we should apply a high discount rate. But as we develop deeper customer insight, we can lower the discount rate applied.

This is an extremely important aspect of calculating Return on Customer, because when we lower the discount rate we are in effect raising our estimate of the firm's customer equity, and so we are raising the firm's overall value. In other words, deeper and more accurate customer insight drives customer equity higher. Deeper insight also has an important benefit in terms of leveraging the tools that managers can apply to generate higher levels of customer equity. Obviously, if future revenues are being discounted less, because of more insight (that is, lower risk of error), then the value created by long-term behaviors such as customer loyalty go up, relative to the value created by short-term behaviors such as acquisition cost. Indeed, the Columbia study cited previously noted that

> "...the impact of retention on customer value is significantly higher at lower discount rates. This suggests that companies in mature and low-risk businesses should pay even more attention to customer retention."

Appendix 5
Full Disclosure

We have referred in this book to dozens of organizations in an effort to illustrate the points we have been making. Over the years, Peppers & Rogers Group and parent company Carlson Marketing Group have had the privilege of assisting numerous companies in the development of customer-based business strategies and the execution of a broad range of marketing initiatives, and some of the many companies we have mentioned have been our clients.

The presence or absence of a client relationship has not influenced our decision to include or exclude a discussion of those companies in our work. Nonetheless, in the spirit of full disclosure, we are here listing companies cited in the book that are (or have been) clients of Peppers & Rogers Group and/or Carlson Marketing Group within the three years prior to initial publication in 2005:

- 3M Company
- AB Volvo
- Acxiom Corporation
- Agilent Technologies, Inc.
- Amazon.com, Inc.
- America Online, Inc.
- Best Buy Co., Inc.
- BMW (Bayerische Motoren Werke AG)
- Boise Office Solutions
- British Airways Plc
- Canadian Imperial Bank of Commerce
- Capital One Financial Corporation
- Cisco Systems, Inc.

- Citigroup, Inc.
- E*TRADE Financial Corp.
- eBay, Inc.
- Eli Lilly and Company
- Ford Motor Company
- General Electric Company
- General Motors Corporation
- IMS Health Incorporated
- Inland Revenue
- International Business Machines Corporation
- Johnson & Johnson
- Oracle Corporation
- Pitney Bowes Inc.
- Royal Bank of Canada
- SAP Aktiengesellschaft
- SAS Institute
- Toyota Motor Corporation
- Toys "R" Us, Inc.
- Tyco International Ltd.
- Verizon Communications Inc.
- WorldCom, Inc.

In addition, Martha Rogers serves on the Board of the Ponemon Institute, and Larry Ponemon has served on the editorial board of *Inside 1to1: Privacy*, an online newsletter published by Peppers & Rogers Group.

Endnotes

Chapter 1

AN OPEN LETTER TO THE FINANCIAL COMMUNITY

page

11 ROC and ROI are each financial metrics designed to track the efficiency with which value is created. ROI measures how much value is created relative to the financial capital employed to create it, while ROC measures how much value is created relative to the "customer capital" employed. If customers are scarcer than capital, then maximizing your ROC on the customers and prospects available is a more efficient way to prioritize your actions than simply maximizing your ROI on the capital available.

11 We take the idea of value creation or destruction very seriously. For lots of companies, the problem with reengineering is not that it didn't save enough money in the short run. It was that, in the long run, reengineering often *destroyed* firm value.

11 The main point of the 2004 executive survey of more than 400 senior financial executives by Duke University and the University of Washington, is this: Ironically, the Sarbanes-Oxley Act, enacted by the American government in the wake of scandals involving managed earnings and financial manipulations, and imposing tough new restrictions on corporations' ability to adjust their accounting to manage their earnings, has probably resulted in increased willingness on the part of executives to sacrifice value. Because a firm is no longer able to manipulate its accounting to smooth its earnings, 78% of the executives surveyed said they would actually change policies and give up long-term value in exchange for smoothing out short-term earnings. As reported in "Study: Executives sacrifice shareholder value to please Street," February 9, 2004, by Emery P. Dalesio, AP Business Writer, The Associated Press State & Local Wire (press release) and "Anglo-American Lunacy" by John Plender, in the *Financial Times* (London, England), February 16, 2004, London Edition 1, Section: Companies: UK & Ireland; p.20. Also see "Balancing Short-and Long-Term Performance," by Janamitra Devan, Anna Kristina Millan, and Pranav Shirke, in *The McKinsey Quarterly,* 2005, No. 1, pp.31–33.

12 Whenever "the market" reports quarterly earnings, the main reason is to understand and predict the value of a company based on "current" numbers. In point of fact, they are, technically, yesterday's numbers, or last quarter's.

13 Reports abound about personal wealth derived from short-term results. See Ann Davis and John R. Emshwiller, "Enron's in Court, But Wall Street's the One on Trial," *Wall Street Journal*, June 3, 2004, p.C1.

13 R&D = research and development

13 Any listing of trusted or admired companies will generally include mostly large, well-known companies. In that category – large, well-known firms – there are far fewer private companies than publicly-traded ones, yet these "admired" and "trusted" lists nearly always include a larger percentage of private companies than their numbers in the market should warrant. The authors' company, Peppers and Rogers Group, was acquired in 2003 by Carlson Marketing Group of Carlson Companies, a very large and successful privately held, family-owned company. The CEO, Marilyn Carlson Nelson, daughter of the founder, frequently quotes the Carlson Creed:

Whatever you do, do with Integrity
Wherever you go, go as a Leader
Whomever you serve, serve with Caring
Whenever you dream, dream with your All
And never, ever give up.

Curtis Nelson, who serves as third-generation company president, along with Marilyn, are both adamant that Carlson be a great place to work, and ethical as well. Curtis and Marilyn often begin their own analysis of the work Carlson is doing for a customer or a client company with the question "What's in the client's best interest here?"

14 In the discussion on organic growth, the first quote is from Richard Kovacevich, Chairman and CEO, Wells Fargo, quoted in "Wells Fargo Chairman and CEO Interview," CEO *Wire*, December 4, 2003, by Ron Insana and Consuelo Mack. The second quote was from Kennett Burnes of Cabot Corporation, quoted in Ivan Lerner, "Cabot Focuses on Organic Growth to Drive Revenue Gains." *Chemical Market Reporter*, November 24, 2003, Vol. 264, Iss. 18, p.4. Others have also clarified the importance of organic growth, most notably the executives at Enterprise Rent-a-Car, who are dedicated to long term value, and organic growth. Their philosophy? The best capital market may be the one you grow yourself. We'll talk more about Enterprise later in the book.

14 HR = Human Resources, the part of the company that hires and fires people, and manages their benefits and training

14 The poetic and quite accurate reference to organic growth as the "fountain of youth" for a company is from Andre R. van Heemstra, Personnel Director and Member of the Board of Unilever NV, in The Netherlands, told to one of the authors during a business conference in Lausanne, November 13, 2003.

15 ROI = Return on Investment.

17 We heard the story about the magazine's self-destructive behavior from a good friend who is a venture capitalist.

18 Have a look at "Manage Marketing by the Customer Equity Test," *Harvard Business Review*, July–August 1996, by Robert C. Blattberg and John Deighton, pp.136–144.

18 "Managing Strategic Customer Relationships as Assets: Developing Customer Relationship Capital" (2003), by Peter F. Mathias and Noel Capon, mentioned earlier, p.14.

19 Stephen R. Covey speaks often of "the law of the harvest" – based on the biblical notion that you reap what you sow, in agriculture and in life. See Stephen R. Covey, "30 Methods of Influence," *Executive Excellence,* Provo: April 1991, Vol. 8, No. 4, pp.3–4. We think Covey's points apply equally well to our farming analogy of optimization. In farming and in life and in business, you reap what you sow.

19 The "survey" mentioned here is the study of 400 financial executives we cited previously out of Duke University and the University of Washington.

23 When we talk about "shareholder return," we're really talking about the rate at which an enterprise is creating value for its owners. But we're using this term as loosely and generically as possible. If you're in business for yourself, you're THE shareholder for your own enterprise. Shareholder value matters, whether the shareholder meetings are big formal affairs or held over the kitchen table.

23 The definition of TSR came from Value-Based Management.net, at http://www.valuebasedmanagement.net/methods_tsr.html.

23 Cash is king, of course. See Bill McGuinness's book, *Cash Rules Learn & Manage the 7 Cash-Flow Drivers for Your Company's Success*, Washington, DC: Kiplinger, 2000. Our point is that cash and capital value are approximately the same thing.

Chapter 2

MAXIMIZING THE CUSTOMER VALUE PROPOSITION: BUILDING CUSTOMER TRUST

28 The role of "interruption" in marketing ("interruptive techniques," "interruptive messages," "interruptive ads," and "interruptive TV advertising") is credited to Seth Godin in his book *Permission Marketing: Turning Strangers Into Friends And Friends Into Customers* (New York: Simon & Schuster, 1999). In the context of sales training, "interruptive marketing" is discussed by Stephan Schiffman, *Cold Calling Techniques: (That Really Work!)* (Adams Media Corporation, 1999). We realized advertising is truly ubiquitous when we heard that it's not just on the T-shirts our kids wear at school or on the floor graphics at many supermarkets, but also reported by *Business 2.0* as including logos painted, for a week at a time, onto the foreheads of university students in London who collect £88.20 a week for these ForeheADs. (Adam Horowitz, Mark Athitakis, Mark Lasswell, and Owen Thomas, "101 Dumbest Moments in Business," *Business 2.0,* Jan/Feb 2004, Vol. 5, Issue 1, pp.72–82; Parmar, Arundhati, "Final frontier: Maximum exposure; Advertisers use bodies as billboards to up brand visibility," *Marketing News*, September 15, 2003, p.6.)

28 In an article that ran in *Fast Company* in June 2002 (by Robert Simons, Henry Mintzberg, and Kunal Basu, pp.117–121), we read that "in 1997, the Business Roundtable announced that it was making a remarkable U-turn. Its report on corporate governance assigned a new priority to CEOS: Maximize shareholder value. 'The

notion that the board must somehow balance the interests of stockholders against the interests of other stakeholders fundamentally misconstrues the role of directors.'" These authors asked how CEOs who signed this document could think of themselves as leaders? "The answer is simple: They aren't leaders – they're followers. What if a company really tries to put its shareholders first next quarter but alienates its customers next year?" If every company just looks at the short term measures, and views customers as a series of transactions, then customers won't be able to trust any company to do what they say they will, and no one will ever key in a credit card number on the web, or use food after the printed expiration date, or pay insurance premiums, or send a bouquet to a loved one in a distant city. Commerce would be hobbled, and only the lawyers would get rich. See also Robert M. Morgan and Shelby D. Hunt, "The Commitment-Trust Theory of Relationship Marketing," *Journal of Marketing*, July 1994, Vol. 58, pp.20–38. The article outlines antecedents and consequences of relationship marketing, theorizes that successful relationship marketing requires commitment and trust, models this requirement, and tests this key mediating variable in two companies that do and don't have their customers' "trust." Their finding: Trust produces better business results. Also see Ronald J. Alsop, "Corporate Reputation: Anything But Superficial – the deep but fragile nature of corporate reputation," *Journal of Business Strategy*, 2004, 25(6), pp.21–29.

28 We first read about the problems Citibank had in Japan in *The Wall Street Journal*, September 20, 2004, p.A3, "Japan Orders Citibank to Halt Private Banking," by Andrew Morse and Mitchell Pacelle, staff reporters at WSJ.

28 The Citigroup stories continue with an editorial in the *Times* of London, "Moral Bankruptcy," September 20, 2004.

28 More bad news about Citigroup appeared on the AFX News service, September 20, 2004, 2:39 pm, "Citigroup Cut on Ethics Concerns," available at http://www.crmbuyer.com/story/Citigroup-Cut-on-Ethics-Concerns-36793.html. We also saw an article in *The Japan Times*, September 18, 2004, which cited a government official as saying "We found so many rampant and repeated abuses, the punishment had to have considerable weight."

29 The video rental fiasco took place in Waterville, Ohio, in February 2004.

30 Readers will understand when we suggest that we could write a whole book on companies that make a quick buck at the expense of long-term trust and growth in customer equity. We could only shake our heads at these examples, reported in *Business 2.0*, January–February 2004, "101 Dumbest Moments in Business," by Adam Horowitz, Mark Athitakis, Mark Lasswell, and Owen Thomas. We bet you have your own examples to add. Self-interest vs. constituent interest. Short term vs. long term. Success vs. failure.
- Pressured to improve their numbers, a McDonald's outlet in Chicago's Field Museum kept serving food right up until it was closed by health inspectors who discovered that raw sewage was backing up into the food preparation area, and that employees had changed the expiration dates on 200 cartons of milk. *(Business 2.0, 2004.)*
- In our interview with Geoff Colvin, Editor and columnist at *Fortune*, co-anchor of *Wall Street Week with Fortune* on PBS, and co-author, with Larry Selden, of *Angel Customers* and *Demon Customers*, Geoff made an important point: At Scott Paper, Al Dunlap did radical surgery to save the patient's life, but then when he went to Sunbeam, slashing and burning, he played a bit too cavalierly with

numbers and pensions. Charles Nelson provoked the crisis at a Board meeting, when he asked "How's the second quarter?" to which Dunlap retorted, "Do you trust me or not?" Now Dunlap is forcibly retired.

- Only half of the American college-educated opinion leaders with incomes over $75,000/year trust business to "do what's right," according to Paul Cordasco, "Business Begins to Rebuild Consumer Trust," *PR Week*, January 19, 2004. In Europe, roughly two-thirds do not trust American companies. Most trusted brands in the US: UPS, J&J, P&G, IBM, Michelin, Heinz, and Coca-Cola. Most trusted brands in Europe: Michelin, Amnesty International, World Wildlife Fund, IBM, Danone; Most trusted in China: Coca-Cola, Samsung, HSBC, and in Brazil: J&J, Danone, Ford, Greenpeace, Michelin.

You can find a great treatise on this subject, from the "marketing" perspective, in Richard W. Buchanan, *When Customers Think We Don't Care: Ending Actions that Self-Destruct Companies, Customer Service, and Jobs,* McGraw-Hill Australia 2002.

30   Joe Pine wrote *Mass Customization* in 1993 (Boston, MA: Harvard Business School Press) and more recently *The Experience Economy* coauthored with Jim Gilmore (Boston, MA: Harvard Business School Press, 1999). The two now work together at Pine and Gilmore.

32   We realize we have been a little hard on AOL here, and we are hoping that not everyone at America Online is content with the "finders-keepers" approach that comes across to customers. We pledge here and now that if AOL changes its culture, its approach, and its reputation – and starts to build trust by thinking about the value of customer *relationships* and not just *transactions*, that we will write positively about them in our articles or a future book, and we genuinely look forward to it. At that point, we may even buy stock in the parent company.

      People go out of their way to tell us stories about AOL, and none of them are good. The facts in our story about AOL came from several sources: *PC Magazine*, May 18, 2004, p.55. Ed Maxell reports that the phone rep at AOL would not cancel his deceased brother's account and would not give the cancellation number until after the complete do-not-cancel pitch, claiming that it was an FCC requirement. Mr. Maxell wrote a letter to AOL, "suggesting that a more sensitive method be used for death cancellations – like faxing a death certificate." Also see "Arresting News for AOL," by Mike Musgrave and David A. Vise, staff reporters, *Washington Post*, June 25, 2004, p.E01. The "sucks" survey figures are from websites visited September 21, 2004.

32   James Schwartz was referring especially to Fair Air, a company no longer in business, and was quoted in Douglas Quinby and Kenneth Kiesnoski, "Fair Air Option," *Leisure Travel News*, March 12, 2001, Vol. 17, No. 10, p.1.

33   The consumer quote is from the 1998 *Harvard Business Review* article "Preventing the Premature Death of Relationship Marketing," in the January–February issue, by Susan Fournier, Susan Dobscha, and David Glen Mick.

34   We've been working with Kay Lemon on measuring the value of the company to the customer. See Katherine Lemon, Don Peppers and Martha Rogers, "Managing the Customer Lifetime Value: The Role of Learning Relationships," working paper.

34   Article by Robert Winnett and Zoe Thomas, "Are You a Second Class Consumer?" *Sunday Times* (London), October 19, 2003, Home News, p.9.

35 Charles Green coauthored *The Trusted* Advisor with David Maister and Rob Galford, Free Press, October 2000. You can find a summary of these ideas in "The Trust Equation: Generating Customer Trust" in *Managing Customer Relationships: A Strategic Framework,* Wiley, 2004, pp.72–77. Green is president of Trusted Advisor Associates.

36 J&J's stock price made an equally impressive recovery. On the day preceding the first death (Tuesday, September 28, 1982), the closing price of the stock was $47–1/8. On the first business day following the last death (Monday, October 4, 1982), the stock closed at $41–2/8 – a 12.5% decline. But the stock rose to a record high of $51.25 after just three months.

36 The Johnson & Johnson story was widely reported in 1984 and 1985. We looked to Mark L. Mitchell, "The Impact of External Parties on Brand-Name Capital: The 1982 Tylenol Poisonings and Subsequent Cases," *Economic Inquiry*, October, 1989, 27(4), pp.601–618 for source of basic facts of the incident, and change in market share. We got the stock price facts from "Tylenol Maker in Doldrums," *The New York Times*, January 31, 1984, section D, p.8. To understand the number of bottles recalled and the magnitude of the decision, we looked at Jason Richardson and Eric Bolesh, "Toward the See-Through Corporation," *Pharmaceutical Executive*, November, 2002, 22(11), pp.54–60. The James Burke quote came from Daniel F. Cuff, "Making a Difference," *The New York Times*, February 9, 1992, section 3, p.12.

36 In addition to religion, ethical philosophers almost uniformly embrace the principle of reciprocity. Immanuel Kant's "Categorical Imperative" is a restatement of it. And John Rawls's "just society" is based on the actors having to make decisions about how the society should be set up from behind a "veil of ignorance," meaning that they must not know which roles they will play, but that a just society will be based on rules that would be fair to everyone, whether prince or pauper. This, in effect, operates as a "social" version of the principal of reciprocity.

37 USAA uses SAS technology for much of the relationship building capability.

37 See Forrester's report on customer service among financial institutions, which has USAA at the very top. Bill Doyle, "What Satisfies Financial Services Consumers," *The Forrester Report*, June 2, 2004. These quotes are from Forrester's press release, "New Research Unveils Financial Services Winners And Losers In Customer Advocacy Ranking," June 10, 2004.

37 We wrote about USAA in Don Peppers and Martha Rogers, *The One to One Manager: Real-World Lessons in Customer Relationship Management*, Currency/Doubleday, 1999, pp.93–102. Compare the employee empowerment – and accountability – at USAA with that of a major American airline that momentarily (for an hour) lost a piece of luggage belonging to one of the authors, delaying departure from the airport to the hotel du jour. The customer service representative for the airline, feeling bad for the customer and not allowed to help this frequent flyer in any other way, looked carefully for dings and dents once the suitcase was found, and announced, "This suitcase needs replacing. I'll send you a new one." The suitcase was not hopelessly battered, and the customer would have been happier with extra frequent flyer miles, but the service representative did the only thing she was empowered to do – buy the customer a new bag.

38 The great story about trustworthy managers at hotels came from Tony Simons, "The High Cost of Lost Trust," *Harvard Business Review,* September 2002, pp.18–19.

38   The core purpose and values of Tesco are certainly consistent with our discussion, and the reader may find it interesting to note the Tesco Statement of Purpose, as of 2004 (http://www.tesco.com/recruitment/html/careers/comInfo/values.htm, accessed July 2005):

Our Core Purpose is all about customers.
"Creating value for customers, to earn their lifetime loyalty."
This statement is at the centre of all we do.
Our two values drive the way we do business.
No one tries harder for customers:
Understand customers better than anyone
Be energetic, be innovative and be first for customers
Use our strengths to deliver unbeatable values to our customers
Look after our people so they can look after our customers
Treat people how we like to be treated:
All retailers, there's one team...The Tesco Team
Give support to each other and praise more than criticise
Ask more than tell and share knowledge so that it can be used
Trust and respect each other
Strive to do our very best
Enjoy work, celebrate success and learn from experience

(Source: http://81.201.142.254/companyInfo/businessStrategy.asp?section=1)

Also see *Scoring Points: How Tesco is Winning Customer Loyalty*, by Clive Humby and Terry Hunt (Kogan Page, Philadelphia, 2004) for a historical summary of the financial performance of Tesco, including revenue, income, and employee growth statistics (1997 – 2003). Tesco "Company Overview – At a glance" (see http://81.201.142.254/companyInfo/ataglance.asp?section=1) also contains growth statistics for number of stores and selling space (1999 – 2003). Also see "BOGOF and Hopefully You Will Come Back for More," *Brand Strategy*, January 2, 2003, p.10.

38   "Trust Strategy Drives Business at Intel," Don Peppers and Martha Rogers, *Inside 1to1*, October 18, 2004. Research showed that website improvements drove trust values up, which in turn positively affected the number of downloads and – at the same time – saved Intel millions of dollars in customer-support costs. The research was centered around eight "trust cues" – specific elements that have positive or negative effects on user trust, such as navigation, friendliness, touch and feel, and personas, among others. Individual rating scores were then averaged to create an overall trust measure.

39   We first reported the GM story in *1to1 Magazine*, October 2003, p.19, J. B. King, "Big Business Bets on Its Customers," *1to1 Magazine*, October 2003, pp.18–19.

40   Scott Adams coined the phrase "the stupid rich" and used it in his 1996 book, *The Dilbert Principle* (New York, NY: HarperCollins Publishers, Inc.). Adams describes a market segment known as the "'Stupid Rich,' so named because of their tendency to buy anything that's new regardless of the cost or usefulness" (p.133).

40   Lack of knowledge on the part of customers has traditionally played a role in economic theory. In strict economic terms, the absence of perfect information is indeed one of the key drivers of higher margin. The more difficult it is for a customer to make valid comparisons, or to identify substitutes, or to understand the costs that go into a product, the more likely the producer is to be able to secure a higher price, and

when sales to customers are seen as isolated, independent events involving a more or less infinite supply of potential new customers. However, in reality customers are scarce in number, and with today's technology a firm can track its transactions with each customer over time. As a result, when the firm assists a customer in obtaining the data needed to make more informed buying decisions, the customer's trust of the firm will increase and ROC will increase, too.

41   The authors did in fact meet personally with executives at one major airline who said this is what their firm and several other airlines do. They were unhappy about it, sensing that it creates mistrust among customers, but didn't know what else to do to fill planes.

42   Peter Blau, president of Customer Growth, commented to us in an email September 20, 2004, about the airline industry.

42   Forrester's report: Bill Doyle, "What Satisfies Financial Services Consumers," The Forrester Report, June 2, 2004.

43   See http://www.fortune.com/fortune/ceo/articles/0,15114,749318,00.html for Jeffrey Immelt's list of the four things needed to keep GE on top."Virtue" is first on his list. See "Money and Morals at GE," by Marc Gunther, *Fortune,* November 15, 2004, 150(10), p.176, reprinted on the GE website, at:
http://www.ge.com/en/company/investor/ge_social_responsibility_and_citizenship.htm

44   Happily, proof abounds that leaders and companies can succeed when they act in the customer's interest as well as their own. If you've never had a chance to read these books, check them out:
•   Tom Peters *Re-imagine!* London: Dorling Kindersley Limited, 2003.
•   Tom Chappell, the president of Tom's of Maine, wrote *The Soul of a Business: Managing for Profit and the Common Good*, New York, Bantam, 1993. In 2003, the company had "more than $35 million in annual sales." The company relocated to a new building in 2004 because "We are bursting at the seams." Quim, Beth, "Tom's of Maine Relocating," *Portland Press Herald*, February 24, 2004, p.1A. Standard & Poor's reported sales of $20 million (August 13, 2004).
•   Ken Blanchard and Mark Miller, *The Secret: What Great Leaders Know – And Do,* San Francisco: Berrett-Koehler Publishers, Inc., 2004.
•   Jim Kouzes and Barry Posner, *The Leadership Challenge*, New York: Jossey-Bass, 2002.

44   While we were thinking about Enron and companies like it, we found it useful to see an article taken from Trusted Advisor Website, Oct 2003, "What Should Enron Have Taught Us?" Trusted Advisor Associates, 2002, http://www.trustedadvisor.com.

Chapter 3

BUILDING THE FIRM'S VALUE BY TAKING THE CUSTOMER'S PERSPECTIVE

45   Larry Selden and Geoffrey Colvin published "Five Rules for Finding the Next Dell," in *Fortune,* July 12, 2004, p.102.

46   A more complete discussion of Dell appears in: Don Peppers and Martha Rogers, *One to One B2B: Customer Development Strategies for the Business-to-Business World*, New York: Currency/Doubleday, 2001 (pp.67–105). You'll find additional material in Don Peppers and Martha Rogers, "Success One Account At a Time," *Business 2.0*, April 17, 2001 6(8), p.60; Peppers, Don and Martha Rogers, "Lessons from the front," *Marketing Tools*, January/February 1998, 5(1), p.38ff.

46   See our more complete case study on Royal Bank of Canada in Don Peppers and Martha Rogers, *The One to One Manager: Real-World Lessons in Customer Relationship Management,* New York: Currency/Doubleday, 1999 (pages 121–129). More about RBC appears in: Martha Rogers, "Show Me the ROI," *Inside 1to1*, October 29, 2001; Martha Rogers, "CRM Dividends for Royal Bank of Canada," *Inside 1to1*, April 27, 2000; and Martha Rogers, "Royal Bank's 9 Million Loyal Customers," *Inside 1to1*, September 30, 1999.

46   See "Best Buy Accelerates Customer Centricity Transformation; Insights Gained from 32 Lab Stores Fuel Decision to Launch Customer Centricity at up to 110 Additional U.S. Best Buy Stores During Fiscal 2005," Business Wire, Minneapolis, MN, May 3, 2004 (p.2).

46   Balter, Gary, and Brian Nagel, "Best Buy Co., Inc.; Best Buy Shaping Up to Become One of Retail's Great Companies" (UBS Investment Research, May 5, 2004). The first quote about Best Buy is from p.3 and the second quote is from p.4. We also used a Best Buy press release: "Best Buy Second-Quarter Earning per Share from Continuing Operations Increase 10% to 46 Cents, After Charges of 7 Cents; Robust Revenue Drove Results," Business Wire, Minneapolis, MN, September 15, 2004. The quote from Brad Anderson came from this release.

48   We've been working with Kay Lemon on measuring the value of the company to the customer. See Katherine Lemon, Don Peppers and Martha Rogers, "Managing the Customer Lifetime Value: The Role of Learning Relationships," working paper.

48   Let's not be confused about what we mean by "needs." When we say "needs," we do not mean demographics, or product features, or a customer's transaction history, or anything that is, at best, a piece of the puzzle. Instead, we mean beliefs, preferences, whims, vague appetites, deep-rooted wants, fundamental predispositions. These are harder to collect and synthesize, but once we do, we have a much greater advantage over a competitor who only knows zip code area or age group. We found it useful to see Robert B. Woodruff and Sarah F. Gardial, *Know Your Customer: New Approaches to Understanding Customer Value and Satisfaction,* Blackwell, 1996, as well as Jill Dyche, *e-Data: Turning Data into Information with Data Warehousing,* Addison-Wesley, 2000, B. Joseph Pine II and James H. Gilmore, *The Experience Economy: Work is Theatre & Every Business A Stage*, Harvard Business School Press, 1999, and Ronald S. Swift, *Accelerating Customer Relationships: Using CRM and Relationship Technologies,* Prentice-Hall, 2001.

51   See Marji McClure, "Energy Companies Spark Customer Relationships at Reduced Costs," *Inside 1to1*, June 28, 2003.

51   See Don Peppers and Martha Rogers, *One to One B2B: Customer Development Strategies for the Business-to-Business World*, New York: Currency/Doubleday, 2001, Chapter 3, for a comprehensive case study of the innovative Dell Premier Pages program.

52   See Degussa Web site at www.degussa.com. Much of this comes from Vandenbosch, Mark and Niraj Dawar, "Beyond Better Products: Capturing Value in Customer Interactions," *MIT Sloan Management Review*, Summer 2002, 43(4), pp.35–42. Vandenbosch wrote about Master Builders in 2002, but they changed their name in June, 2004, to Degussa Admixtures.

53   For more on Cisco, see "Feedback Helps Cisco Satisfy Customer Needs," by Don Peppers, *Inside 1to1*, March 3, 2003.

54   "311 Answers the Call for Customer Service," by Don Peppers, *Inside 1to1*, January 26, 2004. We've seen some excellent work done on these 311 systems, and had a stimulating conversation in early 2004 with Shep Parke at Accenture about the work they have done in the 311 system for New York City.

55   Professor Eric Von Hippel was quoted in *Inside 1to1*, "Why Pitney Bowes Needs Needs Research," by Martha Rogers, Ph.D., January 24, 2005.

56   We believe customers do not want to have to choose (unless they're out browsing for pleasure). They will choose if that is the only way to get what they want. See "The Burden of Choice" in Chapter 6 of Don Peppers and Martha Rogers, *Enterprise One to One: Tools for Competing in the Interactive Age,* Currency/Doubleday, 1997, pp.136–138.

56   The story about St. George Bank is anecdotal. We heard it on a recent trip to the land down under. But we know this capability is also available from National Australia Bank, known for its customer centricity, (See Martha Rogers, "Analytics Drive Results for National Australia Bank," *Inside 1to1*, March 1, 2004.)

58   The key to meeting a customer's needs is a successful Learning Relationship. It works like this: If you're my customer, and I get you to interact with me, then I learn something about what you need that my competitors don't know, and then I can do something for you my competitors can't do. See Joseph E. Pine II, Don Peppers, and Martha Rogers, "Do You Want to Keep Your Customers Forever?" *Harvard Business Review*, March/April 1995, pp.103–114 and Don Peppers and Martha Rogers, *Managing Customer Relationships: A Strategic Framework,* Wiley, 2004.

58   We first addressed the idea about brands being equivalent to problem solutions in a subscriber-based study: *Supply Chain Responses in a Consumer-Centric Marketplace*, White Paper, Institute for the Future and Peppers and Rogers Group, June, 2001, p.20.

59   We found it useful to see "Why Brand Strategy is Critical for the Next Generation of CRM," Accenture White Paper, downloaded from Accenture's Web site, May 2004, by Stephen F. Dull. Also see Erich Joachimsthaler and David A. Aaker, "Building Brands without Mass Media," *Harvard Business Review*, January–February 1997, pp.42–50.

60   Tesco launched the Clubcard on February 13, 1995. (See Clive Humby and Terry Hunt with Tim Phillips, *Scoring Points: How Tesco is Winning Customer Loyalty*, London: Kogan Page Limited, 2003, p.1.)

60   Britton Manasco, writing in Corante *Tech News*, 28 April 2004, asserted the £100 million figure.

61   While it might seem like great consumer convenience, home delivery of groceries is not necessarily an easy business to run profitably. The majority of independent online grocery delivery operations launched during the dot-com boom are now bust. Groceries delivered to an online shopper generally are picked and packed at a local Tesco retail operation, rather than in a larger, more centralized warehouse. The company's consolidated record of an individual's online and offline shopping history allows it to improve its online home-delivery service substantially. For instance, if the brand a consumer ordered online is temporarily out of stock, the customer's second-most-purchased brand could be substituted into the delivery. We agree with David Bell and Rajiv Lal, "The Impact of Frequent Shopper Programs in Grocery Retailing," white paper, March 2003, which suggests that most frequent shopper programs in grocery stores fail to differentiate by value, and thus the programs often have the greatest impact on the behavior of the least valuable customers.

61   A report on tesco.com reads "In 2000 tesco.com, covering all Tesco e-commerce business for customers, was launched. 2000 also saw the start of tesco.com, the grocery homeshopping service, which has since become the largest grocery homeshopping business in the world . . ." Numbers came from a report by Devon Wylie, "CRM Case Study #14." Seklemian/Newell, November 4, 2003, *http://222.loyalty.vg/pages/CRM/cas_study_14_Tesco.htm*. According to Martin Veith ("Rival E-Grocer Takes On Tesco." VNU Net (April 15, 2003): 9), "Online sales remain a tiny fraction of Tesco's business but the growth curve is sharp. Tesco.com sales for the year ending 23 February grew by 50 percent to £356m and the operation is profitable excepting US startup costs; but the Internet division represents just 1.5 percent of Tesco's business."

TESCO.COM

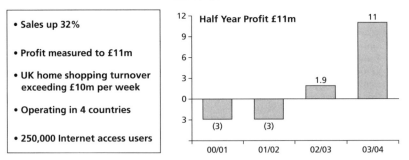

Goodroe, Steve and Clive Humby, in "Are You Delivering What Your Customers Want?....The Tesco Case Study," at the John Yeck Center for Advanced Studies in Direct and Interactive Marketing, Direct Marketing: Managing the Interactive Future, conducted by The Direct Marketing Educational Foundation, Tarrytown House, Tarrytown, New York, June 10, 2004. See also p.244 in Clive Humby and Terry Hunt with Tim Phillips, *Scoring Points: How Tesco is Winning Customer Loyalty*, London:

Kogan Page Limited, 2003. Moreover, nearly 40% of Tesco's customers have given the company their email address, according to Goodroe and Humby.

62 Over just the last few years, by using technology to expand its relationships with customers under the shelter of a powerful brand, Tesco has dramatically increased its growth potential, and as a result its publicly traded share price has grown commensurately, if not consistently.

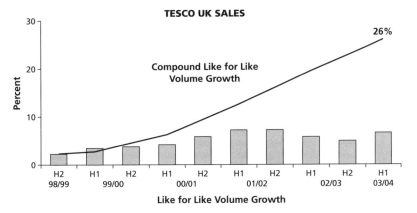

TESCO UK SALES

Source: Leahy, Terry. "Interim Results 2003." Webcast presented on September 16, 2003.

Chapter 4

ROC AROUND THE CLOCK

65 Thanks to Christian Neckermann at Peppers & Rogers Group for helping us think through many of the issues with respect to making ROC-based decisions.

66 It's not our goal in this book to delve into the specifics of calculating customer lifetime values, or LTVs, using the intricately capable modeling and forecasting tools now available to help companies predict the future behaviors of their customers. See Appendix 2.

66 According to Grizzard Performance Group report No. 20, only 24% of firms segmented their customers by LTV in 2002.

66 Both SPSS and SAS Institute, the two most prominent customer analytics software firms, regularly invoke the term "predictive analytics" to describe their software capabilities, as do a variety of other firms.

66 See Rajendra K. Srivastava, Tasadduq A. Shervani, and Liam Fahey, "Market-Based Assets and Shareholder Value: A Framework for Analysis," *Journal of Marketing*, January 1998, Vol. 62, pp.2–18.

68   "Going the distance with telecom customers," *The McKinsey Quarterly*, 2003
     Number 4, pp.83–93 by Adam Braff, William J. Passmore, and Michael Simpson
     provided many of the details for this section about telecom companies, and these
     authors serve as the "group of industry experts" we mention.

69   Balancing short-term and long-term helps us to see whether our deeply held
     assumptions are correct. It was useful for us to see Werner J. Reinartz and V. Kumar,
     "On the Profitability of Long-Life Customers in a Non-Contractual Setting: An
     Empirical Investigation and Implications for Marketing," *Journal of Marketing,* Vol. 64
     (October 2000), pp.17–35.

71   This dilemma – balancing retention and acquisition budgets – was in fact the subject
     of Blattberg and Deighton's marvelously insightful and prescient HBR piece ("Manage
     Marketing by the Customer Equity T Test," *Harvard Business Review*, July–August
     1996, by Robert C. Blattberg and John Deighton, pp.136–144).

72   Thanks to Simon Jury at Peppers & Rogers Group for his help with the acquisition-
     retention graph.

73   The example in our sidebar on "ROC and Tactical Decision Making" was provided and
     analyzed for us by Patrick Winterbottom.

73   The LTV, or lifetime value, equation for different businesses can be written differently.
     Almost all lifetime value equations, however, will involve some variation on all or most
     of the following seven variables, and the variables themselves overlap somewhat:
     acquisition cost, margin, frequency of purchase, tenure of relationship, share of cus-
     tomer, customer growth, and cost to serve.

75   Our thanks to Scott Cook at Intuit for pointing out the fact that if customers were not
     scarce, Treatment 1 would be the best course of action for the department store
     retailer.

76   We found helpful the report of the survey of American households in "Customer
     retention is not enough," by Stephanie Coyles and Timothy C. Gokey, *McKinsey
     Quarterly*, July 2004. We also look forward to the full report based on a proposal
     funded by the Teradata CRM Center at Duke University: "Defection Detection:
     Improving Predictive Accuracy of Customer Churn Models" by Scott Neslin,
     Dartmouth College; Sunil Gupta, Columbia University; Wagner Kamakura, Duke
     University, Junxiang Lu, Comerica Bank; and Charlotte Mason, UNC-Chapel Hill.

76   Thanks to Linda Vytlacil at Carlson Marketing Group for this discussion of how to
     think about customer retention, attrition, and defection.

77   You'll find a more thorough discussion of customer "vintages" in *Enterprise 1to1:
     Tools for Competing in the Interactive Age*, Currency/Doubleday, 1997, pp.365–366.
     Although we're not attempting to cover the acquisition topic thoroughly in this book,
     we should mention that for a company using ROC as a basis for management, acqui-
     sition will often take the approach of lookalike prospecting based on your MVCS, or
     Most Valuable Customers.

Chapter 5

BUILDING ENTERPRISE VALUE, ONE ROC AT A TIME

83 The idea of "treating different customers differently" is commonly referred to as "differentiating customers," and is an important part of the Identify-Differentiate-Interact-Customize framework. See *Managing Customer Relationships: A Strategic Framework*, by Don Peppers and Martha Rogers (New York: Wiley), 2004.

84 See the discussions of "Learning Relationships" in Don Peppers, Martha Rogers, Ph.D., and Bob Dorf, *The One to One Fieldbook,* 1999, 97–98, and in B. Joseph Pine II, Don Peppers and Martha Rogers, "Do You Want to Keep Your Customers Forever?" *Harvard Business Review*, March–April 1995, reprint # 95209.

86 See the box in Chapter 4, **"What is the Value Today of a Customer You Don't Yet Have?"** for more discussion. "Potential value" is formally defined as the net present value of the maximum reasonable future financial contributions from the designated customer, if the company were to succeed in applying an optimum proactive strategy for changing that customer's otherwise expected behavior. We define "actual value" (that is, LTV) as: The net present value of future financial contributions from the designated customer, behaving in the way he is expected to behave, knowing what we know now, with no significant unanticipated change in the customer's needs, in the competitive landscape, or in the company's planned strategy.

90 We've written extensively about how to handle BZS before. The main point is that the sooner we can help them up in value or out into the arms of our competitors, the sooner we will help not only our own bottom line, but also our best customers, who – as the folks keeping us in business – are paying the freight when we serve customers who will always destroy value. Also see recent additional thinking from Larry Selden and Geoffrey Colvin, *Angel Customers and Demon Customers*: *Discover Which is Which and Turbo-Charge Your Stock*, Penguin, 2003.

90 See "Going the distance with telecom customers," *The McKinsey Quarterly*, 2003 Number 4, 83–93 by Adam Braff, William J. Passmore, and Michael Simpson.

91 Documentation of the bottom-line benefits of loyal customers is abundant. The place to begin is Frederick F. Reichheld and W. Sasser, "Zero Defections: Quality Comes to Services," *Harvard Business Review*, September–October, 1990, pp.105–111; Frederick F. Reichheld, "Loyalty-Based Management," *Harvard Business Review*, March, 1993, pp.64–73; Frederick F. Reichheld, *The Loyalty Effect: The Hidden Force Behind Growth, Profits, and Lasting Value*, Boston: Harvard Business School Press, 1996; and Frederick Newell, *loyalty.com: Customer Relationship Management in the New Era of Internet Marketing*, New York: McGraw-Hill, 2000. You may also want to consider:

- In Carol Krol's article titled "Study quantifies bottom-line value of loyalty," she quotes Michael DeSanto, VP-Marketing Communications at Indianapolis-based Walker Information: "When you're a loyalty leader, customers are more willing to purchase more, more willing to recommend you and less eager to look hard at competitors," *B to B*, October 11, 2004, 89(11), p.4.
- "Research by the firm found that a mere 5% reduction in customer defections translates into a 25% increase in profitability . . ." according to a study conducted by Tower Group described in an article by Denny Coote, "Life changers and long-term profitability," *Bank Marketing International*, October 26, 2001, p.12.

- Mark Rechtin cites an important finding in his article, "Study finds loyal buyers will pay," *Automotive News*, August 4, 1997, No. 5725, p.8: "Buyers who remain loyal to a brand or automaker pay an average transaction price $1,200 higher than those who have to be conquested, according to a survey to be released today, August 4, by J.D. Power and Associates."

91   The retailer study was reported in Werner J. Reinartz and V. Kumar, "On the Profitability of Long-Life Customers in a Noncontractual Setting: An Empirical Investigation and Implications for Marketing," *Journal of Marketing*, 2000, 64(4), pp.17–35; also see Werner J. Reinartz & V. Kumar, "The Mismanagement of Customer Loyalty," *Harvard Business Review*, July, 2002, pp.86–94. And see Grahame R. Dowling and Mark Uncles, "Do Customer Loyalty Programs Really Work?" *Sloan Management Review*, 1997, 38(4), pp.71–82; and Julia Mohs, "Frequency Marketing," in *Retail Report*, 1999, Vol. 12, No. 4, published by David F. Miller Center for Retailing Education and Research, University of Florida. Note: The Reinartz & Kumar study specifically excluded customer acquisition costs when comparing profit margins from transactional and relational buyers.

92   One white paper, "Managing Strategic Customer Relationships as Assets: Developing Customer Relationship Capital" (2003), by Peter F. Mathias and Noel Capon, examines the importance of "strategic" customer relationships for businesses and concludes that the first task in building greater relationship capital in such situations is to "identify customer potential" (p.4). Specifically, the study urges B2B firms to evaluate customer growth potential in order to identify the right "customers of the future" – the "future winners" who will continue to grow and make a profit themselves.

92   Insurance graphic given to one of the authors at a conference. We modified it to protect the company.

92   The idea that usage of more than one product reduces churn was reinforced in a presentation by David Pugliese, VP of Product Marketing and Management for Cox Communications. He stated: "Bundling reduces churn as much as 50% in three-product homes."

97   We first wrote about this concept (collaborative filtering) in *Enterprise One to One*, (New York: Currency/Doubleday, 1997) calling it "community knowledge." The term "collaborative filtering" has become more common now, though. Whatever you call it, learning from all your customers to help you decide what to offer each one next is a very different way to think about grouping customers than, say, demographic segmentation or zip code prospecting. You can find a comprehensive review of collaborative filtering in *The Economist* magazine, March 12–18, 2005, "United We Find," pp.21–23 of the Technology section.

97   One company that did some research into this issue with respect to their own customers found they could improve the accuracy of their customer classifications by about 50%, through using direct interactions rather than simple outward characteristics. This firm's customer base consists mostly of professionals and small business owners. The company first fielded a survey and, using statistical analysis, grouped their customers by needs and values. (The outward characteristics model correctly classified 54% of customers, while the interaction model correctly classified 75%. Based on work by Swantje Drescher.) For additional information on "golden questions," see Don Peppers and Martha Rogers, *Managing Customer Relationships: A Strategic Framework*, Hoboken, NJ: John Wiley & Sons, 2004, pp.180–181.

98   There is an important sales and human psychology story with the vacation club, too. You might think that when there are only two or three simple categories of customers the firm should simply ask a prospective investor whether they planned to vacation themselves at the property, or to trade it for other stays at other places. But there are several problems with doing this: First, it requires a prospect to choose, and people don't like to be made to choose. Choice is not the same, and not as attractive, as customization. People will choose if it's the only way to get what they want, but fundamentally the element of choice can be a burden in the buying process. In addition, having a salesperson introduce product or service features that are truly relevant to a customer has a very favorable effect on the customer's attitude toward the salesperson. Asking the customer outright would give up that benefit. But finally, the prospect or customer himself might not actually know whether or not he will want to trade his property for other vacation spots. So gaining insight into the actual needs of a customer through the use of a "Golden Question" provides a company with a useful way to anticipate that customer's needs.

98   Information about the health care company was gathered from interviews with company executives.

Chapter 6

PREDICTING THE FUTURE

100 The Will Rogers quote shown is reprinted from a website, http://www.zwire.com/site/news.cfm?brd=2256&pag=460&dept_ID=457707, but many different variants of this quotation have appeared in publications and writings. Another site quotes Will Rogers this way: "The stock market is easy. Buy stocks that go up. If they don't go up, don't buy them." (http://www.tradingsmarts.com/stocks.htm). And Will Rogers is quoted in *Gales Quotations: Who Said What* [CD-ROM] Gale Research. Detroit, MI: 1995): "Don't gamble; take all your savings and buy some good stock and hold it till it goes up, then sell it. If it don't go up, don't buy it."

101 Of course, it's not clear that all the companies measuring the value of their customers are using the standards we are discussing here. We used numbers from a Grizzard survey, cited in "Survey: Current Customers Get Renewed Corporate Focus," by Melissa Campanelli, Senior Editor, *DM News*, October 1, 2004.

103 The information from the large consumer service business is proprietary, but was documented for us in an email from a colleague sent to the authors in May 2004 that included this statement we've been allowed to share: "For a very high level summary of the LTV [lifetime value] calculation, we ran a regression to see what independent variables affect a [customer's] likelihood of returning. We then used the coefficients of the successful variables to create a formula for predicting future revenue for each [customer]. At least one of these was external – something like consumer confidence. Finally we applied the historical contribution of each [customer] to get to future contribution. Our LTV calculation contains only future expected contribution. We applied the formula to historical customer data to get LTV from previous years."

103 See Appendix 3 for a more complete review of customer lifetime valuation.

104 We've already discussed the elements of a lifetime value equation in great detail, but there is an increasing level of academic interest in this issue. Some of this discussion and research is driven by an effort to explain the Internet stock bubble. For example, one study of business-to-consumer Internet companies found that a website's reach and "stickiness" (that is, visitor retention) were closely correlated with genuine market value, as evidenced by the fact that those dot-com firms whose websites had relatively less reach and stickiness tended to lose a great deal more of their value when the bubble burst. "A Rude Awakening: Internet Shakeout in 2000," in *Review of Accounting Studies*, 2001, 6, pp.331–359.

104 For the study on Ameritrade, E*TRADE, eBay, Amazon, and Capital One, see "Valuing Customers" by Sunil Gupta, Donald R. Lehmann, and Jennifer Ames Stuart, *Journal of Marketing Research* , Vol. 41, No. 1, February 2004, pp.7–18.

104 In addition to these companies' rapid growth as high-profile Internet companies creating their own, self-fulfilling stock-market valuation, another possibility, suggested by Gupta, Lehmann, and Stuart in the case of eBay, is that the nature of eBay's business might have some hidden, intrinsic value in itself – either because of network externalities, or because the business involves earning money from both buyers and sellers at once, clouding the definition of "customer."

105 Profit margin on sales, usually referred to as "sales margin," measures the immediate, fully allocated profit earned on the sale of a product or service.

105 Gartner Research notes that "high costs are associated with owning data, and Gartner believes that having bad data can increase these costs by a factor of 10 when one considers the costs arising from bad business decisions and poor CRM based on such data" (see S. Nelson, R. Singhai, W. Janowski, and N. Frey, "Customer Data Quality and Integration: The Foundation of Successful CRM," Gartner Research, *Strategic Analysis Report* R-14-7181, November 26, 2001). Also see Don Hinman and Bob Wallach. "High Cholesterol Databases – Is Your Data Quality Slowly Killing Your Business?" Webcast presented on December 18, 2003, AMA Marketing Effectiveness Online Seminar Series, http://www.acxiom.com/subimages/1218200324918highcholesterolslidepres.ppt

107 Hang onto your hat. Here we are, all trying to be quite serious about the development of usable and increasingly refined predictors of human behavior, but just when we were all convinced that devining future human behavior would forever remain in the realm of predictive modeling, based on just the kind of leading indicators we're talking about here, along come the "pioneer neuroeconomists," who are using frontal-lobe brain research to predict the decisions a "customer" in a lab setting is about to make. We can't make this stuff up! According to Eric Roston ("The Why of Buy," *Time*, New York, March 8, 2004, Vol. 163, Issue 10, p.80), "The trouble with homo economicus is that he has little to do with his emotional, dimwitted half-brother, homo sapiens, who bought Petsmart.com on a hunch." Like the weather, humans are predictable, but never perfectly.

108 Royal Bank of Canada uses Teradata to drive customer-specific decisions. The bank deserves its own book for its innovative thinking, culture of customer-centricity, focused management, and serving as a world-class example of the business case for building customer value on purpose. See Don Peppers and Martha Rogers, Ph.D., *The One to One Manager: Real-World Lessons in Customer Relationship Management* (Currency/Doubleday: New York), 1999, pp.121–129.

109 The details here on Royal Bank of Canada are from Cathy Burrows' presentation to the Executive Education Program on "Managing Customer Value" at Fuqua School of Business at Duke University, September 13, 2004, and from a subsequent telephone interview with Burrows and Mark Vermeersch at Centra Bank.

109 Customer attitudes, like other "soft" (non-financial) measures, have proven to be the epicenter of a controversy. On one side are those who believe that customer attitudes, brand value, employee turnover, and other non-financial measures will prove to be clear predictors of future performance, and on the other side are those who maintain that a lot of what we believe, such as "customer satisfaction adds value," and "reduced employee turnover reduces costs," is simply folklore. See Robert Bruce, "Non Financial Measures Just Don't Add Up," *Financial Times*, March 29, 2004, p.10. You may also want to see other recent work, including:

- Capon, Noel, John U. Farley, and Scott Hoenig, "Determinants of Financial Performance: A Meta-Analysis," *Management Science*, 36 (10), 1990, pp.1143–1159.
- Danaher, Peter J. and Roland T. Rust, "Indirect Financial Benefits from Service Quality," *Quality Management Journal*, 1996, (3), pp.63–75.
- Gitomer, Jeffrey, *Customer Satisfaction is Worthless; Customer Loyalty is Priceless*, Bard Press, 1998.
- Ittner, Christopher, and David F. Larcker, "Are Non-Financial Measures Leading Indicators of Financial Performance? An Analysis of Customer Satisfaction," *Journal of Accounting Research*, Vol. 36, 1998, pp.1–36. A careful documentation of the different analyses conducted or reviewed by the authors, regarding customer satisfaction and its relationship to financial success. Finds "a positive and statistically significant relation between stock prices and ACSI scores; however, this significance is much lower than that of the recorded assets and liabilities." As we read it, the article looks at customer satisfaction measured at the customer level, the business unit level, and the enterprise level, and statistically correlates the customer satisfaction index, or CSI, to financial success using a number of different variables. What the authors found is that CSI is indeed highly correlated to *future* financial performance up to a point, after which there is a leveling off – that is, moving from .6 to .7 is clearly beneficial, but going from .7 to .8 is less so and going from .8 to .9 or higher may provide no help at all (or even cost more than it returns), and thus go beyond the "optimization" we've been discussing. This validates the work of Ray Kordupleski and others which notes that if it is to be correlated with business performance, then customer satisfaction must be measured *relative* to the competitive set ("I can be happy with you but still leave and go somewhere else where I'll also be happy.") Certainly, as quality becomes ubiquitously available it is less compelling in terms of keeping customers loyal. The point Ittner and Larcker lay out here and elsewhere is that making 75% of your customers highly satisfied instead of 50% is almost certainly a worthy goal, but going from, say, 90% to 95% will probably cost more in extra services and expense than it will return in value. See also Raymond E. Kordupleski and Roger W. Gallagher, *Customer Value Management – The CVA 2000 Collection*. Customer Value Management New Zealand Ltd., 1999.
- Matthew Thomson, Deborah J. MacInnis, and C. Whan park, "The Ties That Bind: Measuring the Strength of Consumers' Emotional Attachments to Brands," *Journal of Consumer Psychology*, 15 (1), pp. 77–91.
- Itamar Simonson, "Determinants of Customers' Response to Customized Offers: Conceptual Framework and Research Propositions," *Journal of Marketing*, Winter 2005, pp. 32–51.

- Richard Lambert, "Customer Satisfaction and Future Financial Performance, A Discussion: Are Non-Financial Measures Leading Indicators of Financial Performance? An Analysis of Customer Satisfaction," *Journal of Accounting Research*, Vol. 36, 1998, pp.37–46. Discussion of Ittner and Larcker's 1998 paper on non-financial measures. Lambert notes that a review of the literature revealed conflicting evidence.
- Christopher D. Ittner and David F. Larcker laments the fact that businesses are measuring all sorts of financial metrics but are doing so willy-nilly, without paying attention to the "causal mode" connecting the metric to actual value creation. Have a look at "Coming Up Short on Nonfinancial Performance Measurement," *Harvard Business Review* (Nov. 2003), pp.88–95. This article is a must-read, for its sheer entertainment value. It documents a riotous corporate metrics environment at many firms (most unnamed). Larcker says companies need to know *how* a non-financial metric can be expected to add value. We suggest, modestly, that ROC is **the** causal model.
- Anderson, Eugene W., Claes Fornell, and Donald R. Lehmann, "Customer Satisfaction, Market Share, and Profitability: Findings from Sweden," *Journal of Marketing*, July 1994, 58, pp. 53–66.
- Banker, Rajiv D., Gordon Potter, Shinu Srinivasan, "An Empirical Investigation of an Incentive Plan that includes Nonfinancial Performance Measures," *The Accounting Review*, January 2000, 75 (I), pp. 65–92.
- Foster, George, and Mahendra Gupta, "Marketing, Cost Management and Management Accounting," *Journal of Management Accounting Research*, Fall 1994, 6, pp. 44–77.

110 But measuring customer satisfaction is not as straightforward as it might sound. See the discussion in Don Peppers and Martha Rogers, Ph.D., *Enterprise One to One: Tools for Competing in the Interactive Age,* Doubleday/Currency, 1997, p.116 ff. Although we know "customer satisfaction" has ardent supporters for lots of good reasons, in our mind, the greatest criterion for its value as a metric is whether or not it is a good predictor of future customer value.

110 See Ittner, Christopher, and David F. Larcker, "Are Non-Financial Measures Leading Indicators of Financial Performance? An Analysis of Customer Satisfaction," *Journal of Accounting Research*, Vol. 36, 1998, pp.1–36. Also see Ellen Garbarino & Mark S. Johnson, "The Different Roles of Satisfaction, Trust and Commitment in Customer Relationships," *Journal of Marketing,* April 1999, Vol. 63, pp.70–87. These researchers found that for low-relational customers, satisfaction is a better predictor of future behavior, but for high relational customers, trust and commitment are more important.

110 The National Quality Research Center finding was cited in "No-Frills CRM," by Viren Doshi and Richard Verity, in Booz Allen Hamilton's *Resilience Report,* a monthly e-update of *Strategy & Business*, found online at http://www.strategy-business.com/resilience/rr00009, also found in *Strategy& Business,* Fall 2004, pp.8–10.

110 For more about the Roper Starch and Peppers and Rogers Group study, see "Customer Relationship Management in Financial Services: A National Perspective," Roper Starch Worldwide, CNO-385, September, 2000. For an in-depth description of the research, see: Brookner, Jonathan and Julien Beresford, "One to One in Retail Financial Services: New Strategies for Creating Value Through Customer Relationships," Peppers and Rogers Group and LOMA (Life Office Management Association, Inc.), 2001.

110 In one article, David Myron notes that ". . . bundling two services usually reduces customer churn by 25%. Bundling a third product reduces it by an additional 13%, and a fourth product reduces churn by an additional 6%." ("Telecoms Focus on Services, Not Price, to Reduce Churn," *Customer Relationship Management*, May, 2004, p.18). Susana Schwartz reported that "in fact, Yankee Group finds that tying two services together causes churn to fall by one-quarter; tying three causes it to fall another eighth; and adding a forth leads to churn rates falling an additional sixteenth" in her article, "The Race to Bundle Voice, Data and Video," *Billing World and OSS Today*, June, 2004, pp.20-26. And Michelle L. Hankins asserts that ". . . churn costs the telecom industry $10 billion a year. On average it costs a provider $60 to retain a customer but $350 to $400 to acquire a new one . . ." and that "every time you cross-sell a service to a customer, you decrease churn by one-third," in her article, "Carriers Struggle to Control Churn," *Billing World and OSS Today*, January, 2003, pp.36–40.

110 Carlson Marketing Group is the parent company of Peppers and Rogers Group.

111 RSx is a proprietary framework for measuring relationship strength, developed by Dr. Thomas D. Lacki, Linda Vytlacil, and Jeffery M. Weiner of Carlson Marketing Group in close collaboration with Dr. Robert M. Morgan at the University of Alabama. The reported results were generated by a series of three pilot studies conducted by Carlson Marketing Group between May 2000 and October 2001.

113 An additional by-product of the British Airways initiative was that career paths for the Executive Club Member Services agents were improved, allowing the carrier to attract and retain higher-quality agents. Today there is, in fact, virtually no turnover among those agents. Our information about British Airways came from an internal Carlson Marketing Group report, confirmed in e-mails with BAUSA employees.

113 We introduced the term "ROC Dashboard" in 2004. See Don Peppers and Martha Rogers Ph.D., "Reading the ROC Dashboard," *Inside 1to1 Strategy* (online newsletter available at www.1to1.com).

114 We pulled the quote about leading indicators from Paul D. Berger, Ruth N. Bolton, Douglas Bowman, Elten Briggs, V. Kumar, A. Parasuraman, Creed Terry, "Marketing Actions and the Value of Customer Assets: A Framework for Customer Asset Management," *Journal of Service Research*, Vol. 5, No. 1, August 2002, pp.39–54. Develops a framework for assessing how marketing actions affect customer LTV (emphasis added).

114 By remembering that maximizing ROC is an optimization problem, we can think more clearly about the true economic cost vs. benefit tradeoff inherent in various types of interruptive marketing, including telemarketing, direct mail, email, and other forms of outbound marketing messages. Research by advertising and direct marketing agencies, as well as by academic investigators, has shown that it often requires more than one "hit" to communicate a message to, or elicit a response from, a consumer. A television ad, for instance, might require three to five exposures before most consumers actually absorb it and can "play back" its central message for a researcher, but after certain number of exposures, there is no increase in recall. See Krugman, Herbert, "Why Three Exposures May Be Enough," *Journal of Advertising Research*, 1972, 12, pp.11–14.

114 We pulled the Kaplan and Norton quoted from the website: http://www.balancedscorecard.org/basics/bsc1.html, 12 January 2004.

116 Thanks to Christian Neckermann for the pharma optimization curve illustration.

116 Information about imsHealth pulled from their website, *imsHealth.com*:
     http://www.imshealth.com/ims/portal/front/articleC/0,2777,6599_18731_40198214,00.html.

Chapter 7

STRATEGY: ROC IN A HOSTILE ENVIRONMENT

120 ABB's corporate website, *www.ABB.com* October 2004. For more about ABB, see
     "Beyond Better Products: Capturing Value in Customer Interactions," by Mark
     Vandenbosch and Niraj Dawar, *MIT Sloan Management Review*, Summer 2002, Vol.
     43, No. 4, 35–42.

120 Too many companies choose to benchmark, sometimes slavishly, in order to learn
     and reproduce "best practices." While an understanding of successful players is
     important, copying the strategies of others, rather than developing a unique com-
     petitive advantage, can result in "a race to the bottom." See Philipp M. Nattermann,
     "Best Practice Does Not Equal Best Strategy," *The McKinsey Quarterly*, 17 August
     2004.

120 For more about Orica, see "Deriving Value from Customer Relations," *Financial Times*
     supplement, Mastering Innovation, October 1, 2004 (UK edition), by Mark
     Vandenbosch and Niraj Dawar, pp.6–8. See also "Beyond Better Products: Capturing
     Value in Customer Interactions," by Mark Vandenbosch and Niraj Dawar, *MIT Sloan
     Management Review*, Summer 2002, Vol. 43, No. 4, pp.35–42.

122 Michael Porter frequently cites Southwest as an example of clear strategic execution,
     for example. See *Competitive Advantage: Creating and Sustaining Superior
     Performance,* New York: Free Press, 1985, pp.107–109.

123 Southwest focuses on keeping costs – and prices – low. See:

   • Southwest Airlines, "Customer Service Commitment," November 14, 2003: "To
     keep our fares low, we do not serve or sell prepared meals onboard any of our
     flights," and "To keep our fares low by maintaining the efficiency of our own
     operation, Southwest Airlines makes reservations and sells tickets exclusively
     for travel on our airline and over our routes," and "We do not share flight num-
     bers, issue tickets, transfer Customers, transfer baggage, or accept reservations
     for travel on any other airline".
   • McKenzie, Daniel, "Southwest Airlines Co." Citigroup Global Markets, April 20,
     2004, via Thomson Research/Investext : "…because Southwest does not go
     after connecting traffic, the carrier does not interline with other airlines" and "all
     seating is one class," and "because each plane sits parked only for about 25
     minutes on average between flights (versus about 50 minutes to an hour for its
     hub-and-spoke peers), its planes are up in the sky collecting revenues more fre-
     quently than those of its hub-and-spoke peers."
   • O'Brian, Bridget, "Flying on the Cheap: Southwest Airlines Is A Rare Air Carrier:
     It Still Makes Money – Proficient at Its Short Hops, It Keeps Fares So Low It
     Competes With Buses – Lots of Jokes but No Meals," *Wall Street Journal*.
     October 26, 1992. p.A.1: "Travel agents won't find Southwest in any of the big
     reservations computers because it deems booking fees too costly" and "…at

Southwest: 80% of its 1,300 flights a day get into the air as quickly as Flight 944" [i.e., "in less than 15 minutes"].

- Trottman, Melanie, "New Atmosphere: Inside Southwest Airlines, Storied Culture Feels Strains; Spirit of Fun and Hard Work Is Clouded by Picketing And Employee Complaints; No Longer the Underdog," *The Wall Street Journal*, July 11, 2003, p.A1: "By offering a generous profit-sharing and stock-option plan, and creating a "we're all family" culture with office parties and advancement opportunities, Southwest has spurred its employees to continually boost productivity and profits. And it has engendered a fiercely loyal and competitive work force along the way." The article does discuss the fact that the "culture is showing signs of strain", Southwest is "seeing more problems as it moves from adolescence to adulthood."

123 Michael Porter points out that a successful strategy does not rely on a single strength or feature of the business, such as a "core" competency or a "key" success factor, but is instead based on a network of interlocking policies and unique activities that fit together to block competitors from mimicking the strategy. The more interlocking components there are to a strategy, the stronger and more effective the strategy will be. See "What is Strategy?" in *Harvard Business Review*, November–December 1996, pp.61–78, at p.70. Also see Michael E. Porter, Michael E. *Competitive Advantage: Creating and Sustaining Superior Performance.* New York: The Free Press, 1985 and Michael E. Porter, *Competitive Strategy: Techniques for Analyzing Industries and Competitors.* New York: The Free Press, 1980.

123 FedEx is the name of today's company, but it began life as "Federal Express."

123 See more about FedEx in *Competitive Advantage*, Michael Porter, 1985, p.109.

124 The Canadian professors are Mark Vandenbosch and Niraj Dawar. See "Deriving Value from Customer Relations," *Financial Times* supplement, Mastering Innovation, October 1, 2004 (UK edition), by Mark Vandenbosch and Niraj Dawar, pp.6–8. See also "Beyond Better Products: Capturing Value in Customer Interactions," by Mark Vandenbosch and Niraj Dawar, MIT *Sloan Management Review*, Summer 2002, Vol. 43, No. 4, pp.35–42.

125 We introduced the phrase "learning relationship" in Pine, Joseph B., Don Peppers, and Martha Rogers, "Do You Want to Keep Your Customers Forever?" *Harvard Business Review*, March–April, 1995, pp.103–114. The concept was expanded in Don Peppers, Martha Rogers, and Bob Dorf, *The One to One Fieldbook: The Complete Toolkit for Implementing a 1to1 Marketing Program.* New York: Doubleday, 1999.

127 See Michael Treacy and Fred Wiersema, *The Discipline of Market Leaders: Choose Your Customers, Narrow Your Focus, Dominate Your Market,* Reading, MA: Addison-Wesley Publishing Company, 1995. The "disciplines" themes in Treacy and Wiersema's book build on prior work by Michael Porter (*Competitive Advantage: Creating and Sustaining Superior Performance,* New York: The Free Press, 1985 and *Competitive Strategy: Techniques for Analyzing Industries and Competitors.* New York: The Free Press, 1980). For a description of the intellectual bridge between the work of Treacy and Wiersema and Porter, see: Phillip Sadler, "The success formula," *Director*, October 1995, p.101; and Howard R. Gold, "Paths to Greatness," *Barron's*, February 27, 1995, p.52.

129 One example of how customer insight can boost a product innovator's strategy is Perdigão, a consumer goods company in Brazil, which has focused on product quality and innovation since it started as a small grocery store run by Italian immigrants 69 years ago. Until recently customer contact consisted of inbound calls to the service center, and contact from the sales agent. In 2002, Perdigão installed my SAP CRM in order to automate, track, and simplify the resolution process. Results: Average 30-day improvement in response time to customer complaints, and predicted 52% improvement on internal rate of return. See a more complete report in Tom Spitale and Laura Cococcia, "Don't Sacrifice Product Innovation for Customer Insight," *Inside 1to1,* June 14, 2004.

130 While structural issues require a firm to concentrate primarily on providing one benefit or another in order to succeed competitively, the customers themselves want all three benefits – best product, most complete service, lowest price. *Every customer* wants good products at low prices with complete service, even though they may vary in their willingness to trade off one benefit for another. As a result, many firms buy from and ally themselves with other firms, as necessary to satisfy customer demands.

132 We pulled the "loyalty" quote from the Enterprise website: (http://aboutus.enterprise.com/who_we_are/mission.html, accessed March 2005).

132 Thanks to Bob Langer, Tom Spitale, Vernon Tirey, Steve Skinner, and Lorenz Esguerra for their perspectives on the issues in this section on "tough customers." The term "oppressive-but-necessary customers" is from Tom Spitale.

133 We pulled the corporate information about Magna from Magna.com in September 2004. "Magna employs approximately 81,000 people at 219 manufacturing divisions and 49 product development and engineering centers throughout North and South America, Mexico, Europe and Asia." See http://www.magna.com/magnaWeb.nsf/webpages/Company+Info?OpenDocument.

133 For more about Magna, see "Beyond Better Products: Capturing Value in Customer Interactions," by Mark Vandenbosch and Niraj Dawar, MIT *Sloan Management Review*, Summer 2002, Vol. 43, No. 4, pp.35–42.

Chapter 8

MAKING IT HAPPEN: THE ADOPTION CHALLENGE

138 We pulled the first opening quotation in the chapter from: http://home.att.net/~quotations/motivation.html, October 2004.

138 We pulled the second opening quotation from: http://home.att.net/~quotesexchange/yogiberra.html, October 2004.

138 Thanks to Peter Zencke, member of the executive team at SAP, for this enterprise-wide perspective of ROC.

142 When "customer relationship management" initiatives don't meet their objectives, there are basically three reasons:

1   The "strategy" problem, or not having a clear understanding of what the customer strategy should accomplish for the company (Ready-fire-aim!).

2   The "information" problem, which results from disconnected information about any one customer (Your customer has one view of your company. Do you have a single view of your customer?).

3   The "adoption" problem (Customer initiatives can't be installed. They must be adopted.).

See "When Information Becomes a Problem," Don Peppers and Martha Rogers, *Inside 1to1 Strategy*, February 2003.

144 Although they include issues in addition to those related to adoption and organization, we found it very useful to see David Bell, John Deighton, Werner J. Reinartz, Roland T. Rust, and Gordon Swartz, "Seven Barriers to Customer Equity Management," *Journal of Services Management*, Vol. 5, No. 1, August 2002, pp.77–85. The seven barriers are: lack of individual-level, enterprise-wide data, failure to track marketing's effects on the balance sheet (not just the income statement), need to model future revenues appropriately, the need to maximize customer lifetime value and not just measure it, the need to align the organization with customer management activities, the imperative of respecting customer information, and the challenge of evolving the chairman from an efficiency tool to a service improvement tool.

Also see Philippe Haspeslagh, Tomo Noda, and Fares Boulos, "Managing for Value: It's Not Just about the Numbers," *Harvard Business Review*, July–August 2001, pp.64–75, and Anupam Agarwal, David P. Harding and Jeffrey R. Schumacher, "Organizing for CRM," *The McKinsey Quarterly*, 20 July 2004. Too few companies pay enough attention to the organizational challenges, must go beyond "vigorous exhortations and heavy handed rollouts" and address fuzzy accountability and resistance to change.

Also see "Mastering CRM," a white paper by Chris Nadherny and Conchita Robinson of Spencer Stuart in Chicago, which examines the elements required for CRM success.

144 Larry Selden, and Geoffrey Colvin. *Angel Customers and Demon Customers: Discover Which is Which and Turbo-charge Your Stock.* New York: Penguin Group 2003. We spoke to Geoff in a phone interview August 13, 2004.

144 John P. Kotter and Dan Cohen *The Heart of Change*. Boston: Harvard Business School Press, 2002. Also see Tom Rothand Donald O. Clifton, *How Full Is Your Bucket?*, Gallup Press, 2004, excerpted in "Are Your Employees Scaring Off Customers?" by Tom Roth and Donald O. Clifton, *The Gallup Management Journal*, September 9, 2004. And see Simon Knox, Stan Maklan, Adrian Payne, Joe Peppard, and Lynette Ryals, *Customer Relationship Management: Perspectives from the Marketplace*, Butterworth/Heinemann, 2003.

145 Thanks to Marijo Puleo at Carlson Marketing Group, and the Peppers and Rogers Group Organizational Transformation Center of Excellence for helping us to think through these ideas.

145 Trilogy, the consulting firm assisting Tesco with the initiative, has won awards from Guardian Newspapers and from the Management Consultancies Association for

their work. See web links:
http://www.mca.org.uk/MCA/News/NewsArticle.aspx?NewsID=64
and http://www.interactiontraining.com/p/results1.html. Also *Guardian* Unlimited
(UK) (02/19/04), p.6.

145 See Philippe Haspeslagh, Tomo Noda, and Fares Boulos, "Managing for Value: It's Not Just About the Numbers," *Harvard Business Review*, July–August 2001, pp.64–75.

146 The story about Boise is based on Peppers and Rogers Group work, as well as an article from Alice Dragoon's article in *Darwin* magazine, "This Changes Everything," March 2002, pp.30–42. Also thanks to Dave Johnson for his input.

148 Another key, ground-breaking adoption effort at Boise dealt with a problem that many organizations face in attempting to implement customer-facing strategies – the need for business units and the IT organization to work together closely, quickly, and effectively. In the customer-facing arena, the need is acute because of the requirement for rapid iterations of business process, data, and technology change leading to a final solution. This is further compounded by the ever-changing business requirements in a customer-facing solution. Boise effectively bridged this gap through a series of adoption mechanisms, including formal cross-functional teams, establishment of common performance measurements, and links to compensation. The final result was a high-speed implementation of the overall solution. As Dave Goudge noted, "The organization in essence learned a whole new way to do projects, which we have carried over to other initiatives." By adopting these combined business/IT principles, Boise was able to achieve objectives in less than a year – a performance far beyond the capabilities of many other firms.

149 We had a chance to catch up with Dave Goudge in September 2004. He shared some of the Boise details with us.

149 Customer-retention information from Alice Dragoon's article in *Darwin* magazine, "This Changes Everything," March 2002, pp.30–42.

149 The Boise customer quotation came from "JH," a Key Accounts Manager for a "major vendor" for Boise, provided for us by Dave Goudge.

150 See *Doing CRM right: What it takes to be successful with CRM*, a white paper by IBM Business Consulting Services, April 2004, quoted at p.3 and p.5.

152 See "Gartner Attendees: Cost is King," by Thomas Hoffman, in *ComputerWorld*, October 8, 2002. It could easily be argued that a large, established airline such as United or Delta will *never* be able to duplicate what JetBlue has done, because the work rules imposed by their unionized workforces have ossified each company's employee culture. In such cases, it might just be better to start over – with an entirely new organization, such as Ted or Song.

153 Julie Strickland was quoted in a Blue Pumpkin press release, October 14, 2002 ("Blue Pumpkin and JetBlue Airways Reinvent Customer Service," PR Newswire).

Chapter 9

DELIVERING VALUE *TO* CUSTOMERS TO BUILD ROC

157 The Ritz ladies and gentlemen quotation is cited online at http://www.expert-magazine.com/EMOnline/RC/part2.htm in an article entitled "My Pleasure: The Ritz-Carlton Hotel PART II," by Bill Lampton, Ph.D. Also see *First, Break All the Rules: What the World's Greatest Managers Do Differently*, by Marcus Buckingham and Curt Coffman, which identifies the needs of employees, and is formulated in a sort of Maslow's needs hierarchy (New York: Simon & Schuster, 1999).

158 Federal Express Corporation won the Baldrige National Quality Program award in 1999. For a listing of award winners, please see: National Institute of Standards and Technology, "1988–2004 Award Recipients' Contacts and Profiles," http://www.quality.nist.gov/Contacts_Profiles.htm.

158 For further information about CRM at FedEx, please see: Yvonne Guzman, "FedEx delivers CRM," SearchCRM.com, April 14, 2004, accessed February 2005, as well as FedEx Corporation, "FedEx Corporation Facts", FedEx Company Web site, http://fedex.com/us/about/today/companies/corporation/facts.html, accessed February 2005.

158 We interviewed officials at Stena by phone in August 2003, including Dan Sten Olsson, CEO; Maude Weideman, Olsson's personal assistant; and Alan Gordon, managing director of the Irish Sea operation.

159 Not only is Southwest Airlines a low-cost carrier but, not unlike some other low-price carriers (Virgin Atlantic and JetBlue, for instance), it enjoys a reputation for very good customer service in the industry. See, for example, National Academy of Science, Transit Cooperative Research Program TCRP Project J–7, Synthesis of Transit Practice 45 – Customer-Focused Transit (2004).

159 Stew Leonard's company still operates in an extremely customer-oriented fashion, under the leadership of CEO Stew Leonard, Jr.

160 For the study by the two New Zealand professors, see "Implementing a Customer Relationship Strategy: The Asymmetric Impact of Poor Versus Excellent Execution," Mark R. Colgate and Peter J. Danaher, in *Journal of the Academy of Marketing Science* (2000), Vol. 28, No. 3, pp.375–387.

161 We've already seen (with the RSx curve in Chapter 6) how a poorly balanced effort can actually erode the effectiveness of a relationship.

163 Thanks to Sophie Vlessing at Peppers and Rogers Group for helping us get the details right in this story about BMW.

161 Information about BMW's "dealer modules" based on interviews with Mike Sachs, Customer Experience Development Manager at BMW and Sophie Vlessing at Peppers and Rogers Group in November 2004. Mike Sachs doesn't refer to BMW as a "manufacturer." He calls BMW the OEM – or original equipment manufacturer.

166 Thanks to Richard Hornby at Peppers and Rogers Group and Julia Beeton at Zurich UK Commercial for helping us to get the facts right on this story about Zurich.

166 One report of the Wharton study appeared as "The Anatomy of a Superior Customer Capability," by George S. Day, *1to1 Magazine*, October 2003.

169 For a lot of the information in this section, thanks to Bill Millar and Chris Helm, as well as a white paper available from SAP: "Supply Chain and Demand Chain Integration: The Pathway to Profit and Competitive Advantage," 2003.

169 This recounting of the occurrences at Volvo is from Hau Lee, "Ultimate Enterprise Value Creation," a white paper for the Stanford Global Supply Chain Management Forum, September 2001. Cited in "Supply Chain and Demand Chain Integration: The Pathway to Profit and Competitive Advantage." See http://www.sap.com/solutions/business-suite/crm/pdf/Misc_Pathway_to_Profit.pdf.

169 We use the term "demand chain" to refer to the "pull" effect of those further down the supply chain – the ones who are buying from *you* or those you sell to. Just as the head end of the supply chain is the miner who extracts ore from the earth and sells to a manufacturer, the head end of the demand chain is an individual consumer.

170 Facts about SPAR drawn from company website April 2004 as well as a telephone interview we had with Gordon Campbell, CEO of SPAR, on Feb 10, 2003, and on information received from Dr. Dieter Dornauer, Managing Director of SPAR Austria.

170 Deloitte Research, "Consumer Business Digital Loyalty Networks: Increasing Shareholder Value Through Customer Loyalty and Network Efficiency" Deloitte and Touche (2002). Italics added in the quotation. Also see a 2001 white paper authored by Prof. Hau L. Lee, director of the Stanford Global Supply Chain Management Forum, which documents several additional examples of companies that have used customer insight to drive more efficient and flexible supply-chain activities, with profitable results. Zara, for instance, an apparel giant in Spain, has achieved a sales growth of 20% in consecutive years since 1990, and its profit margin of 10% is the highest in its competitive set. Lee says these results stemmed from Zara's "extensive use of sales and demographics data to create new products on a rolling basis, price their products aggressively, and quickly make products obsolete in response to market signals."

Chapter 10

ROC AND THE ECONOMICS OF YOUR ENTERPRISE

174 EVA® and Economic Value Added are trademarked terms of Stern Stewart & Co. What is perhaps most important about the EVA concept is the issue of measurement itself. Whether you are a manager, a CEO, or a financial analyst, if you measure, as HSBC did one period, the 11% return on assets, but fail to measure the 13% cost of capital, then your company is always in danger of destroying its own value even while appearing to be profitable and healthy. If you don't track EVA, you and your investors may not even notice the damage being done to your capital base until it is too late. Just as EVA helps a company's managers understand the real cost of capital, ROC *helps those managers understand the real cost of current revenues.*

174 See *Every Manager's Guide to Business Processes* (1995), by Peter G. W. Keen and Ellen M. Knapp. An IT consultant and the author of several books on the topic of how best to deploy and exploit information, Peter Keen has also published *Decision Support Systems* (Addison-Wesley, 1978), and *The Process Edge: Creating Value Where It Counts* (Harvard Business School Press, 1997).

174 One limitation of the traditional EVA metric, however, is that it is a current-period measure. Long-term value can still be sacrificed in exchange for short-term EVA-measured performance.

174 Arthur Andersen LLP, founded in 1913, separated Andersen Consulting (Accenture) from Andersen, in 2000. Andersen's client Enron Corporation passed muster in February 2001 when Andersen stated Enron's financial statements "presented fairly" the client's financial position – a month before Enron entered the largest bankruptcy in history. Andersen, convicted of a felony count of obstruction of justice after shredding thousands of documents, closed its doors for good in August 2002. See David F. Hawkins, and Jacob Cohen, "Arthur Andersen LLP," HBS Case No. 9-103-061. Boston: Harvard Business School Publishing, February 13, 2003. See Joseph Radigan, "Closing the Books on Arthur Andersen," CFO.com, August 30, 2002, http://www.cfo.com/printable/article.cfm/3006242?f=options, accessed February, 2005; James W. Semple., "Accountants' liability after Enron," *FDCC Quarterly*, Fall 2002, 53(1), pp.85–98; Jennifer M. Niece and Gregory M. Trompeter, "The Demise of Arthur Andersen's One-Firm Concept: A Case Study in Corporate Governance," *Business and Society Review*, 2004, 109(2), pp.183–207.

180 In the hypothetical investment example for units K and L, we are assuming that each business unit's Year 2 profit will grow in the same proportion as its Year 2 customer equity has grown.

Chapter 11

ROC THE GOVERNMENT

184 We found the time consistency of economic policy discussion particularly relevant and interesting. See "Edward Prescott and Finn Kydland Win Nobel Economics Prize," Bloomberg newswire, 11 October 2004. Also see "A Nobel Tiger in the Tail," by David R. Henderson, *Wall Street Journal*, October 12, 2004, p.A22, and "Edward Prescott bio," October 12, 2004, Minneapolis *Star Tribune*, cited online at http://www.startribune.com/stories/535/5027745.html.

185 Many thanks to Tim Shorrocks for his insight into how government agencies have come to be so keenly interested in customer-oriented initiatives, and for his advice on the programs being implemented by Inland Revenue, specifically.

185 Utilitarian economics can sound brutal, but it is a field with increasing credibility. To the economist, the questions to ask might be: What is the economic benefit when one person is helped off of unemployment and put to productive work by a government agency's action? How many lives do lower speed limits save, compared to how many extra man-hours are wasted in cars driving more slowly?

186 See "Can Personalization Work for Government?" by Martha Rogers, *Inside 1to1*, April 29, 2002.

186 Accenture ranks Canada as the world's most advanced government when it comes to e-thinking in the white paper *E-Government Leadership: Engaging the Customer*, Accenture, 2003.

187 The quote about Canada's GOL is from their website, http://www.gol-ged.gc.ca/.

187 For further information about Inland Revenue, please see: Mila D'Antonio and Marji McClure, "Customer Crusaders," *1to1 Magazine*, April, 2004, 6(3), pp.17–25; and Don Peppers and Martha Rogers, "Who's Leading the Customer Revolution?" *Inside 1to1*, April 19, 2004.

Chapter 12

VIOLATE YOUR CUSTOMER'S TRUST AND KISS YOUR ASSET GOOD-BYE

191 See Margaret Webb Pressler, "So Close at the Hairdresser's," *The Washington Post*, August 1, 2004.

193 Many firms act as though there is a "parallel universe" for business. For the original discussion about the "parallel universe," see Chapter 2.

193 Learn more about the Ponemon Institute at www.ponemon.org. One of the authors serves on the Board.

193 Although we only mention "privacy legislation" in passing, we are very concerned about it. Unfortunately, the bad guys make it necessary to legislate parameters for use of customer data, but we need more expert input into these measures. Gramm-Leach-Bliley is a flop.So we have to ask: At what point does legislation create more problems for consumers that it solves? If all companies are highly regulated and compliance makes all companies look the same from a "privacy" perspective, then will customers lose the potential to evaluate the trustworthiness of companies from the most visitable manifestation? Right now, differences in creating and rationalizing privacy policies can tell a customer a lot about which company to do business with. If all privacy policies look the same, won't trust for all companies, ironically, decline? A report from Forrester Research ("Who Consumers Trust with Personal Data," Technographics Research North America, June 7, 2002), by Jed Kolko and Gillian DeMoulin, indicates that "consumers are overwhelmingly skeptical about companies' promises that they won't misuse personal data." The results of the study can be summarized in three points:

● Consumers are wary of companies' privacy claims.
● Confidence is not gained easily.
● Consumers don't trust service firms, especially ISP, phone, cable, and wireless companies.

195 Yahoo! sent the following message to one of the authors (**emphasis added**):

Your privacy is very important to us here at Yahoo!. We are sending you this email to let you know that we have updated our Privacy Policy. You can read our updated Privacy Policy by visiting Yahoo!'s comprehensive Privacy Center.

Our commitment to privacy hasn't changed. We believe that you should understand what we do with your information and what choices you have. So why are we revising our Privacy Policy? To streamline it and make changes to address several important topics.

In recent years, we have added a Children's Privacy Policy and Privacy Information for users of Yahoo!'s financial products and services, in accordance with requirements of federal legislation. We at Yahoo! have become increasingly aware of questions about how data is treated when a user's safety may be at risk, when fraud or illegal activities may be occurring, or when companies are combined. We feel that the time is right to streamline our privacy policies into a single, comprehensive policy and to address these and other issues in the process. Please take a moment to visit our Privacy Center and read our updated Privacy Policy. (Note: The Yahooligans! Privacy Policy, for our children's website, has not changed. Although the format and some parts of the Yahoo! Privacy Policy have been updated, our collection, use, and treatment of information from kids under age 13 remains unchanged.)

In order to keep you up to date about our many new products and services and how they might be of use to you, we have created a new Marketing Preferences page within the Account Information area. It is designed to make it easier for you to manage the marketing communications you receive from Yahoo! and ensure you get the latest relevant information to meet your needs. **We have reset your marketing preferences and, unless you decide to change these preferences, you may begin receiving marketing messages from Yahoo!** *about ways to enhance your Yahoo! experience, including special offers and new features. Your new marketing preferences will not take effect until 60 days after the date of this mailing, so you have plenty of time to decide what you want to receive and what you don't. To change your preferences, go to the Marketing Preferences page.*

Yahoo! recognizes that while we've grown and changed, things in your life have probably also changed. You may have a new job, a different email address, a new house, or different interests. We invite you to take this opportunity to update your personal information so you can continue to receive content and advertising that is most relevant and interesting to you. **Please do not reply to this message. If you have any questions about these changes, please visit our Frequently Asked Questions page.**

Thank you,

The Yahoo! Team

197 We got the quotes about disseminating information from "The devil's in Pac Bell's phone bill details," by David Lazarus, *San Francisco Chronicle*, November 27, 2002.

197 Lesson learned: A friend received a call late one Friday evening from her pension company – a major American financial institution. The caller offered to perform a simple, useful task, and asked for a piece of information to accomplish the mission. Our friend gave it, and immediately regretted it, realizing that the caller might not be

from the company. As soon as the call ended, she went to the company's website to find the number to call to check on and secure her account. Result? There isn't one that she could call at 9 pm on Friday. She'd have to wait until Monday morning to speak to a representative! Very worried, she pulled her paper file, dug through the many documents and mailings, and finally discovered a number where she could leave a message – that was the "Special Security" number. She also did everything she could to send an email, just to notify the company of a potential problem. She called her attorney. On Monday morning, she was relieved to discover there was no problem, and that the company had taken measures to make sure no third party could have tampered with her account. But she tried to convince them that taking those measures was not enough. Protecting her data and her accounts was not enough. She needed a way to communicate whenever she needed to about her data's security, and her privacy.

197 See Yankelovich, 2004, *A Crisis of Confidence: Rebuilding the Bonds of Trust/State of Consumer Trust*, by Craig Wood, presentation, June 2–4, Chicago, IL: 10th Annual Fred Newell CRM conference.

197 More insight from Yankelovich, Inc. 2004.

197 The survey, conducted by TNS on behalf of Accenture, polled 1,000 American adults. It was designed to determine the level of customer satisfaction and loyalty across 17 industries (see "Two-Thirds of U.S. Consumers Would Pay More in Exchange for Better-Valued Services, Accenture Survey Finds," *Business Wire*, August 5, 2004). Also see William C. Taylor, "Companies Find They Can't Buy Love with Bargains," *The New York Times,* August 8, 2004, Sunday Business section, p.5.

198 The story about Gateway is from *Inside 1to1*, August 30, 2004, "Do You Practice What You Preach?" by Mike Spinney, www.1to1.com. Gateway Learning Corp.is in no way connected with the better-known computer company with a similar name.

199 We got this great quote from a telephone interview with Jennifer Barrett August 11, 2004.

200 Note: Responsible Information Stewardship®, or RIS®, is a registered service mark of Peppers and Rogers Group. See "Privacy: Beyond Compliance: Responsible Information Stewardship." Peppers & Rogers Group, White Paper. Norwalk: Peppers & Rogers Group, 2003. http://www.1to1.com/DocumentDownload.aspx?DOC_ID=26320, accessed December 2004. Also see Larry Ponemon "Exceed Customer Expectations with Responsible Information Management," *Inside 1to1*, February 17, 2003, http://www.1to1.com/View.aspx?DocID=25988, accessed February 2005 as well as Cheryl Krivda, "Privacy Principles Pay Off," *Business 2.0*, May, 2003, 4(4), p.40.

200 We pulled the "elements" of privacy from www.1to1.com and from Larry Ponemon, "Responsible Information Management: It's a Matter of Trust," *1to1 Magazine*, March, 2003, pp.43–44.

201 "Why Consumers Trust Certain Companies," *Inside 1to1: Privacy,* January 15, 2004 lists the 10 characteristics of the most trusted companies, based on a perception study by the Ponemon Institute:
1   Strong commitment to honoring their privacy obligation to customers, employees, and other stakeholders.
2   A belief that the value proposition of good privacy is more than compliance with laws and regulations.

3   Communication of privacy obligations to consumers in a clear and concise way.
4   Extra steps to control, manage and limit third-party data sharing through legal agreements as well as due diligence.
5   A formal redress program and clear channel for raising questions and concerns.
6   Websites have limited "required" fields from customers.
7   Early adopters of enabling technologies for privacy and information security.
8   Seal programs such as TRUSTe or BBB.Online to verify and demonstrate online compliance.
9   Consistent privacy policies in both the online and offline universe, consistent around the world.
10   Proactivity in improving their information management practices. They tend to keep a low profile about these improvements.

Chapter 13

MANAGING PORTFOLIOS OF CUSTOMERS TO BUILD ENTERPRISE

202 We've heard all the objections to the term "customer management," or "customer relationship management." The argument we hear is that customers don't want to be managed, thank you very much, and we agree. When we talk about managing customers or groups of customers, when we use the terms "relationship management" or "portfolio management," we are referring to making managerial decision to build greater value to customers so they will deliver greater value to the firm.

202 Regardless of whether brands are organized around a constellation of products or of customers, *brand success* can still be measured by ROC, which serves as a great unifier of brand management and relationship management. Customer Portfolio Management will lead to *current payoff and continuous and sustainable payoff*. This is not about scraping by this quarter, or about get-rich-quick. It's about get-rich-and-stay-rich.

203 One question that comes up again and again is this: Your customer has a single view of your entire organization. Do you have a single view of your entire customer? See "Don't Just Measure Customer Value. Manage It", by Christian Neckermann, *Inside 1to1*, August 11, 2004. Also see a cogent article from *The Journal of the Academy of Marketing Science*, by Mark R. Colgate and Peter J. Danaher, "Implementing a Customer Relationship Strategy: The Asymmetric Impact of Poor Versus Excellent Execution" (Vol. 28, No. 3, pp.375–387, Summer 2000) which concludes that a relationship building strategy implemented well can increase satisfaction and loyalty but executing a strategy poorly is worse than not implementing one at all, and the negative effects can exceed the positive benefits of an excellent implementation. We also found it useful to see Neil Woodcock, "Does how customers are managed impact on business performance?" *Interactive Marketing*, Vol. 1, No. 4, pp.375–389, April/June 2000. Initial report from an ongoing study on the impact of CRM on business performance. Hypothesis: "Customers that Manage Customers Well Achieve Better Business Performance Than Those That Do Not." Studied 21 businesses – all top-500 in Europe – and found very high positive correlations between whether a company has developed a set of sensible, observable, well-implemented business practices are very likely to be best-in-class business performers. Not surprisingly, the reverse is also true. If you haven't seen them yet, read *Execution: The Discipline of*

Getting Things Done, by Larry Bossidy, Ram Charan, and Charles Burck Crown Business, 2002, and *Good to Great: Why Some Companies Make the Leap...And Others Don't,* by Jim Collins, Harper Business, 2001.

204 We first used the term "customer portfolio" in 1993, with the publication of *The One to One Future* (Don Peppers and Martha Rogers, Currency/Doubleday), in order to delineate clearly the type of individual customer management we were advocating from the more traditional forms of market segmentation. Since that time, however, some have used the term to suggest a form of risk-spreading, as in modern portfolio theory. In *The Marketing Information Revolution* (1994), edited by Robert C. Blattberg, Rashi Glazer, and John D.C. Little, and published by Harvard Business School Press, Stephan Haeckel wrote a piece suggesting that the information revolution would lead to "customer portfolio management," by which he meant tracking good and bad customers in order to balance the risk and reward of managing each type, "measuring and ensuring the quality of a firm's customer base..." (p.338). Then, in 2003 Ravi Dhar and Rashi Glazer wrote about the same concept in their *Harvard Business Review* article, "Hedging Customers" (May, 2003, p.86). While we acknowledge that portfolio risk is a legitimate concern for managers of large groups of customers, when we employ the term we are not talking about portfolio risk, but portfolio management – specifically, the management of non-overlapping groups of individual customers.

204 See Neil Woodcock, "Does How Customers Are Managed Impact on Business Performance?" *Interactive Marketing*, Vol. 1, No. 4, pp.375–389, April/June 2000.

206 Thanks to Axel Heinemann at Hannover Life Re for helping us tell the Hannover Life Re story. We confirmed details via e-mail in February 2005.

208 It may be useful to see the white paper, *From Interaction to Profit: Customer Experience Management that Drives Results*, prepared by Peppers and Rogers Group, sponsored by Hewlett-Packard, March 2004.

210 For a more comprehensive description of the mass-customization process itself and how it can be applied to facilitate treating different customers differently, see Joe Pine's books on mass customization: *Mass Customization: The New Frontier in Business Competition,* Harvard Business School Press, 1993, by B. Joseph Pine II, revised and reprinted with Stan Davis in 1999; B. Joseph Pine II and James H. Gilmore, *Markets of One: Creating Customer-Unique Value through Mass Customization,* Harvard Business School Press, 2000. Also see Don Peppers and Martha Rogers, *Managing Customer Relationships: A Strategic Framework* (Wiley 2004), Chapter 10, and Don Peppers and Martha Rogers, *Enterprise One to One* (Currency/Doubleday 1997), Chapter 6.

212 The term "capabilities manager" was coined by Joe Pein in his 1993 book *Mass Customization*, mentioned earlier.

214 Our CIBC story is based on our telephone interview with John Moore, CIBC's Senior VP, Personal Banking and Customer Insight Relationship Marketing, August 30, 2004, and on "Improving Growth and Profits through Relationship Marketing," published by APQC and Carlson, 2002, pp.96–106. Thanks to Tom Lacki, one of the coauthors of the white paper.

219 We get a lot of questions about "segments" and "portfolios," so here's a little tutorial on groups of customers, as we see them:

First: the simplest, shortest possible definition of a *customer portfolio*:

A portfolio of customers is a group of customers under management.

"Under management" means a manager has been assigned as traffic cop for these customers, having the authority to determine how each customer is treated by the firm, no matter what medium is used or what product is being promoted.

> *Because the customers in a portfolio are under management, portfolios them-selves* must *be non-overlapping. No customer can have two different traffic cops coordinating for them, because that undermines the whole concept of "management."*

> *Because the customers are under management, the customers* must *be indi-vidually identified and at least a large portion of their interactions and transac-tions must be trackable. Otherwise, it would be impossible to coordinate how the firm treats any single customer.*

We *suggest* holding portfolio managers responsible for maximizing ROC, or at least for considering customer LTVs as well as current profits from customers. This is because the very purpose of coordinating the various transactions with any single customer is to improve the customer's LTV. We suggest this, but it is not a *require-ment* before customers can be considered "under management."

We *suggest* grouping portfolios of customers in terms of similar needs and values. However, this is not a requirement – a portfolio might be composed simply of MVCs, with no needs differentiation, or it might be composed of customers who all frequent a particular sales channel, or it could be some other criterion.

OK, now let's define the concept of a *market "segment"*:

**A market segment is a non-random customer group
selected from a larger market.**

Case closed, no further elaboration required. However we choose to select cus-tomers from a larger market population and place them into a group, provided it's not completely at random, we can then call that group a segment. In practice, everyone uses the terms "market segment" and "customer segment" interchangeably, but in a purely literal sense, looking at a customer segment wouldn't be very pretty.

Here are the implications:

1   Portfolios are market segments under management.

2   A "needs-based group" of customers is a market segment, as is a value tier. MVCs (most valuable customers), MGCs (most growable customers), migrators (we're still figuring out their value) and BZs (below zero customers) can all be market seg-ments, as are demographic and psychographic groups, clusters, and all other categories of customers that are related in any non-random way.

3   Customers can be placed into only one portfolio at a time, but they can be placed into many different market segments simultaneously.

4   Both segments and portfolios are groups of customers with at least something in common – and perhaps a great deal in common. But customers in a portfolio do not necessarily have more (or less) in common with one another than do customers in a segment.

5   Although it's useful to visualize a portfolio as being built one customer at a time, by adding another, then another, it could just as easily be composed of customers all placed under management at the same time, or with the same company decision or policy.

6   A key account manager in a sales organization and a portfolio manager responsible for a portfolio have the same *authority* over their customers. In more progressive sales organizations, the sales manager will be judged by roughly the same criteria, also – that is, a balance of long-term customer value as well as short-term profit results.

7   A "segment manager" differs from a "portfolio manager" in these ways:
    a. He is not a traffic cop, having no actual authority over how the whole enterprise treats the customers in his segment.
    b. His customers are not necessarily individually identified and trackable – although some or all of them might be.
    c. He is most likely judged based on sales or current-period profit, although there is no reason he shouldn't be held accountable for average LTV within his segment, also.

8   Finally, it's been our observation that customers in "segments" are considered to be a marketing responsibility, whereas customers under portfolio management are recognized as the firm's primary asset at enterprise level. In other words, "segments" tend to be a marketing issue and "portfolios" are a boardroom issue. The main role of a Customer Portfolio Manager is to increase the value, today, of current and future customers in his portfolio, and thus his success tracks directly to the success of the firm.

221   One way to think about customer management's natural progression: A company starts with product managers → sales managers/account managers → segment managers. Some of these segment managers are basically customer insight experts and omsbudsmen, whereas others have line authority and accountability and thus become portfolio managers.

222   Our story about Company J came from company executives and consultants working with the company.

Chapter 14

WHO MOVED MY ROI? SHAREHOLDER VALUE, INVESTING, AND CUSTOMER TRUST

225   The Oscar Wilde quote is cited in *Michael Moncur's (Cynical) Quotations* (online reference: http://www.quotationspage.com/quote/27594.html).

228 Bill Dreher was quoted in "The Costco Way," by Stanley Holmes and Wendy Zellner, *BusinessWeek*, April 12, 2004, p.76.

229 For the SEC's intervention on "customers," see "SEC Dials 411 on Telecom Math: Agency Asks Many Companies How They Count Subscribers To Check for Signs of Inflation," by Randall Smith, Shawn Young, and Jesse Drucker, *The Wall Street Journal*, July 1, 2004; p.C1. See also "SEC Probes Hazy Notion of 'Customer,'" by Shawn Young and Peter Grant, *The Wall Street Journal*, July 6, 2004, p.A21, and "SEC Probing Telecoms' Accounting," by *Stephen Taub*, CFO.com, July 6, 2004, cited at http://www.cfo.com/article.cfm/3015039/c_3042606?f=archives&origin=archive.

229 Facts on Lilly ratings came from Elizabeth Kountze and Carla Fried, Steven T. Goldberg, David Landis, Anne Kates Smith, and J. Alex Tarquinio, "Trends You Can Bank On," Kiplinger's Personal Finance, July 2004, 58(7), pp.38–45.

230 This is the same article we quoted earlier: "The Costco Way," by Stanley Holmes and Wendy Zellner, *BusinessWeek*, April 12, 2004, p.76.

Appendix 3

LIFETIME VALUE EQUATIONS AND EXAMPLES

238 See "Customer Lifetime Value: Marketing Models and Applications," by Paul D. Berger and Nada I. Nasr, in *Journal of Interactive Marketing*, Vol. 12, No. 1, Winter 1998, pp.17–30, for a fairly comprehensive set of LTV models for different types of industry structures.

242 *Economist* Magazine, "In Praise of Bayes," September 30, 2000, cited online at http://www.cs.ubc.ca/~murphyk/Bayes/economist.html.

Appendix 4

THE ECONOMICS OF CUSTOMER EQUITY

250 You can learn more about Bass Diffusion Theory in "A New Product Growth Model for Consumer Durables," by Frank M. Bass, 1969 *Management Science* (15)5, pp.215–227.

250 For the study on Ameritrade, E*TRADE, eBay, Amazon, and Capital One, see "Valuing Customers", by Sunil Gupta, Donald R. Lehmann, and Jennifer Ames Stuart, *Journal of Marketing Research*, Vol. 41, No. 1, February 2004, pp.7–18.

251 Thanks to Chris Bassler at Peppers & Rogers Group for his very smart suggestions regarding the relationship between discount rate and customer insight. The work of Rajendra K. Srivastava has also been invaluable: See "Market-Based Assets and Shareholder Value: A Framework for Analysis," by Rajendra K. Srivastava, Tasadduq A. Shervani, and Liam Fahey, in *Journal of Marketing,* January 1998 pp.2–18 for conceptual framework for the marketing-finance interface, and a discussion of how

market-based assets (customer, channel, and partner relationships) increase share-holder value by accelerating and enhancing cash flows, reducing the volatility of cash flows, and increasing the residual value of cash flows.

251 The quotation comes from "Valuing Customers", by Sunil Gupta, Donald R. Lehmann, and Jennifer Ames Stuart, *Journal of Marketing Research,* Vol. 41, No. 1, February 2004, pp.7–18.

Index

After a page number, "fig." indicates a figure, or figure and text; "n" indicates a note; "tab." indicates a table, or table and text.